Doing Sociolinguistics

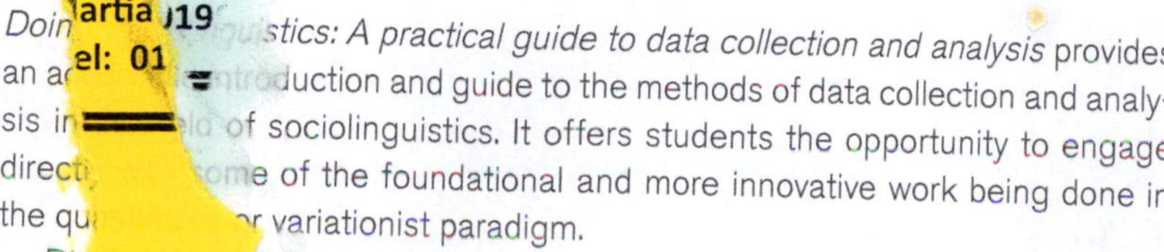

Doin[illegible]*stics: A practical guide to data collection and analysis* provides an a[illegible]ntroduction and guide to the methods of data collection and analysis i[illegible]eld of sociolinguistics. It offers students the opportunity to engage direct[illegible]ome of the foundational and more innovative work being done in the qu[illegible]r variationist paradigm.

Di[illegible]6 short chapters, *Doing Sociolinguistics*:

- c[illegible]as a core text in class or as an easy reference whilst undertaking[illegible];
- w[illegible]rs through the different phases of a sociolinguistic project, provi[illegible]nowledge and skills training students will need to conduct their ow[illegible] of language;
- fe[illegible]rpts from key research articles, exercises with real data from the[illegible]wn research and further reading;
- is [illegible]y the Routledge Sociolinguistics companion website (www.rou[illegible]m/textbooks/meyerhoff) and will feature further exercises and sa[illegible]ers.

Designed [illegible]ction as both a standard text for methods classes in sociolinguistics and a[illegible]mpan[illegible] to the Routledge textbook *Introducing Sociolinguistics, 2nd edi*[illegible] this book will be essential reading for all students studying and research[illegible]g in this area.

Miria[illegible] is [illegible]sor of Linguistics at Victoria University of Wellington, New Ze[illegible]and.

Erik Schleef is [illegible] Lecturer in the Division of Linguistics and English Language at the University of Manchester, UK.

Laurel MacKenzie is Lecturer in the Division of Linguistics and English Language at the University of Manchester, UK.

Doing Sociolinguistics

A practical guide to data collection and analysis

Miriam Meyerhoff, Erik Schleef and Laurel MacKenzie

LONDON AND NEW YORK

First published 2015
by Routledge
2 Park Square, Milton Park, Abingdon, Oxon OX14 4RN

and by Routledge
711 Third Avenue, New York, NY 10017

Routledge is an imprint of the Taylor & Francis Group, an informa business

British Library Cataloguing-in-Publication Data
A catalogue record for this book is available from the British Library

Library of Congress Cataloging-in-Publication Data
A catalog record for this book has been requested

ISBN: 978-0-415-69821-4 (hbk)
ISBN: 978-0-415-69820-7 (pbk)
ISBN: 978-1-315-72316-7 (ebk)

Typeset in Akzidenz and Eurostile
by Keystroke, Station Road, Codsall, Wolverhampton
Printed by Ashford Colour Press Ltd.

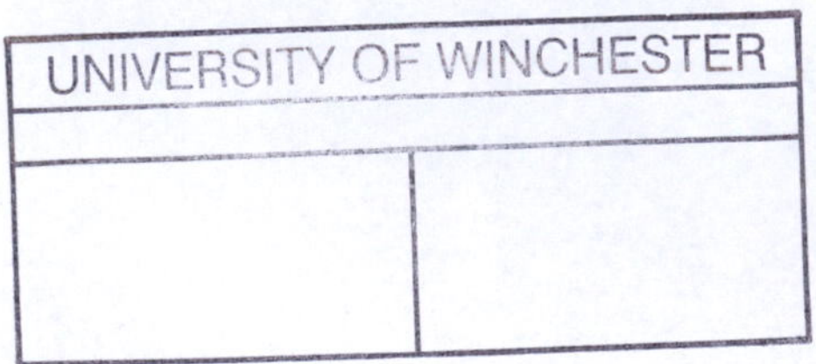

Contents

Figures

Tables

Preface and user guide

This book is intended to serve as an accessible guide, a reliable companion and a clear and casual conversation on methods of data collection and analysis in the field of sociolinguistics. The book outlines important principles that inform the collection of sociolinguistic data, how such data is handled and analysed once it has been collected and how it is then related to other work. *Doing Sociolinguistics: A practical guide to data collection and analysis* (*DS*) offers readers an opportunity to engage directly with some of the foundational and more innovative work being done in what is broadly known as quantitative or variationist sociolinguistics. While this is not to the exclusion of studies that examine sociolinguistics using more qualitative methods, it is a useful perspective to foreground, as it emphasises connections between the methods and principles required for the general study of language structure and the study of the socially situated uses of language.

The book can be used as a stand-alone text in introductory methods classes or an easy reference to different methodological issues, e.g. questionnaire design or transcription. Yet, it may be helpful for a methods book to be supported with another text that can spell out current issues and central principles in the field. We have written *DS* with particular companion textbooks in mind: the Routledge textbook *Introducing Sociolinguistics, 2nd edition* (Meyerhoff 2011) and *The Routledge Sociolinguistics Reader* (Meyerhoff and Schleef 2010). But experienced teachers will see ways in which *DS* could be supplemented with readings from other introductory volumes. *DS* was written in such a way that it can also be used in more specialised sociolinguistics classes that require students to learn about methods in order to prepare them for their own research. Thus, it also provides the scaffolding on which a teacher can build a coherent course of study.

This book reflects on many conversations we've had with our students and we have written it in a 'can do' style, as we realise that student researchers are often limited by time and resources in what they can achieve. We take this to heart when providing ideas and practical guidance, often discussing what could ideally happen but what may still be acceptable practice if circumstances are difficult. We offer a positive attitude that students working under time pressure in a one-semester course will especially appreciate. *DS* was written by three people, but since we intensively reviewed and edited each others' writing, it speaks with a single authorial voice. Our book is a snappy distillation of what we have learnt as researchers and teachers. This means there are no gaps in the guidance on process: we have worked through each step as we do with our own students and in our own work.

We have divided *DS* into two parts: data collection and data analysis, and our 16 chapters reflect the knowledge and skills necessary to conduct sociolinguistic analyses of language. The book walks the readers through the different phases of a sociolinguistic project and can be read as a coherent 'story'. Users of *DS* who work through each part in turn will find that their journey takes them from guidance on how to find a research topic to collecting and analysing the data and writing up the final report.

Each of the 16 chapters consists of three parts: (1) a clear yet brief introduction to the issues involved, (2) exercises and (3) an informative list of further reading and references. These suggestions for further reading allow more advanced users or users with very specific and clearly focused research questions to get a quick start creating a 'master class' of their own.

The exercises we provide at the end of each chapter probe a little further; they explore more complicated issues, they reinforce the content of each chapter and offer ideas for research topics to the user. We have tried as much as possible to make these exercises 'hands on' and data-based. Where this was not possible, we have tried to raise awareness of our research culture and the complex and intellectually rewarding field of sociolinguistics by providing examples and excerpts from some of the writing that we have found most inspirational. We hope we have been sensitive in our treatment of their original ideas. Where we have omitted something from the original text, we show this with ellipsis, so: [. . .]. Likewise, any editorial comments of our own are enclosed in square brackets.

Exercises are supplemented on our companion website (www.routledge.com/textbooks/meyerhoff) with brief notes on what we were thinking about when we created them. This is not to say they are answers; in fact, we tried to resist the temptation to offer answers. Instead, we have used the notes as a way of suggesting how you might go about addressing the exercises and where you might look for relevant information. Our companion website also contains some additional material and exercises relevant to the topics covered in *DS*. Links to the companion website are scattered throughout the book.

The idea for this book goes back to a 'how-to' methods chapter Miriam and Erik wrote for *The Routledge Sociolinguistics Reader* in 2009. That chapter itself started out as a two-hour workshop for (post-)graduate students, who might or might not be already working in sociolinguistics. It has subsequently been adapted to the needs of various audiences. It made sense to turn this into a short book that introduces methods in sociolinguistics clearly, straightforwardly and in a 'how-to' spirit that enables students to start their own research. We all bring differing expertise to the book and while we wrote many chapters together, some were initially written by one person and then edited by the team later on. It is fundamentally invidious to try to carve up our contributions in what is pre-eminently a collective work, and doing so undermines the well-known capacity for scholarly collaboration to generate something that is more than a sum of its parts. Nevertheless, we are compelled to recognise the climate of evaluation and its impact, particularly on emerging scholars. We therefore acknowledge (with regret) first authorship for the chapters as follows: Miriam and Erik co-wrote chapters 1, 2 and 10; Miriam wrote chapters 3, 5, 11 and 15; Erik wrote chapters 4, 6, 8, 9 and 16 and Laurel wrote chapters 7, 12, 13 and 14. There was a lot of give and take in the process, though, and ideas were free-floating from chapter to chapter. Miriam edited the whole manuscript to ensure a coherent style.

We hope that we have done a satisfactory job and that you will enjoy *DS*, as it stands. But we particularly hope that our chapters here inspire you to conduct your own research, make your own contribution to the field of sociolinguistics and, most importantly, that your journey will take you much beyond the modest guidance that we have provided here.

Miriam Meyerhoff
Wellington, 2014

Erik Schleef
Manchester, 2014

Laurel MacKenzie
Manchester, 2014

Acknowledgements

We are very grateful to all those many friends and colleagues who have offered us advice and have answered so many of our questions in the writing process, particularly Maciej Baranowski, Tine Breban, Richard Cameron, Stefan Dollinger, Josef Fruehwald, Kyle Gorman, Yuni Kim, Andrew Koontz-Garboden, William Labov, Naomi Nagy, Peter Patrick, Hilary Prichard, Meredith Tamminga, Danielle Turton, George Walkden and Nuria Yañez-Bouza. Our thanks also go to the reviewers of our original book proposal and to those who provided us with comments on many of our chapters, especially Nuria Yañez-Bouza and the members of the 2014 Perceptions and Attitudes Directed Reading Group at the University of Manchester. The insights of all these people have enriched this book tremendously.

Many friends and colleagues have sent us material for inclusion in the book. The data of exercise 2 in Chapter 1 have been reproduced with the kind permission of Nick Wilson. Scenarios in exercise 1 in Chapter 3 are adapted from ones created by Yuni Kim and are reproduced with her permission. The example of exercise 1 in Chapter 9 was sent to us by Nuria Yañez-Bouza. Terri Mackeigan and Stephen Muth have kindly given us permission to use their unpublished figure of a thread passing network, which we have reproduced as Figure 4.1. We are grateful to Naomi Proszynska for sharing the findings of her study of Victoria Beckham's /l/-vocalisation, reproduced in Chapter 14. We would also like to thank William Labov for giving us permission to make a set of his interview modules available on our companion website, as well as Adam Schembri, Jordan Fenlon and Kearsy Cormier for allowing us to put up their BSL information sheet and consent form on our site.

For academic support, we thank the University of Auckland, which enabled Erik to spend four months of a British autumn and winter in a summery New Zealand. We would also like to thank the staff at Routledge – Rachel Daw, Louisa Semlyen and Helen Tredget – for their invaluable support, but in particular Nadia Seemungal, who had the initial idea for this book and who has been terribly patient and supportive, even when our plans kept changing.

The authors and publishers would like to thank the following copyright holders for permission to reprint the material listed here:

Extract from pages 51–52 in Rajah-Carrim, Aaliya. 2007. Mauritian Creole and language attitudes in the education system of multi-ethnic and multilingual Mauritius. *Journal of Multilingual and Multicultural Development* 28: 51–71. © Taylor and Francis 2007, reproduced with permission.

Extract from pages 221–222 in Stuart-Smith, Jane, Claire Timmins and Fiona Tweedie. 2007. "Talkin' Jockney?" Variation and change in Glaswegian accent. *Journal of Sociolinguistics* 11: 221–260. © Wiley 2007, reproduced with permission.

Extract from pages 399–400 in Sharma, Devyani and Lavanya Sankaran. 2011. Cognitive and social forces in dialect shift: Gradual change in London Asian speech. *Language Variation and Change* 23: 399–428. © Cambridge University Press 2011, reproduced with permission.

Extract from pages 471–472 in Eckert, Penelope. 2008. Variation and the indexical field. *Journal of Sociolinguistics* 12: 453–476. © Wiley 2008, reproduced with permission.

Extract from pages 402–403 in Llamas, Carmen, Dominic Watt and Daniel Ezra Johnson. 2009. Linguistic accommodation and the salience of national identity markers in a border town. *Journal of Language and Social Psychology* 28: 381–407. © Sage 2009, reproduced with permission.

Table on page xv in Baranowski, Maciej. 2007. *Phonological Variation in the Dialect of Charleston, South Carolina*. Raleigh, NC: Duke University Press. © Duke University Press 2007, reproduced with permission.

Table on page 26 in Meyerhoff, Miriam and Erik Schleef. 2010. *The Routledge Sociolinguistics Reader*. London: Routledge. © Routledge 2010, reproduced with permission.

Extract from page 8 in Skarabela, Barbora, Shanley E.M. Allen and Thomas C. Scott-Phillips. 2013. Joint attention helps explain why children omit new referents. *Journal of Pragmatics* 56: 5–14. © Elsevier 2013, reproduced with permission.

Extract from pages 211–212 in Schleef, Erik, Miriam Meyerhoff and Lynn Clark. 2011. Teenagers' acquisition of variation: A comparison of locally-born and migrant teens' realisation of English (ing) in Edinburgh and London. *English World-Wide* 32: 206–236. © John Benjamins 2011, reproduced with permission.

Figure 5.1 in Labov, William. 2001. The anatomy of style-shifting. In Penelope Eckert and John R. Rickford (eds) *Style and Sociolinguistic Variation*. Cambridge: Cambridge University Press, 85–108. © Cambridge University Press 2001, reproduced with permission.

Extract from pages 68–70 in Smith, Jennifer, Mercedes Durham and Liane Fortune. 2007. "Mam, my trousers is fa' doon!": Community, caregiver, and child in the acquisition of variation in a Scottish dialect. *Language Variation and Change* 19: 63–99. © Cambridge University Press 2007, reproduced with permission.

Sample from an online survey on page 441 in Campbell-Kibler, Kathryn. 2011. The sociolinguistic variant as a carrier of social meaning. *Language Variation and Change* 22: 423–441. © Cambridge University Press 2011, reproduced with permission.

Table 9 in Dollinger, Stefan. 2012. The written questionnaire as a sociolinguistic data gathering tool: Testing its validity. *Journal of English Linguistics* 40: 74–110. © Sage 2012, reproduced with permission.

Figure 8 in Labov, William, Sharon Ash, Maya Ravindranath, Tracey Weldon, Maciej Baranowski and Naomi Nagy. 2011. Properties of the sociolinguistic monitor. *Journal of Sociolinguistics* 15: 431–463. © Wiley 2011, reproduced with permission.

Map 1 in Duhamel, Marie-France and Miriam Meyerhoff. 2014. An end of egalitarianism? Social evaluations of language difference in New Zealand. *Linguistic Vanguard* 1, December 2014 DOI:10.1515/lingvan-2014-1005. © Marie-France Duhamel and Miriam Meyerhoff, reproduced with permission.

Excerpt 8 in Heritage, John. 2012. Epistemics in action: Action formation and territories of knowledge. *Research on Language and Social Interaction* 45: 1–29. © Taylor and Francis 2012, reproduced with permission.

Comic strips from page 71 in Bell, Steve. 1985. *The Unrepeatable If...* London: Methuen. © Steve Bell 1985, reproduced with permission.

Transcription conventions on page 51 in Holmes, Janet and Stephanie Schnurr. 2006. 'Doing femininity' at work: More than just relational practice. *Journal of Sociolinguistics* 10: 31–51. © Wiley 2006, reproduced with permission.

Transcription conventions on pages 221–222 in Bucholtz, Mary. 1999. "Why be normal?" Language and identity practice in a community of nerd girls. *Language in Society* 28: 203–223. © Cambridge University Press 1999, reproduced with permission.

Figure 6 in Labov, William. 1990. The intersection of sex and social class in the course of linguistic change. *Language Variation and Change* 2: 205–254. © Cambridge University Press 1990, reproduced with permission.

Figure 1 in Foulkes, Paul, Gerard Docherty, and Dominic Watt. 2005. Phonological variation in child-directed speech. *Language* 81: 177–206. © Linguistic Society of America 1990, reproduced with permission.

Figure 3 in Milroy, James, and Lesley Milroy. 1985. Linguistic change, social network and speaker innovation. *Journal of Linguistics* 21: 339–384. © Cambridge University Press 1985, reproduced with permission.

Figure 3 in Gorman, Kyle. 2010. The consequences of multicollinearity among socioeconomic predictors of negative concord in Philadelphia. *University of Pennsylvania Working Papers in Linguistics* 16: 66–75. © Kyle Gorman 2010, reproduced with permission.

Figure 8 in D'Arcy, Alexandra, Bill Haddican, Hazel Richards, Sali A. Tagliamonte and Ann Taylor. 2013. Asymmetrical trajectories: The past and present of *–body/–one*. *Language Variation and Change* 25: 287–310. © Cambridge University Press 2013, reproduced with permission.

Extract from pages 380–381 in Haddican, Bill, Paul Foulkes, Vincent Hughes, and Hazel Richards. 2013. Interaction of social and linguistic constraints on two vowel changes in northern England. *Language Variation and Change* 25: 371–403. © Cambridge University Press 2013, reproduced with permission.

Extract from pages 93–95 in Eckert, Penelope. 2011. Language and power in the preadolescent heterosexual market. *American Speech* 86: 85–97. © Duke University Press 2011, reproduced with permission.

Figure 1 in Eckert, Penelope. 2011. Language and power in the preadolescent heterosexual market. *American Speech* 86: 85–97. © Duke University Press 2011, reproduced with permission.

Extract from pages 18–19 in Johnstone, Barbara and Scott F. Kiesling. 2008. Indexicality and experience: Exploring the meaning of /aw/-monophthongization in Pittsburgh. *Journal of Sociolinguistics* 12: 5–33. © Wiley 2008, reproduced with permission.

Extract from pages 231–232 in Meyerhoff, Miriam. 1999. Sorry in the Pacific: Defining communities, defining practices. *Language in Society* 28: 225–238. © Cambridge University Press 1999, reproduced with permission.

Table 2 in Meyerhoff, Miriam. 1999. Sorry in the Pacific: Defining communities, defining practices. *Language in Society* 28: 225–238. © Cambridge University Press 1999, reproduced with permission.

Figure 10 in Swales, John. 1990. *Genre Analysis: English in Academic and Research Settings.* Cambridge: Cambridge University Press. © Cambridge University Press 1990, reproduced with permission.

Extract from pages 305–306 in Trudgill, Peter. 2004. Linguistic and social typology: The Austronesian migrations and phoneme inventories. *Linguistic Typology* 8: 305–320. © Walter de Gruyter 2004, reproduced with permission.

Extract from page 355 in King, Ruth and Terry Nadasdi. 1999. The expression of evidentiality in French-English bilingual discourse. *Language in Society* 28: 355–365. © Cambridge University Press 1999, reproduced with permission.

Every effort has been made to obtain permission to reproduce copyright material. If any proper acknowledgement has not been made, or permission not received, we would invite copyright holders to inform us of this oversight.

Part I
Data collection

1 Finding a topic

Sometimes the hardest part of doing research is deciding on the topic. The task of honing a good topic is threefold: the topic has to appeal to you; you have to make it appeal to others; it has to be doable given the time and resources you have at your disposal.

We are going to start this book by running through some principles that will help you with each of these challenges. We'll discuss how you might formulate a research topic, how you might motivate your research topic and how you might implement your research topic with a research plan. (Of course, the bulk of the rest of this book is devoted to how you might implement a topic, so in this chapter we'll keep that part to the point.)

Formulating a research topic

There are six main ways researchers use to identify a satisfying research topic. One way to remember them is: *career*, *idea*, *'not found here' (observation)*, *conflict*, *theory* and *further research*.

Career

A lot of the angsting over choosing a research topic can be forestalled once you realise that the main reason for undertaking a research project is to benefit some kind of professional or career goal.

If you are simply looking for a research topic for a course you're enrolled in, you might ask yourself what you plan to do with yourself after you finish this course (or, indeed, finish this degree). Are there skills that you would want to have to make these goals possible? If you have more substantial intellectual ambitions, you might ask yourself what you want to contribute to your subject area or what you want to learn more about within your discipline or across disciplines. How you answer these questions can play a major role in how you frame your research topic.

For example, suppose that you want to work in the media or do graduate training in journalism, you might decide that it would demonstrate interest and commitment if you were to analyse an example of mediated discourse, let's say the structure and content of question-answer sequences in radio interviews. Or you might decide that it will be useful to be able to demonstrate skills in interviewing people.

If, on the other hand, you want to do speech and language therapy later on you might instead find it more interesting and helpful to analyse the discourse of doctor-patient interactions. Alternatively, you might want to undertake a detailed description of what's normative speech for a minority speech community, e.g. how exactly are back vowels in Asian English pronounced (this sort of question is important because we need the norms of typically developing speakers to assess the emergence of atypical or pathological habits). Another option might be to do an acquisition study, where you track the development of one child over several months.

SKILLS VALUED IN LINGUISTICS GRADUATES

Sometimes people are not at all sure where they want to go next, but work by college and university careers offices tell us that Humanities and Social Science graduates are valued for:

- presentation and communication skills (effective written and spoken language);
- planning and management skills (planning a project, managing and completing it on time);
- problem-solving skills (being critical in analysing problems, flexibility in devising solutions and evaluating them);
- teamwork, collaboration and interpersonal skills (working effectively in a team, negotiation of planning, management and completion of a project, engaging with others and establishing rapport);
- leadership skills (learning to lead others effectively by understanding their strengths and needs);
- mastering information communications technology (word and data-processing to specialised software skills);
- data collection (e.g. designing and undertaking interviews, questionnaires, systematic observation, etc.);
- qualitative and quantitative skills of data processing and analysis (e.g. data analysis and at least some basic skills in inferential statistics);
- self-reliance, self-reflection, self-motivation and self-confidence.

Idea

Some research projects start with a very general idea. "I don't know what to do. I think I'm interested in gender, like, in how women and men talk differently from each other."

This is not a good topic as it stands – it's far too broad. If you have an idea like this, the next step is to go to the literature and see what people have *recently* claimed, and make sure you define a topic that reflects recent developments in the field.

You might find, for instance, that some researchers (e.g. Cameron 2014; Freed 2014) have suggested that our obsession with gender differences tells us more about society than about language. Assuming that's true, then you might pick a research topic where you analyse how the media builds up an ideology of language differences based on speaker sex/gender.

A study of recent work on gender and language should also highlight how much research questions in the field have changed over time. Researchers now are more concerned with finding out when, why and how different women and men use particular linguistic strategies. This might help shape more specific and tractable research questions. You could start from generalisations that have been made in the literature or the popular press (e.g. women give compliments/talk more than men; women lead certain sound changes and men follow) and you could see whether this holds in specific contexts or in a specific group of speakers you have access to.

Observation ('Not found here')

Another route that often leads to an engaging research topic is when the researcher has noticed something that occurs 'here' but not 'there'. That is, it occurs in one context or with one speaker but not in others. For example, one of Erik's students had noticed that people in Manchester sometimes produce a tap for their /r/ when it is intervocalic. Now she'd like to know whether everyone does this, whether it only occurs intervocalically and whether it is a change taking place in Manchester.

LOOK AND LISTEN

You may be surprised how generous your immediate community is in giving you research topics: pay attention to how people use language and how language is used around you.

Assessing conflicting claims

Another productive source of research questions is when you notice that two sources make competing claims. Does the data you have access to support one or the other? Are some claims associated with certain kinds of data? If so, what different data sources could help to assess the validity of that claim?

Testing theory

Some linguistic, social or cognitive theories lend themselves to quite specific theory-internal questions about the way we use language. For example, some researchers have asked how a generative theory of syntax could accommodate variation (Adger 2006; Embick 2008). Others have asked whether listeners' expectations about the social attributes of a speaker affect what they 'hear' (Niedzielski 1999; Campbell-Kibler 2009). Different theories of human cognition model the way we share attention to forms and derive norms on the basis of that shared attention. Testing a theory that focuses on interaction might require that you frame a research topic so that it makes reference to social and visual channels of information. Testing theories that emphasise frequency of exposure might require you to have larger corpora so you can explore different measures of frequency.

Further research: jumping to conclusions

A final source of ideas for research topics may be the conclusion section in previously published papers. When they outline their conclusions, some researchers are as open and direct about what they haven't addressed as about what they *have* addressed. These sorts of topics can be deeply satisfying because they allow you to make a meaningful contribution towards advancing a research tradition. Previous researchers do not always answer all their questions fully, or they may not be able to consider all factors that may influence language use. Sometimes open questions remain and researchers often highlight these gaps themselves in their data analysis and conclusion, so pay attention to these little hints researchers give you in their writing and follow them up. For example, Drager analyses factors influencing the phonetic realisation of discourse *like*. She includes a large number of variables in her statistical analysis, and these give us a good idea of what may influence the realisation of *like*. However, she does admit that an analysis of prosodic features may give additional depth to her analysis, so exploring the prosodic positions of *like* tokens may help explain differences in realisations of *like* across its different functions (Drager 2011: 705).

Motivating your research topic

For every research project, it is important to choose a topic because you think it will be fun. This may sound flip, but it really is important. It can sometimes be the crucial difference between pressing on and trying to finish (especially a longer project, like a PhD) and throwing in the towel and sitting the exams for law school, or the civil service.

But this is never all it can be. A good research topic must fill some sort of research niche. If you chose your topic because you had identified competing claims or the predictions about the way language can pattern internally, the niche is filled from the start. So the step of motivating your topic has to be foregrounded when your topic has been defined based on *Career*, *Idea* and *Not found here* topics.

Again, you will do this much better if you motivate your topic choice in the light of *recent* developments in the field. One of the most common flaws we have seen in students working with us is someone who has gone back to what was a key piece of literature in, say, 1975 and used that as the basis for formulating their research topic. Although it is very important to read the classic literature on a specific topic, sometimes this is a research topic that has been thoroughly outdated by developments in the field. The more recent literature on the topic may suggest new topics and these are much more satisfying for the researcher and their audience.

Drawing up a research plan

The final step in identifying a good research topic is to think about how much time you have and decide how much of that time you think you'll need for data collection, analysis and write-up (all subjects of later chapters in this book). Before you start, it can be very helpful to have a rough idea about how long you can devote to the different stages in your project. This allows you to make principled adjustments to the scope of your research topic if, for some reason, you find yourself short on time.

EXERCISES

Exercise 1 – finding a topic and motivating it

Consider the following introductions, which have been extracted from research articles published in peer-reviewed journals. How did the authors find their research topic and how do they make a case for their research being interesting and important?

Mauritian Creole and language attitudes

On creole-speaking multilingual Mauritius, languages act as important markers of identity (Eriksen, 1998; Stein, 1982). In fact, most of the 12 languages present on the island are associated with specific ethnic and/

or religious groups. The various languages can broadly be divided into three groups: ancestral languages (Indian and Chinese languages) whose usage is limited, colonial languages (English and French) and language of everyday interactions (Mauritian Creole/Kreol – see Note 1) (Rajah-Carrim, 2005). While most of these languages have a place in the education sector – as medium of instruction or subject – the native language of most Mauritians, Kreol, tends to be excluded from the classroom.

The teaching of languages has become a highly politicised issue in Mauritius. In 2004, the Minister of Education declared that Kreol would be officially introduced in the education system in the coming years. The new political leaders who came to power in 2005 are also committed to the promotion of Kreol. But how do the Mauritians themselves feel about the introduction of Kreol in the school system? In this paper, I discuss attitudes to the use of Kreol in the education sector based on a survey conducted in Mauritius. In the first section, I describe the demographic and linguistic situations of Mauritius. This is followed by a description of the national education system. I then show how the language-in-education issue is not unique to Mauritius and is tied to ideologies of identity and power. In the fifth section, I discuss the questions related to the school domain in the survey. In the next two sections, I analyse responses to the survey questions. The final section consists of a brief summary and conclusion.

Source: Rajah-Carrim (2007)

Variation and change in Glaswegian

. . . In the late 1990s, preliminary results from a study of Glaswegian accent indicated that working-class adolescents, with few apparent opportunities for contact outside the city, were both using features usually associated with southern English (e.g. TH-fronting, the use of [f] for /θ/ in e.g. *think*), and at the same time, not showing expected 'Scottish' features (e.g. production of postvocalic /r/ in e.g. *car*). These findings led to a flurry of media reports which jokingly dubbed the 'new' dialect 'Jockney' ('Jock' = Scot + 'Cockney'), and which speculated that another possible cause for such patterns of variation was watching London-based TV soap operas, such as the popular show, *EastEnders*.

This paper presents the first integrated account of the linguistic facts behind such reports. Here we describe the main patterns of variation observed in a socially stratified sample of Glaswegian collected in 1997, and we account for them in terms of evidence which directly relates to the corpus itself, the recent social history of Glasgow, and indications of local language ideologies constructed about this history. Using univariate and multivariate statistical analysis, we look at the use of a range of consonant variables in speakers from two neighbouring areas of Glasgow, representing distinct points on the sociolinguistic continuum of Glaswegian English. [. . .]

Our young innovators are using a consonantal system which in many respects is more similar to that of London English, but at the same time, they are exploiting 'non-local' variation in such a way that it is used, and feels to them to be, thoroughly local. This then provides further support for the notion that constructing identity through linguistic variation is crucially connected to the local context (e.g. Labov 1963; Eckert 2000; Dyer 2002; see also Meyerhoff and Niedzielski 2003).

Source: Stuart-Smith, Timmins and Tweedie (2007)

Cognitive and social forces in dialect shift

In situations of migration, severe disparities between parent and peer dialects can arise for local-born individuals, who may have parents who are non-native speakers as well as peers who are native speakers of the local language. For such cases, Chambers (2002) proposes a strong peer-orientation mechanism: an innate accent filter that blocks parental non-native features and leads local-born children to exclusively acquire the local dialect. However, numerous studies have found that foreign phonetic features introduced via in-migration are not always lost in local-born speech (Sankoff, 2002). A "weak" view of dialect assimilation in migration might propose that, rather than being entirely lost, foreign traits can be retained and functionally reallocated.

Both the strong and weak views often treat nativeness as a major boundary. Accent traits are expected to be either absent (strong version) or immediately reallocated by the first set of individuals to acquire the local dialect natively (weak version). Incremental stages of intergenerational accent change have not been studied closely enough in immigrant groups to move beyond speculation, however, and the following question remains largely unresolved: How quickly and how completely do local-born generations acquire a local dialect and lose exogenous traits, and is this rate and degree of shift governed by largely cognitive (e.g. nativeness) or social (e.g. demographic) factors?

Source: Sharma and Sankaran (2011)

Exercise 2 – finding a topic based on observation and/or theory

Consider the following transcriptions of recordings made by Nick Wilson (University of Cardiff) as part of his MSc studying language variation in a rugby club in Edinburgh. How could this data serve as the basis for a linguistic research topic? Try to find a topic based on something you see in the data below and/or linguistic theory. Below are some questions that you may want to ask yourself in your attempt to find a research topic based on the data provided.

Quantitative analysis

What features in the extracts would be amenable to quantitative analysis? Identify as many potential variables as you can. State what you believe the important variants are (you can draw on your wider linguistic knowledge in this, as the transcripts are pretty close to Standard English orthography). What kinds of features would you expect to investigate as potential constraints on the variables? How could you imagine making your findings about these variables relevant to linguistic theory?

Qualitative analysis

What kinds of information do these recordings offer for the sociolinguist who is more interested in qualitative analysis? Where might you go next to find supplementary sources of data? How might this information inform debates about, and questions in, linguistic theory?

Rugby training sessions

This data is reproduced with the kind permission of Nick Wilson.

Example 1 [Training session 16/01/2007; time stamp 00:21:30–00:24:16]

Coach: Right okay eh- tonight we are [. . .] gonna be focusin on one key area
which eh- for everyone's important but more so for the guys who'll play
against East Kilbride on Saturday it'll be very important. [. . .]
Eh- traditionally, East Kilbride eh-
having played against them, will try tae be eh- fairly ruthless up-front
they'll be generally pretty big and they'll try and keep eh- keep teams
on their feet.
Eh- so to combat that we're gonna look at our eh- body position and

our height eh- carryin the ball into contact. That's gonnae be the real focus for us tonight eh leadin intae Thursday and transferrin that intae the game on Saturday. So that's gonnae be our major focus tonight. Eh- [. . .]

So what we've got set up to start off wi- just continuin our warm-up but gettin used tae comin through the gates, we've got eh- we've got a blue start point and a green start point if we can just split into two groups, even at either end we only need one ball just now. (1.3) Couple more up this end. Okay so what'll happen is Mark's gonna come through the cones here [. . .] an he's passin it tae John not wi a pop but I want him to ram it in the gut. So it's a gut pass. Okay and then John'll be comin through and we're just shuttlin backwards and forwards [. . .] but there is enough width in this middle section here tae get two guys past so you're gonnae have tae get your timin right as well.

Example 2 [Training session 16/01/2007; time stamp 01:10:01–01:10:44]

Coach: So Thursday, be more of the same lookin at body shape and body height. We'll split, eh- we'll do our eh- our units work, come tae-gither, team run and hopefully that should stand us in guid stead for Saturday. Is there anyone not able tae train on Thursday?
(2.1)
Neil: Ah've got a dinner, Ah'm tryin to get out of it- for work- (supposed to have) a dinner but I'm tryin [to get out of it.
Coach: [Anyone not available to play on Saturday? There will be a second team game as well=
Scott: =>I'm not available.<
Coach: You fuckin better be.
Scott: I'm not.
Coach: You're kiddin. Ohohoh [no ((sarcastic laughter))
Sam: [Going to a (chic) dinner party?
Scott: Aye well- ((nervous laughter)) Aye kinda.
Coach: Kinda, right okay.=
Scott: =Well it's ma mate's thirtieth
Coach: =Right okay, right anyway that doesn't matter we've got people who can step in eh- ((sarcastic laughter))

Example 3 [Training session 16/01/2007; time stamp 01:11:10–01:11:53]

Euan: Ah was just wonderin, like. For the twos and everythin. How
ready- honestly, how ready do you think ah am. Ah mean uh- can ye
at least see me progressin?
From when ah ┌came
Coach: └Well ye can make a tackle (1.3) and ye can clear
out in a ruck. Ah think ye should be thinkin about havin a run now.
Euan: Cos ah- ah feel- ah feel reasonably comfortable ye know?
Coach: The biggest- eh- the biggest issue would've been the contact stuff,
the tacklin, the- the clearin out, but to be honest you know, your doin
it as well as a couple of other guys who play so I wouldn't worry about
that too much. Ah think ye should think about maybe getting a run
this Saturday, so if you want to make yourself available we'll put you
in the squad yeah? ┌Guid man.
Euan: └Well-

Exercise 3 – identifying further research options

Consider the following conclusions, which have been extracted from research articles published in peer-reviewed journals. What topics for further investigation do the authors suggest? What would you need to pursue these topics?

Variation and the indexical field

Labov's introduction of class into the study of language was a landmark of immense importance. But his view of the class hierarchy, and of the relation of standard and vernacular language to that hierarchy, is only the beginning of a theory of the social value of variation. The social is not just a set of *constraints* on variation – it is not simply a set of categories that determine what variants a speaker will use – it is a meaning making enterprise. And while one's place in the political economy has an important constraining effect on how one makes meaning, and on the kinds of meanings one engages with, this place cannot be defined in terms of a simple model. A theory of variation ultimately must deal with meaning, and not only does a view of meaning in variation as predetermined and static seriously undershoot human capacity, it cannot even account in any principled way for the changes in correlations that have been observed over the lifetime of a sound change (e.g. Labov 2001: chapter 9). Ultimately, all change unfolds in the course of day-to-day exchange, and that exchange involves constant local reinterpretation and repositioning. Ultimately, it is in this action that we can get at the meaning-making that gives life to variation. While the larger patterns of variation can profitably be seen in terms of a static social landscape, this is only a distant reflection of what is happening moment to moment on the ground.

Source: Eckert (2008)

Linguistic accommodation and national identity markers

This article has presented the results of a study designed to test the extent of speakers' linguistic accommodation to members of putative in-groups and out-groups in a border locality, where such categorizations can be said to be particularly accentuated. Findings were considered in terms of their implications for the notion of salience, the evidence required for claims of phonological convergence and divergence, and the interviewer effect in the compilation of data sets for use in quantitative studies of phonological variation and change. [. . .]

As regards compelling evidence for phonological divergence in intergroup short term contact interactions, it appeared that to interpret patterns of variation in such a way, it would be necessary to identify a set of default production patterns, presumably those corresponding to a vernacular speech style, from which the speaker would move. It is not clear that this identification is possible. [. . .]

More work is necessary on the central notions of interspeaker convergence and divergence in short-term contact situations, which are so often invoked in the interpretation of patterns of phonological variation and change. The potential they contain as explanations of motivations for variable linguistic behavior implies that better understanding of such processes permits us to comprehend more fully the dynamics of language change more generally.

Source: Llamas, Watt and Johnson (2009)

Exercise 4 – identifying further research options

Go back to the breakout box listing the kinds of skills valued in linguistics graduates. Decide which ones you think you have mastered well and which ones you haven't. (You might like to ask a friend or family member who knows you fairly well to assess you on these criteria too – sometimes we are a bit hard on ourselves.) How could the results of this skills assessment influence topic selection?

References

Adger, David. 2006. Combinatorial variability. *Journal of Linguistics* 42: 503–530.

Cameron, Deborah. 2014. Gender and language ideologies. In Susan Ehrlich, Miriam Meyerhoff and Janet Holmes (eds) *The Handbook of Language, Gender and Sexuality*, 2nd edition. Oxford: Wiley Blackwell, 281–296.

Campbell-Kibler, Kathryn. 2009. The nature of sociolinguistic perception. *Language Variation and Change* 21: 135–156.

Drager, Katie K. 2011. Sociophonetic variation and the lemma. *Journal of Phonetics* 39: 694–707.

Eckert, Penelope. 2008. Variation and the indexical field. *Journal of Sociolinguistics* 12: 453–476.

Embick, David. 2008. Variation and morphosyntactic theory: Competition fractionated. *Language and Linguistics Compass* 2: 59–78.

Freed, Alice F. 2014. The public view of language and gender: Still wrong after all these years. In Susan Ehrlich, Miriam Meyerhoff and Janet Holmes (eds) *The Handbook of Language, Gender and Sexuality*, 2nd edition. Oxford: Wiley Blackwell, 625–645.

Llamas, Carmen, Dominic Watt and Daniel Ezra Johnson. 2009. Linguistic accommodation and the salience of national identity markers in a border town. *Journal of Language and Social Psychology* 28: 381–407.

Niedzielski, Nancy. 1999. The effect of social information on the perception of sociolinguistic variables. *Journal of Language and Social Psychology* 18: 62–85.

Rajah-Carrim, Aaliya. 2007. Mauritian Creole and language attitudes in the education system of multi-ethnic and multilingual Mauritius. *Journal of Multilingual and Multicultural Development* 28: 51–71.

Sharma, Devyani and Lavanya Sankaran. 2011. Cognitive and social forces in dialect shift: Gradual change in London Asian speech. *Language Variation and Change* 23: 399–428.

Stuart-Smith, Jane, Claire Timmins and Fiona Tweedie. 2007. 'Talkin' Jockney'? Variation and change in Glaswegian accent. *Journal of Sociolinguistics* 11: 221–260.

Further reading

Llamas, Carmen, Louise Mullany and Peter Stockwell (eds). 2007. *The Routledge Companion to Sociolinguistics*. London and New York: Routledge.

Milroy, Lesley and Matthew Gordon. 2003. *Sociolinguistics: Method and Interpretation*. Malden and Oxford: Blackwell.

Schleef, Erik and Miriam Meyerhoff. 2010. Sociolinguistic methods for data collection and interpretation. In Miriam Meyerhoff and Erik Schleef (eds) *The Routledge Sociolinguistics Reader.* London and New York: Routledge, 1–26.

Tagliamonte, Sali A. 2006. *Analysing Sociolinguistic Variation.* Cambridge: Cambridge University Press.

Walker, James. 2010. *Analyzing Linguistic Variation.* London and New York: Routledge.

Wolfram, Walt. 1993. Identifying and interpreting variables. In Dennis R. Preston et al. (eds) *American Dialect Research.* Amsterdam: John Benjamins, 193–221.

2 Sample design and the envelope of variation

What exactly am I looking at?

Whether you are doing qualitative or quantitative analysis, you need to decide pretty early on what you are focusing on. We can call this *defining your variable*. Let's agree that a linguistic variable is any feature that has forms or denotations that vary in different contexts.

THE TERM *VARIABLE*

The term *variable* is used in other disciplines (e.g. mathematics) and other subfields of linguistics (e.g. formal linguistics) as well, where it has different meanings in each case. So depending on what kind of academic you're talking to, they may use the word in a way that's specific to their field. It is interesting, though, how ubiquitous the concept is in language!

Qualitative and discourse analyses don't usually use the word *variable* but actually the concept is not entirely ill-suited even for qualitative research. For example, a qualitative analysis might ask in what kind of conversational routines people use the word *love* or *dude* as an address term, or it might explore the kind of attitudes and speech acts that seem to bundle with the use of different address terms. Even if they don't use the term *variable*, you can see that a qualitative study has to decide which forms will trigger a more detailed analysis. You then have to decide whether to look only at the linguistic context or whether you'll look outside the text for information on how to interpret usage.

For quantitative analysis, the notion of the variable is more restrictively defined. The variable is the abstract representation of what you're investigating – how it gets realised is in the form of different *variants*.

Defining variables and variants

When we are looking at variation in sounds and changes in pronunciation over time, the abstract of the variable corresponds to the abstract phoneme. There is a frustrating amount of notational variation in how people represent variables. Some researchers use the IPA (International Phonetic Alphabet), some use a modified IPA, some use Wells' (1982) lexical sets. A convention established early in sociolinguistics was to place the variable within parentheses – e.g. (i) represents the variable realisation of the vowel in words like *cheese* and *please*. This notation system was useful because it distinguished variables from phonemes (represented with oblique slashes – /i/) and phonetic realisations of the phoneme (in square brackets – [i̝], [əi], [ɨ] etc.). We will follow these conventions in this book though we may sometimes use examples from Wells' lexical sets (here, FLEECE, note the use of small capitals) if it helps provide clarity.

ANAE VOWEL NOTATIONS

Vowel notations used in *The Atlas of North American English* (Labov, Ash and Boberg 2006, Chapter 2) are based on a modified IPA. They highlight the structural connections between vowels of the same subsystem, and we have reproduced here the tables published in Baranowski (2007: xv). Single symbols represent short vowels and two symbols represent long vowels phonemically.

	SHORT		LONG					
			Upgliding				Ingliding	
			Front upgliding		Back upgliding			
Nucleus	front	back	front	back	front	back	unrounded	rounded
High	**/i/** *bit*	**/u/** *put*	**/iy/** *beat*		**/iw/** *suit*	**/uw/** *boot*		
Mid	**/e/** *bet*	**/ʌ/** *but*	**/ey/** *bait*	**/oy/** *boy*		**/ow/** *boat*		**/oh/** *bought*
Low	**/æ/** *bat*	**/o/** *cot*		**/ay/** *bite*		**/aw/** *bout*	**/ah/** *balm*	

	V+/r/	
Nucleus	front	back
High	**/ihr/** *fear*	
Mid	**/ehr/** *fair*	**/ohr/** *four*
Low		**/ɔhr/** *for*

Before you start coding your data, it is terribly important to determine what your variants are. This can be easier for some types of variables than for others. The variants that realise a *phonological* variable are free of any semantic meaning (they do not distinguish minimal pairs) and in this respect, they are like allophones of a phoneme. The difference between variants and allophones is that variants are distributed probabilistically across different contexts and different types of speakers, while allophones are predictable in context and their use is not dependent on non-linguistic facts.

Even though variants of a variable do not semantically distinguish minimal pairs, they do have other kinds of meaning. And the task of sociolinguists is to elucidate what those meanings are – whether they signal a caring or positive affect, whether they occur in extremely mannered and careful speech, whether they probabilistically mark different word classes, etc.

For non-phonic variables, this notion of semantic equivalence has to be relaxed, since word order alternations (2a), the use of periphrastic versus inflected forms of a tense (2b), the presence of an overt subject pronoun (2c) and the choice of a verb of quotation (2d) all make some kind of contribution to the semantics of the clause. There have been arguments about whether such alternations count as sociolinguistic variables since the inception of the field (e.g. Lavandera 1978; Dines 1980; Milroy 1987). But these arguments seem to have been resolved with an agreement that we can justify treating forms like these as variants of some underlying morphological, syntactic or discourse variable because even though they do not have strict semantic equivalence, they have functional and distributional equivalence (Walker 2010 discusses this in more detail).

(2a) V Aux O
þæt he *friðian* wolde **þa leasan wudewan**
that he make-peace-with would the false widow
'that he would make peace with the false widow'

Aux V O
swa þæt heo bið *forloren* **þam ecan life**
so that it is lost the eternal life
'so that it is lost to the eternal life'

(Taylor & Pintzuk 2012, examples 1b, d)

(2b) *Aussitôt qu'il* ***va y avoir*** *des postes ouverts* ***j'appliquerai*** *pour un poste régulier.*
'As soon as there are [lit. 'are going to have'] posts available I'll apply for a regular position.' (Sankoff & Wagner 2006, example 1)

(2c) *olgeta oli stap yusum fasin blong bifo yet.*
'They still do things the old way.'

Ø oli karem wan trak blong olgeta finis.
'They've got a truck for themselves already.' (Meyerhoff, field recordings in Bislama)

(2d) I can remember the sound of that-- that 'fzsssssssss'
yeah that was a sweet and **I was like** '*u::rh*' ha ha ha ha
and I **thought** '*wow* that might be *interesting*' (*italics = voice effect*)
And now kids, they'll **say** 'well, that just flew by'. (Buchstaller 2014: 61)

You will have at least some idea before you start of what the most likely variants are for the variable you have chosen (remember, you did all that homework and wider reading recommended in Chapter 1). However, it is still possible that once you start exploring your data, you will find that there are variants you hadn't expected to find. Sometimes these are variants that are dialect specific. For instance, all dialects of English have an [ɪn]~[ɪŋ] alternation for words with an unstressed <ing> syllable, but not all have the additional option of [ɪŋk] or [ɪŋg].

Defining the envelope of variation

A very important tenet of sociolinguistics is that if you are going to be doing quantitative analysis, you have to count all and every instance of your variable and *in every place it could occur*. This is what's known as the envelope of variation (or for some people, circumscribing the variable context). This is terribly important in order to accurately reveal the patterns of variation constrained by linguistic and social factors because these are often very subtle effects.

To determine what your envelope of variation is, you can rely on previous literature and on your own observation. When you count your tokens, you want to make sure you exclude contexts that aren't actually variable. For example, when investigating t-glottalling, there's no point in including words with word-initial (t), such as *table*, because this is not a context where this phenomenon normally occurs. Word-initial (t) is not within your envelope of variation. In London, t-glottalling can occur after a preceding sonorant in coda (e.g. *hot*) or non-foot-initial onset position, the latter referring to cases where the syllable stress that follows (t) is less than that of the syllable preceding (t) (Tollfree 1999: 171–172), e.g. in *better* and *guilty*. Where these conditions apply, t-glottalling may occur variably, influenced by a set of further linguistic and social factors. Finding out what these factors are is the goal of a variationist study.

The previous example is a relatively easy one to deal with when it comes to determining variants and the envelope of variation (although this is not at all the whole story). However, things can become more complicated. Sometimes finding your variants in a specific context means you will be looking for 'nothing' – places where the form you are interested in fails to show up as expected. So although automated searches for text strings (e.g. "Find me all the instances where a word ends in <ing> or <t>") can sometimes help you quickly identify all the instances of your variable, unless you have a well annotated corpus, this may not be possible for more abstract variables (e.g. "Find me every time a subject follows the finite verb"), in which case, there is no choice but to do it manually. If one of your variants is phonetically null, it may well not be noted in a transcription. You will simply have to go looking for cases where, say, a pronoun could have appeared in subject position, or there could have been a quotative verb introducing some reported discourse.

It's a bit tiresome doing this but it's very important. If you don't count all and every place where your variable can occur, your analysis will be skewed. Here's what we mean by 'skewed': imagine that people often use zero quotative verbs when there's no change in speaker, but the other quotatives are roughly evenly distributed where there is a speaker change and where the same speaker continues. If you haven't counted the zeroes, you'll fail to see that continuing with the same subject is a significant constraint on one of the choices speakers make.

And here's another, very important, example of how things can get complicated: determining the envelope of variation is particularly difficult for discourse structures. Discourse markers (henceforth DMs) often display a startling degree of structural promiscuity. It sometimes appears that they can occur freely virtually anywhere in the clause. Consider the potential distribution of downtoner hedges like *sort of* (Holmes 1988) or the particle *eh* in New Zealand English (Meyerhoff 1994). This structural promiscuity poses a variationist problem of a somewhat different order to the equivalence problem that had to be resolved for grammatical variables. This is because there is no tidy envelope of variation for DMs that the researcher can define. Because of the politeness and intersubjectivity functions they fulfil, they are often optional (e.g. "I really wish I hadn't done that" versus "You know, I really wish I hadn't done that"), and it is often not possible to determine all the separate variants at the level of discourse.

We can try and delimit the variable context as precisely as possible, and a thorough qualitative analysis of DMs that precedes our quantitative study will help us do this. Nonetheless, the problem of not having a clear envelope of variation often remains: what is the denominator going to be when you can't specify all and every place a speaker might choose to express politeness or intersubjective alignment with a DM? Different linguists have dealt with this issue in different ways: by adopting a very large envelope of variation, by using qualitative methods, or a frequency index of particular functions. None of these are perfect.

We can consider a very large envelope of variation, but what does this tell us? For example, expected frequencies of a hedge balloon to ridiculous proportions if we were to try and quantify the occurrence of *sort of* as potentially occurring before any XP (which seems to be its distributional potential in at least some varieties of English). Moreover, even if we were to do this, it is debatable whether it is warranted, as there may be constraints on co-occurrence. For example, a speaker would sound nothing short of pathological if they were to use *like* in every possible slot: **Like I like heard like their like train like is like running like 15 like minutes like late, like* (the asterisk is used to signal this kind of thing is unattested). This means that a model of the variation which starts from the presumption that every slot is potentially fillable is of dubious value. D'Arcy's (2005) analysis of *like* in Canadian English resolves this with sampling: where the envelope of variation is so large as to be difficult to operationalise, she sampled selectively. She extracted 75 randomly selected complementiser phrases per speaker for an analysis of clause-initial *like*. In effect, the position adopted in this approach is to control the denominator in a way that analyses of variation taken from naturally occurring conversations usually cannot, thereby allowing for comparability across speakers. The cost is at the expense of full accountability to the numerator (cf. Schegloff 1993).

Early research on politeness phenomena (Schiffrin 1987: 8, 13; Schegloff 1988; Tannen 1988; Holmes 1988, 1989: 297) resolved the problem somewhat differently, sometimes by adopting qualitative methods of analysis. Another solution, when it may not be possible or practical to specify the denominator accurately or exhaustively, is to create some other form of index that is comparable across speakers. Meyerhoff (1994) quantified the number of tokens of a pragmatic particle over the number of words produced, creating a frequency index. This solution enables us to say something about high and low frequency users (out of the total sample) of a particular DM and high and low frequency functions (relative to all functions of the DM), but since it is at the expense of linguistic detail, we cannot say much about how a DM interacts with the syntax of the rest of the clause. It therefore works well if the primary questions are about the social and transactional meanings of a DM.

How much data do I need?

Once you have decided on a general topic and a plan for action and gained an idea of what the variable, its variants and the envelope of variation are, the next step you might like to take is to decide who you want to collect data from and how many people you'll need. These questions about who and how many fall under the general topic of 'sampling'.

Suppose you decide to investigate several linguistic variables as used by young people between 18 and 28 who live in different neighbourhoods (which more or less overlap with two different socioeconomic classes). Depending on your research question, you might devise a template for sampling speakers as per Table 2.1.

Table 2.1 Example grid for planning the sampling (how many people, what social characteristics) in a study

	Neighbourhood A (Working class)		*Neighbourhood B (Middle class)*	
Age	*Male*	*Female*	*Male*	*Female*
18–23	5	5	5	5
23–28	5	5	5	5
Subtotal	10	10	10	10
				Total: 40

Setting up a data grid like this helps your planning. It's especially useful if you are doing a random sample (see Chapter 4) but even a network study and qualitative discourse analysis (depending on what claims you hope to make) will benefit if you start out with an idea of how many speakers you will need data from.

When conducting a variationist study of language use, it is usually recommended to have at least five or six speakers per cell (see Chapter 8 where we talk about sample size in questionnaire-based studies). This will allow you to make statistically sound generalisations about the speech of (say, in Table 2.1) middle class males between 23 and 28 years old as a group. If you were to add another age group to this grid, your grand total of speakers would rise to 60. This represents quite a substantial increase in work recruiting and recording, and it shows that it's worth thinking about your sample design in advance. You may simply not have the funds and time to collect that much data, not to mention analyse it all at the end. Adding another social factor, such as ethnicity, would increase the grand total by a further order of magnitude.

How much data you need from every individual does of course depend on your research question. If you are looking at phonological variables and only use word lists and reading passages, you may need just 15 minutes per person because your materials are highly structured. If you're after casual speech, you will need substantially more than 15 minutes. Because syntactic variables occur less frequently than most phonological variables, more data is needed to study them.

In Table 2.1, we noted that every time you add a different non-linguistic factor to your investigation, the sample size increases across the board. Note that the same principle applies to token numbers if you are doing a quantitative analysis and want to make generalisations about the effect of, say, word order or following phonological segment. To make quantitative statements about the likely directions and constraints on variation and change, ideally you will have a minimum of 30 tokens for each condition. This is illustrated in Tables 2.2 and 2.3. Guy (1980:

Table 2.2 Example showing ideal number of tokens required to make meaningful quantitative generalisations about final consonant cluster reduction in English (e.g. *past~passed* as [pɑst] vs [pɑs]) across three linguistic contexts (following vowel, consonant and pause)

	Following context			
	–V	*–C*	*– #*	*Total*
–CC	30	30	30	90
–C	30	30	30	90
				180

Table 2.3 Example showing ideal number of tokens required to make meaningful quantitative generalisations about likely presence or absence of subject pronoun in different discourse/syntactic contexts

	Discourse context		*Syntactic context*		
	Same subject as prior clause	*Different subject*	*Preverbal subject*	*Postverbal subject*	*Total*
Pronoun present	30	30	30	30	120
Pronoun absent	30	30	30	30	120
					240

26) established that at least 30 tokens per factor are required for reliable and accurate results. When there were fewer than 30 tokens per cell some of the standard statistical tests used in sociolinguistics are compromised.

You can see that in this case, too, if you add more linguistic contexts, the total number of tokens you will have to collect increases rapidly. And since the contexts in Tables 2.2 and 2.3 are not evenly distributed in naturally occurring speech, the more linguistic contexts you want to explore, the more data you will want to collect. Obviously, the target number of tokens and speakers (Table 2.1) are not independent. These are both desirable minimums, and may be relaxed if, for instance, you had masses of data (hundreds of tokens per cell) from only a few people. And sometimes you can record for hours but you may simply never get 30 tokens of – for argument's sake – negative sentences with second person plural subjects and a stative main verb. Some sounds, too, are not as common as others – you can see this in Table 2.4 which gives the frequency of different segments in Southern British English speech (after D. B. Fry 1947). In that case, you have to take what you can get.

Table 2.4 Frequencies of segments in Southern British English (after D. B. Fry 1947)

Consonants	*%*		*%*	*Vowels*	*%*		*%*
n	7.58	b	1.97	ə	10.74	ʊ	0.86
t	6.42	f	1.79	ɪ	8.33	ɑː	0.79
d	5.14	p	1.78	e	2.97	ɑʊ	0.61
s	4.81	h	1.46	aɪ	1.83	ɜː	0.52
l	3.66	ŋ	1.15	ʌ	1.75	ɛə	0.34
ð	3.56	g	1.05	eɪ	1.71	ɪə	0.21
r	3.51	ʃ	0.96	iː	1.65	ɔɪ	0.14
m	3.22	j	0.88	əʊ	1.51	ʊə	0.06
k	3.09	ʤ	0.60	a	1.45		
w	2.81	ʧ	0.41	ɒ	1.37		
z	2.46	θ	0.37	ɔː	1.24		
v	2.00	ʒ	0.10	uː	1.13		

Just remember: if you are looking at both linguistic and non-linguistic factors quantitatively, then your sample size will have to be big enough to reflect this. If you have relatively little speech from any one speaker, it becomes very likely that differences between individuals will 'swamp' differences between, for example, different following contexts. If you have fewer than the desirable number of tokens in some cells, you can still proceed, but your generalisations should be appropriately hedged.

EXERCISES

Exercise 1

Read the following extract from a paper by Barbora Skarabela and colleagues. The paper examines what the role of shared attention between child and caregiver is in how children acquire linguistic norms in Inuktitut.

1 What is the linguistic variable in this study?
2 What are the variants that realise the variable?

Subject and object omission is frequent and licensed in Inuktitut. This means that all cases of argument omission that we consider are grammatical, and hence are not the consequence of a failure to acquire the target grammar. Indeed, it was the study of null subject languages that highlighted the importance of the wider discourse context to argument realisation in general (Allen et al., 2008).

In order to explore the role of joint attention in how children express new referents, we restricted our analysis to third person arguments only. We excluded first and second person arguments for two reasons: (1) they refer to speech participants 'I' and 'you' and are as such considered always given (Chafe, 1976; DuBois, 1987); (2) they typically represent referents that are produced in the presence of joint attention because interlocutors are usually attending to each other and are aware of that attention. In contrast, third person arguments can refer to new or old information and the referents can be produced in the presence or absence of joint attention.

Third person referents can occur as omitted arguments, as in (6); as demonstratives, as in (7a–b); or as lexical nouns, as in (8). There are no third person pronouns in Inuktitut.

(6) *Ø Ani-si-ju.*
Ø go.out-INCP-PAR.3SS
'(He) is leaving now.' (spoken by Paul's mother)

(7a) *Su-sima-jur-u-na?*
do.what-PERF-PAR.3SS-this.one-ABS.SG
'What did this do?' (spoken by Elijah's mother)

(7b) *U-na* *savi-jua-nngua-lik?*
this.one-ABS.SG knife-big-imitation-item.having
'This one has a big knife?' (spoken by Elijah's mother)

(8) *Itiga-alu-tit* *siura-alu-u-mmata.*
foot-EMPH-ABS.2sdu sand-EMPH-COP-CTG.3PS
'Because your feet are sandy.' (spoken by Elijah's mother)

We included all three categories of referring expressions in this study.

Source: Skarabela, Allen and Scott-Phillips (2013: 8)

Exercise 2

Go back to the extract in Chapter 1 (Nick Wilson's Scottish rugby team data). Consider the pronunciations of *to* or *with* that are represented in the transcript. How often do these alternations apply to these words or similar words? On the basis of that, say what you consider the variable to be, what the envelope of variation is and what the variants are.

Consider the use of personal pronouns in the extracts, especially *we*, *you* and *ye*. Let's call these the variants realising the (you) variable. Define an envelope of variation for the variable. What kinds of linguistic factors seem to be relevant to the use of the different variables? You may also want to draw on your own knowledge about extra-linguistic factors that are likely to be relevant.

References

Baranowski, Maciej. 2007. *Phonological Variation and Change in the Dialect of Charleston, South Carolina*. Durham, NC: Duke University Press.

Buchstaller, Isabelle. 2014. *Quotatives: New Trends and Sociolinguistic Implications*. Oxford: Wiley Blackwell.

D'Arcy, Alexandra. 2005. *Like: Syntax and Development*. Unpublished PhD thesis, University of Toronto.

Dines, Elizabeth R. 1980. Variation in discourse – "and stuff like that". *Language in Society* 9: 13–31.

Fry, D.B. 1947. The frequency of occurrence of speech sounds in Southern English. *Archives Néerlandaises de Phonétique Expérimentales* 20: 103–106.

Guy, Gregory. 1980. Variation in the group and the individual: The case of final stop deletion. In William Labov (ed.) *Locating Language in Time and Space*. New York: Academic Press, 1–36.

Holmes, Janet. 1988. *Sort of* in New Zealand women's and men's speech. *Studia Linguistica* 42: 85–121.

Holmes, Janet. 1989. Review of Bent Preisler, *Linguistic Sex Roles in Conversation*. *Language in Society* 18: 293–299.

Labov, William, Sharon Ash and Charles Boberg. 2006. *The Atlas of North American English*. Berlin and New York: Mouton de Gruyter.

Lavandera, Beatriz R. 1978. Where does the sociolinguistic variable stop? *Language in Society* 7: 171–182.

Meyerhoff, Miriam. 1994. Sounds pretty ethnic, eh?: A pragmatic particle in New Zealand English. *Language in Society* 23: 367–388.

Milroy, Lesley. 1987. *Observing and Analyzing Natural Language*. Oxford: Blackwell.

Sankoff, Gillian and Suzanne Evans Wagner. 2006. Age grading in retrograde movement: The inflected future in Montréal French. *University of Pennsylvania Working Papers in Linguistics* 12: 1–14.

Schegloff, Emanuel A. 1988. Discourse as an interactional achievement, II: An exercise in conversation analysis. In Deborah Tannen (ed.) *Linguistics in Context: Connecting*

Observation and Understanding: Lectures From the 1985 LSA/TESOL and NEH Institutes. Norwood, NJ: Ablex, 135–158.

Schegloff, Emanuel A. 1993. Reflections on quantification in the study of conversation. *Research on Language and Social Interaction* 26: 99–128.

Schiffrin, Deborah. 1987. *Discourse Markers.* Cambridge and New York: Cambridge University Press.

Skarabela, Barbora, Shanley E.M. Allen and Thomas C. Scott-Phillips. 2013. Joint attention helps explain why children omit new referents. *Journal of Pragmatics* 56: 5–14.

Tannen, Deborah (ed.) 1988. *Linguistics in Context: Connecting Observation and Understanding: Lectures From the 1985 LSA/TESOL and NEH Institutes.* Norwood, NJ: Ablex.

Taylor, Ann and Susan Pintzuk. 2012. Verb order, object position and information status in Old English. *York Papers in Linguistics* 12: 29–52.

Tollfree, Laura. 1999. South East London English: Discrete versus continuous modelling of consonantal reduction. In Paul Foulkes and Gerry J. Docherty (eds) *Urban Voices: Accent Studies in the British Isles.* London: Arnold, 163–184.

Walker, James A. 2010. *Variation in Linguistic Systems.* London: Routledge.

Wells, John C. 1982. *Accents of English 1.* Cambridge: Cambridge University Press.

Further reading

Labov, William. 1972. *Sociolinguistic Patterns.* Philadelphia, PA: University of Pennsylvania Press.

Labov, William. 1978. Where does the linguistic variable stop?: A response to Beatriz Lavandera. In Richard Bauman and Joel Sherzer (eds) *Working Papers in Sociolinguistics* 44. Austin: Southwest Educational Development Laboratory.

Tagliamonte, Sali A. 2012. *Variationist Sociolinguistics: Change, Observation, Interpretation.* Oxford: Wiley-Blackwell.

Walker, James A. 2010. *Variation in Linguistic Systems.* London: Routledge.

Wolfram, Walter A. 1991. The linguistic variable: Fact and fantasy. *American Speech* 66: 22–32.

3 Ethics and archiving

Over the last decade or so, the business of applying for and being granted approval to do your research by an ethics board has become an integral part of sociolinguistic research.

The kinds of formal routines you have to go through to obtain ethics approval for your work will depend on the local culture – in some places the processes are shaped by legislative requirements, in some they are shaped by the likelihood of lawsuits, in some they are shaped by specific historic events.

It's impossible for us to cover the wide range of procedures that exist worldwide for gaining ethics approval when working with human participants. But even though the ways in which ethics approval is institutionalised or devolved to individual researchers may differ, they share a concern about researchers' behaviour. So this chapter will focus on exploring the behaviours that are generally considered to be ethical and decent ways of behaving, and that might be relevant to the kind of data collection sociolinguists are likely to undertake.

Because we engage in these behaviours as professionals, it's not surprising that some of the professional organisations that sociolinguists might belong to have useful guidelines for ethical conduct in research situations. So we will also touch on some of the guidelines and resources that are available from those sources.

Finally, we believe that one of the most important decisions that every linguist needs to spend some time thinking about is how the data they collect will be safeguarded or archived for future use. So in this chapter, we also consider some of the choices you might make with regard to archiving your data.

Informed consent when recording

Publicly broadcast talk is fair game for the sociolinguist. If your topic can be addressed with data sampled from public sources such as the internet or other broadcast media, then lucky you. You may have limited ethical issues to deal with.

ETHICS AND THE INTERNET

We don't want to give the impression that the internet is some kind of lawless Wild West. Using data from closed or moderated sites on the internet does raise some issues with obtaining consent and King (2011) discusses these and explains how they can be addressed. Chapter 7 discusses other issues associated with using corpora from the internet and if you want to use data taken from there, you should read that chapter next.

But whenever you record someone yourself you need to make sure that they have given you permission first. Their agreement must constitute what's called *informed consent*, which means that they fully understand what you're doing, what you're going to use the recording for and how and when they can opt out if they want to.

Never record people surreptitiously. Why not? Well, obviously, if you do, they can't possibly have given informed consent. Even if you're pretty sure that your friends and family will be glad to help you out, they have a right to know before you start recording them and they have a right to ask you not to use some or all of what you might record from them. Some people believe that, in the quest to bag the most naturalistic speech possible, it is okay to gain some kind of blanket consent from friends allowing you to record at some unspecified stage in the future. Most professional ethics guidelines do not endorse this. Moreover, in some places, recording someone without their knowledge is not only unethical, it's also illegal. Many jurisdictions have quite strict regulations about recording phone or digital communications (and, unless you are a member of the Five Eyes network, you may come a cropper if you fail to observe these in both the letter and spirit of the law).

DIVERSITY IN LEGAL CONSTRAINTS

The content of this box is not intended as legal advice. It is merely included to illustrate the diversity of legal constraints operating in the area of recording.

The US State of Pennsylvania has what is called a *two-party consent* law. 'Pennsylvania makes it a crime to intercept or record a telephone call or conversation unless all parties to the conversation consent.'[1] This is the case in 12 US states (at the time of writing). In most US states, one-party consent applies – that means as long as one of the participants in the conversation is making the recording, it is legal to record a conversation without other interlocutors' knowledge.

In the UK, several pieces of legislation currently cover recording of telephone and digital communications, so the legal situation is more complex. Fairly simplistically, it seems that in the UK it's legal to record your own phone conversation without telling the other party *but* if you plan to share the recording with anyone else, then you must get the agreement of other participant(s). Effectively, this means that if you were recording off the phone or other communication system in the UK with the intention of using it for linguistic analysis, you have a legal as well as moral obligation to clear it with everyone concerned. That's because your results will be shared with others, and as a good scientist you would be willing to let another bona fide researcher check your analysis against the original recording.

Most universities or colleges in the West require us to devise a form or information sheet that explains the purpose of the research and a consent form that is signed by everyone who agrees to be recorded. The information sheet stays with the participant; the consent form goes into long-term storage.

The purpose of the information sheet is to explain to participants why you're doing your research, who is responsible for conducting it, how you will use the data, how you will store the data and how you will ensure that the data is confidential. When you review the information and consent forms with people, you need to do it in a leisurely way so that participants can be sure they have understood everything and can ask any questions they might want to ask.

Sometimes it may be acceptable to record yourself explaining the purposes of the research to interested parties and keep a copy of your explanation and your participants' questions and agreement in lieu of a signed form.

The information sheet doesn't need to be too detailed about what exactly you are going to analyse for your study. It is also usually the place where you can reassure people that their identity will be confidential. Usually that's achieved by giving a pseudonym or speaker code to the people you record, and storing information about who the actual speaker is apart from the recording itself. Some people may not want their recording to be anonymised when you use it for teaching and research – this might be because they want to retain clear 'ownership' of the information they have passed on to you (this can be the case when you are doing research on language in endangered or minority communities). If you are doing video recording and they agree to allow their image to be shown for teaching or research purposes, this may vitiate any steps towards anonymity.

Finally, the information sheet and consent form need to make it clear that participation is voluntary and that participants are absolutely sure that they agree to take part in your study out of their own free will. Your information sheet should tell people how to access you, the researcher, and the research findings by at least giving your contact details at the end of the form. There may be practical restrictions on when someone can opt out of your project, but in principle it should always be possible. For instance, suppose your data has already been written up and submitted for marking as course work; at that point, it may not be feasible for the data from someone's recording to be excised. (We have put some examples of information sheets and consent forms from our work on this book's website. They may be useful as models for your own application.)

Your department, school or college probably has models for consent forms or information sheets available for you to adapt to your study. If your data collection plans, questionnaires, interview protocols, etc. have to be approved by an official ethics committee, this can take months, so it's a good idea to get started with it as soon as possible. That's one of the reasons we have included it early in this discussion of doing sociolinguistics.

ETHICS SELF-AUDITS

An admirable model is the self-audit ethics checklist developed and administered by the School of Social and Political Science at the University of Edinburgh. The three-step self-assessment process emphasises the individual researcher's responsibility to engage in ethical research practices and it sends only projects that have been identified as higher risk or problematic to independent ethics review. The way the system is administered and the three levels of forms can be viewed at the SSPS website (search: *research ethics SSPS Edinburgh*).

ANONYMOUS RECORDINGS FOR WORK ON SIGN LANGUAGE AND GESTURE

Video recordings of people using sign language and studies of gesture accompanying speech cannot be anonymised fully without losing vital information encoded around and on the face. These issues were resolved in the British Sign Language Corpus Project, where recordings were also made available on an open access website (search: *British sign language corpus project*). If you would like to see and use these information sheets and consent forms as a model you can go to this book's website.

Some institutions may require that you not use video from such projects in public presentations of your research, but others will allow participants the final say. You will need to check this out locally.

Useful resources you can draw on

We have found the professional guidelines available here very helpful:

1 American Anthropological Association Code of Ethics [*Extremely helpful in outlining rights and responsibilities for all parties in longer-term research, or research where the researcher is a member in good standing of the community they are examining.*]
2 British Association for Applied Linguistics – Recommendations on Good Practice [*Useful starting point for most sociolinguistic research.*]
3 British Psychological Society – Code of Conduct [*Well-suited for experiments, including those testing not only linguistic skills but other aspects of cognition and perception.*]
4 The Linguistic Society of America Ethics Statement [*Very useful as a basic, very general, ethical framework for linguists of all subdisciplines.*]

Archiving and long-term storage

A big change in recent years in the way linguists work is that archiving has become a central concern. The researcher's concerns about the storage and use of their data extend beyond the duration of their own project and their own use of the recordings they've made. There's a bit of a tension between whether archives should be open access or controlled – in particular, controlled by the speakers themselves or their descendants. There is some interesting debate on this on the PARADISEC blog on the PARADISEC homepage (PARADISEC is the Pacific and Regional Archive for Digital Sources in Endangered Cultures). But it's clear that the current norms in linguistics are to archive everything as well and as long as possible so data is not lost to the communities of speakers or to future researchers. This means thinking about what will be good file labelling conventions for audio/video files and for the related/derived files you create based on them and what kinds of meta-data you will associate with all your files.

Usually personal information about the people in your recordings will be treated as confidential information. This means it will be kept in a safe place with restricted access. Most people using a corpus will see only pseudonyms of the contributors or speaker ID codes and this will be associated with general demographic information about age, sex, residence, but not details that might uniquely identify them. These ethical guidelines may, of course, be suspended by the speakers themselves: people sometimes want very much to stake their ownership of a story or an experience.

Once you have thought about all of this, made the necessary decisions and prepared all the material, you can finally start collecting your data. That is the topic of the next chapter, where we talk about the business of making contact with the people you might like to record.

EXERCISES

The following exercises are adapted from ones created by Yuni Kim (University of Manchester), and are reproduced with her permission.

Read the scenarios and say whether you think the researchers' actions are ethical. Why, or why not?

Nicole has a part-time job at a nursery. She frequently hears the children there using interesting sentence structures, which she has started writing down informally in a notebook. Several children have shown very interesting paths of development, which she would like to write her dissertation on. She plans to use her notes to date plus several months of continued observation at work.

Karen wants to study the old-time Charleston dialect. She rings up a nursing home in Charleston explaining her project, and the person answering the phone responds enthusiastically, saying that the residents enjoy having visitors. Karen arranges a time to meet one of the nurses, who will introduce her to some of the residents. She prepares a list of questions (hoping to record both a wordlist and spontaneous speech) and brings along a portable digital recorder.

Russell is interested in linguistic politeness strategies that Londoners use when asked for directions to a place whose location they are unfamiliar with. He decides to approach people on the street with a recorder in his pocket, since it will be a quick and formulaic interaction (no possible harm to the subject) and he doesn't think he can remember the exact wordings well enough to accurately write them down afterwards.

Note

1 Retrieved from www.dmlp.org/legal-guide/pennsylvania/pennsylvania-recording-law (last accessed 2 December 2013). And to ensure that people cannot forget they are being recorded on the phone, it is sometimes required that you play a beep while recording.

References

King, Brian. 2011. Language, sexuality and place: The view from cyberspace. *Gender and Language*. 5: 1–30.

www.dmlp.org/legal-guide/pennsylvania/pennsylvania-recording-law (accessed 2 December 2013).

Further reading

Johnstone, Barbara. 2000. *Qualitative Methods in Sociolinguistics*. Oxford: Oxford University Press.

King, Brian. 2011. Language, sexuality and place: The view from cyberspace. *Gender and Language*. 5: 1–30.

Thieberger, Nicholas. 2011. *The Oxford Handbook of Linguistic Fieldwork*. Oxford: Oxford University Press. Especially Chapters 19–21 by Keren Rice, Paul Newman and Monica Macaulay.

4 Sampling techniques and gaining access to speakers

Once you know what you want to find out, you have to ask yourself a very important question: will you be able to access the data you need to answer your question? If you plan to collect new data rather than using a corpus, accessing speakers and finding a way to sample the community are crucial.

Gaining access to speakers and entering the community

Gaining access to participants and entering a community can be quite a challenge. You should always have several backup plans in place and, ideally, test out several ways into the community. Always stay active and keep the ball rolling. Never sit and wait for that one contact who promised to get back to you. Explore other options in the meantime.

THE SPEECH COMMUNITY

What exactly a speech community is, is much debated. Some definitions focus on linguistic criteria, others focus on social aspects. If this becomes an issue in your research, consult some of these sources to follow up on the debate: Labov (1972), Bucholtz (1999), Patrick (2002), Schilling (2013).

There are several ways to contact speakers in a specific community. If you are a member of that community yourself, you can use your insider status to contact individual speakers: a friend, a family member or a former workmate. If you are not a member of the community in question but you know members in that community, you may be able to contact them.

1. A friend or acquaintance. The 'friend of a friend' technique (Milroy and Gordon 2003: 32) has proven to be very useful in data collection. You ask your friend to introduce you to people s/he knows in the community of interest. Ideally, they will in turn introduce you to more people.
2. An official community 'broker'. The term 'broker' is often used to describe people with official community status such as priests, teachers and community leaders. Brokers can facilitate community access tremendously as they have very wide networks. In fact, in some cases it may be impossible to do research without these people's approval. Religious leaders or teachers are essential gate-keepers to certain communities. Nevertheless, there can be hazards in working with a broker. Because brokers may hold positions of social respect, they may be associated with higher degrees of formality, and this association may be extended to the researcher. People with official community status such as priests, teachers and community leaders are also more likely to introduce you to people within their immediate social networks and these may be predominantly speakers who use standard speech styles. So be aware of the kind of networks brokers are introducing you to and try to branch out if this doesn't fully match your goals.
3. If you do not have contacts in a community, you will have to find a way to access speakers in that community yourself. Find a contact by talking to, writing or e-mailing a member of the community you want to study. Some points of contact are particularly worth exploring as they have well-established networks in place that you can use, for example schools, churches, societies or internet interest groups (the 'brokers' mentioned above). Search the internet to find initial points of contact. If you have a clearly delimited task, e.g. filling in a short survey, contacting complete strangers may be appropriate. Places where people gather to spend their free time or social network sites offer good opportunities to contact people. Alternatively, you can become a member of a community yourself. For example, if you're interested in speech and interaction patterns among members of a sports team or a book club, join a sports team or a book club. Volunteer in the community! Miriam got a lot of exposure to very vernacular speech by working in a kitchen in Bequia, and Nick Wilson's rugby data (Chapters 1–2) was collected in the team Nick joined for his fieldwork.

Whichever way you enter the community, always remember that the way you enter may shape your role there. You should have a simple and honest story about who you are and what you do. Also, try not to get too reliant on and identified with one specific group or network within a community. Explore other groups as well. This will enable you to get a wider picture of the linguistic situation in a speech community. Eckert (2000) recommends a useful strategy that keeps you moving between networks: construct a random sample of community members and return to the list at intervals to make contacts with new groups.

Success when making contacts depends a lot on common-sense considerations. Be sincere, polite and interested and do what you can to prepare for meetings and making new friends. Find out about your participants' interests: local football teams, community events, history and most importantly how they talk about their language (for example, do they consider it a language or a dialect). Find out what you can about local values, norms and community structure (see Chapter 11 on 'emic' categories) so you can conduct your research in an atmosphere of mutual respect.

Samples and sampling techniques

How you gain access to participants is intimately tied up with the type of sample you aim for, i.e. the people you collect data from and on which you base your analysis. Below we will outline several types of samples, and the techniques that are usually used to collect data from such a sample. Your decision about sample size and sampling technique depends very much on your research question and the kind of community you're interested in.

Random sampling versus proportionate stratified random sampling

Truly random sampling is hardly ever used in sociolinguistics. It may be an appropriate sampling method when the goal of a study is to provide a description of variation in a city or a town. When selecting your speakers, you will have to use a principled method of selection that gives everyone living there an equal chance of being chosen as a participant in your study. Such a selection method is normally based on some form of existing list of the relevant population (for example telephone or electoral registers). Participants are then selected randomly from those lists. Finding truly representative lists and ensuring selected participants take part in the study is an art in itself. There is also no guarantee that you will tap into speakers in all categories you're interested in. This is particularly the case if segments of the population are unevenly represented, e.g. young people on electoral rolls.

This is where a proportionate stratified random sample has an advantage. Such a sample still uses random selection techniques but the population is divided into strata, i.e. groups of individuals that may be important to the study. A random sample is then collected from each stratum and combined with the samples from other strata to form the full sample. Tagliamonte (2006: 23) proposes that as a minimum requirement a sample should be representative on the basis of age, sex, social class and/or educational level, since these variables prove over and over to be significant in studies of urban speech communities (see Chapter 11 on 'etic' categories). This may be too ambitious for a student project but it's something to be aware of.

RAPID AND ANONYMOUS SURVEYS

These are brief, short-contact anonymous surveys that usually feature randomised speaker selection. Speakers are normally unaware that their speech is the focus of study, and we find out relatively little about the speakers we're polling (except for characteristics such as sex and age that – by and large – can be detected visually). Surveys are conducted in public places such as department stores, streets, coffee shops, etc. Eliciting data in this manner can be done through observation, that is, the researcher places him-/herself in a location where observation of language can take place, e.g. at a service counter or a table near the cash register in a café. Alternatively, the researcher can prompt speech. Gardner-Chloros' (1991) study of codeswitching in a Strasburg department store is an example of the passive technique, while Labov's classic study of language use in three socially stratified department stores in New York City (Labov 1972: 43–69) is an example of prompted speech. Labov randomly selected employees and asked questions that elicited the phrase *fourth floor* twice, which gave four tokens of the variable (r). Usually, audio recording does not take place, partly to avoid ethical issues. This technique requires the researcher to be quick and do several things at the same time: assess the social characteristics of the speaker; make an 'on-the-spot' analysis of the speech sample; note down what was heard. This works well if the variables selected for study are highly targeted and salient, e.g. your prompt always elicits the word *street* and you are interested in whether people say [stɹit] or [ʃtɹit] (see Labov 1984).

Judgement sampling

Judgement sampling is frequently used in sociolinguistics. First, you identify the kinds of speakers you're interested in (e.g. male and female adolescents at a middle-class high school). Then, you collect data from a number of speakers in each group: males, females; possibly also different age groups and ethnicities, if applicable. You should try to capture the basic demographics of whatever population you decide to investigate. This may mean investigating locally important groupings (e.g. nerds, jocks, townies, etc.) in addition to or instead of macro-social categories, such as speaker sex and social class. You'll need to conduct background research and observe for a while before making decisions about categorisations. Also find out about people's attitudes and sense of identity to help you in making decisions about community groupings. Making decisions about social categories is not as straightforward as one may think – Schilling (2013: 46–54) problematises some social categories. As we argue above, it is a good idea to create a data grid (see Chapter 2) and fill the cells, either (a) randomly, (b) by your own judgement or (c) by advancing from speaker to speaker through a social network. Keep in mind, though, that from a statistical point of view a judgement sample is not truly representative as it was not selected randomly. However, linguistic behaviour is much more uniform than other social behaviour (e.g. people's fitness routines, their holiday preferences, etc.), so even a judgement sample allows a certain degree of generalisability (see Schilling 2013: 33).

Social networks and communities of practice

Our assumption so far has been that you want to conduct a study of a speech community. However, there are other frameworks for viewing multiple speakers: social networks and communities of practice (see Dodsworth 2013 for a thorough comparison of these frameworks). They differ from the speech community framework in various respects, for example in how many speakers are considered, the methods used to study them and the assumptions researchers make about social interaction and language. In the speech community framework, composite data is usually investigated and compared across demographic categories. Thinking about sampling is therefore of utmost importance. It's a good approach to use when you are interested in the global distribution of a variable across several external categories within a city or a town.

However, if your focus is highly specific or if you want to find out more about how language is socially embedded within a community, work informed by the traditions of ethnography (see Chapter 6) may be more suited to your research question. Few sociolinguists devote the time for a genuine ethnography, but the practice of immersing yourself in a community for some period of time has been used for studying networks and communities of practice. We will introduce these here briefly. If you work in one of these traditions, it is almost inevitable that you will collect naturally occurring, spontaneously produced speech (see Chapter 6).

The network approach focuses on some pre-existing social network, rather than abstract social categories such as social class or age. Social network analysis finds out who people interact with and how these patterns of interaction relate to language; it is particularly good at shedding light on how features spread or don't spread from person to person and network to network. Researchers attach themselves to such a network and often move from contact to contact using the 'friend of a friend' technique. As you get to know more people in a network, you may become a participant observer within this network of friends and acquaintances (so the work shifts subtly into a more ethnographic mode). What makes such a study a social network study, rather than just a convenient way to collect data, is that some aspect of the structure of the network will also be investigated. Often, an attempt is made to quantify, or at least visualise, this structure. Here are some examples.

Mackeigan and Muth (2006a, b) conducted a social network analysis of Tzotzil Mayan colour terms. They investigated a social network of weavers in Chiapas, Mexico. Some of the weavers collect thread from a central location and then go back into their communities and pass on the thread to other people. Mackeigan and Muth have shown how certain forms of colour terms seem to be transmitted within particular groups within this network. The details of this shall not concern us here, but we'd like to point out the complexity of the network, shown in Figure 4.1.

When attempting to correlate linguistic data with network structure, some measure will have to be found that allows researchers to do this. If the number of people is limited and the linguistic data is not too complex, visual representation may suffice (see Mackeigan and Muth 2006b: 33). However, if a statistical analysis is to be conducted, you can assign a social network score to every individual. Such a score is often a reflection of how dense and multiplex a person's social network ties are. For example, Milroy assigned participants network scores from zero to five and included these in her statistical analyses (Milroy 1987: 141–142). Such a score may be based on participant observation, interview data or a survey.

A social network is still a structure that is, to a certain extent, objective rather than subjective. Sociolinguists are very much interested in how individuals see the world from an even more local perspective. We have, during the last two decades, made increasing use of a construct that allows exactly this: the community of practice (Eckert 1989; Wenger 1998).

Have another look at Figure 4.1. Individuals 1, 2, 3 6, 7, 8, 9, 10 and 13 seem to have dense network connections; so do individuals 27, 28, 50, 60 and 61. To find out whether they are a community of practice we would have to show that there is mutual engagement between all community members, that they're working towards a jointly negotiated enterprise and that there is a shared repertoire. These are the three essential criteria by which communities of practice are defined. Members in a community of practice all interact with each other and they do this by orienting to shared norms and attitudes. For example, a group of close friends may be a community of practice but people who all happen to come together in a carriage on a commuter train are probably not.

Two more aspects are of particular importance in the community of practice approach. First, the community of practice is a useful concept to bridge global and local concerns and to do quantitative as well as qualitative work, i.e. qualitative sociolinguistics or discourse analysis (Holmes and Meyerhoff 1999). You may describe the community of practice and simultaneously locate it in the wider social context which gives it meaning and distinctiveness. This may mean considering larger social categories, such as social class and gender, or working with categories that make sense to informants and are not imposed by the researcher.

Second, the community of practice approach focuses on linguistic (and other) practice, repertoires and values in a small community of speakers, on the social meanings of variables and on how they are used to build up speaker identity.

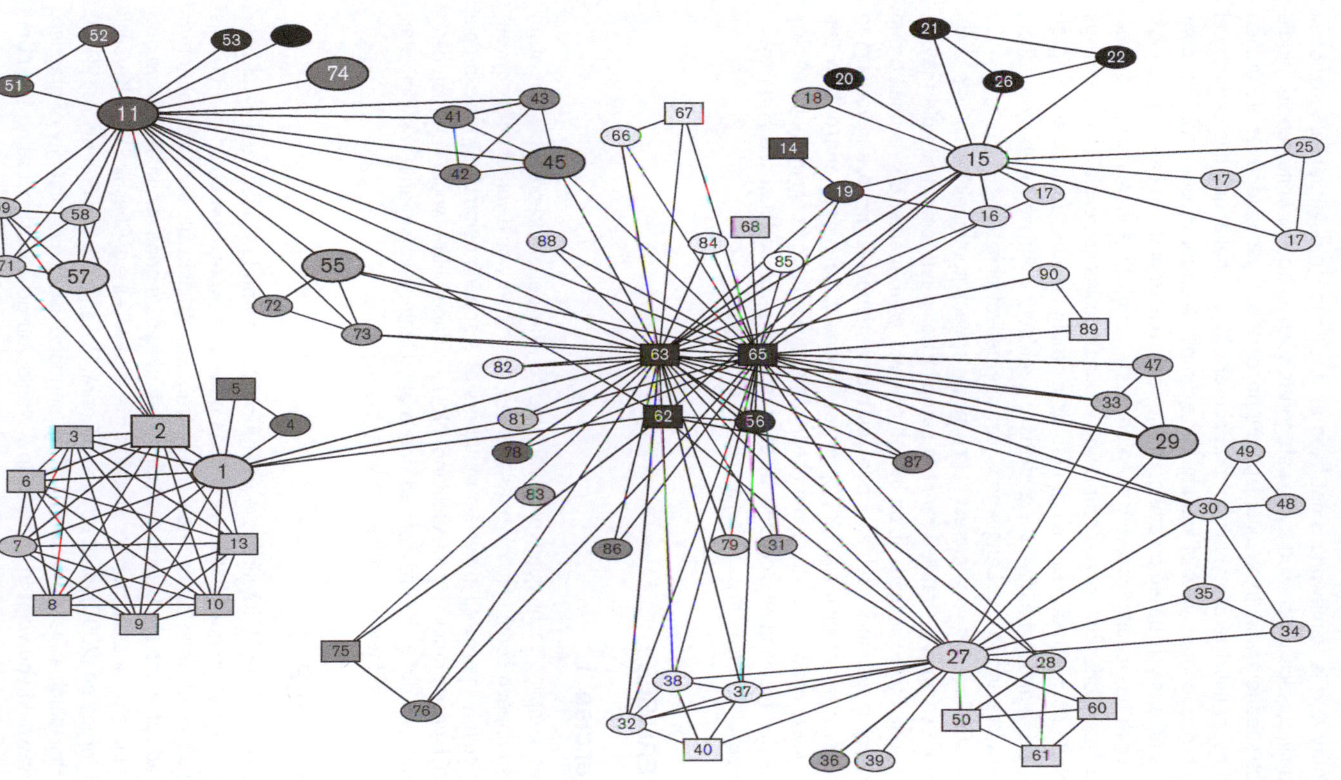

Figure 4.1 Thread passing network

Source: Mackeigan and Muth (2006a), unpublished figure reproduced with permission

Identity, in this framework, is not fixed as it is in much quantitative, variationist sociolinguistics, which works with categories such as adults, white people, middle class speakers, and, to an extent, presupposes that these categories are unified and essential. The community of practice approach challenges this categorical and homogeneous view of identity. For example, Mendoza-Denton (2008) conducts an analysis based on ethnographic research among two Latina girl gangs. Her work has resulted in a very deep understanding of the lives and oppositional social categories of the two groups. She was able to link and explain the meanings behind choices in domains as diverse as clothing colours, Spanish and English use, art, makeup, hairstyles – and that's precisely what we mean by practice, repertoires and values. Language is just one aspect of it.

In conclusion, if your interest is in a larger speech community, such as a town, random sampling, stratified random sampling or a judgement sample may be best suited to your needs. If, on the other hand, your interest is in a small group of specific speakers, such as a book club or a friendship group, and you aim to uncover how variation and other practice is locally meaningful and/or how this practice is used to construct identities, immersive ethnographic methods of data collection focusing on a community of practice may be better suited. You may, of course, also decide to combine sampling techniques.

EXERCISES

Exercise 1

What sampling technique would you use for the general representation of an urban speech community? What sampling technique would you use if you were particularly interested in certain members of a speech community, for example the Chinese community in Auckland, New Zealand? How would your sampling techniques differ if you'd noticed that many Chinese immigrants work in retail, often running their own coffee shop or bistro?

Exercise 2

The community of practice is a useful concept to bridge global and local concerns and to do quantitative as well as qualitative work. How could one do this in practice? Use as an example a relatively well-studied city such as London or Philadelphia and start reading articles that give you a good quantitative base and some useful ideas for further study at the local level, e.g. Cheshire, Fox, Kerswill and Torgersen (2008) for London and Labov, Rosenfelder and Fruehwald (2013) for Philadelphia. Devise a plan to study language use in a community of practice. What would you want to study? How would you go about accessing the community? And why could it be important to do such a study?

Exercise 3

Consider the beginning of the methods section of an article by Schleef, Meyerhoff and Clark (2011), which investigates the acquisition of variation by Polish immigrant adolescents in London, England and Edinburgh, Scotland.

3.1 Data collection

Our study was conducted in two high schools, one in Edinburgh and one in London, where recent immigration has led to an increase in the number of non-locally born students. We interviewed both Polish migrants and teenagers from local British families so as to have a benchmark of the local norms that the teenage migrants were exposed to most frequently. Students volunteered for the study following a presentation from the research assistant about the general nature of the tasks; they were interviewed in friendship pairs in order to facilitate the most casual atmosphere possible given the school-based setting for the interviews (Milroy and Gordon 2003: 66).

The Edinburgh sample consisted of 16 Polish migrants (8 males, 8 females) and 21 Edinburgh-born teenagers. The London sample consisted of 21 Polish migrants (8 males, 13 females) and 24 London-born teenagers. The Polish teenagers were all aged between 12 and 18 with a mean age of 14 in both the London and Edinburgh samples. The length of time that each adolescent had spent in the UK varied from seven months to five years, with an average in both cities of two and a half years in the UK. A locally born female research assistant carried out sociolinguistic interviews in both Edinburgh and London respectively. Recordings were made using the M-AUDIO Microtrack II 2-channel mobile digital recorder and SHURE head-set microphones. The interviews were transcribed orthographically using ELAN (<http://www.lat-mpi.eu/tools/elan/>), resulting in a time-aligned corpus of around 200 000 words.

Source: Schleef, Meyerhoff and Clark (2011)

How was the community (most likely) accessed? What sampling technique was used? Why? What limitations might the researchers have encountered when attempting to collect a large sample of Polish adolescents? Why were English/Scottish students included as well?

References

Bucholtz, Mary. 1999. 'Why be normal?' Language and identity practice in a community of nerd girls. *Language in Society* 28: 203–223.

Cheshire, Jenny, Sue Fox, Paul Kerswill and Eivind Torgersen. 2008. Ethnicity, friendship network and social practices as the motor of dialect change: Linguistic innovation in London. *Sociolinguistica* 22: 1–23.

Dodsworth, Robin. 2013. Speech communities, social networks, and communities of practice. In Janet Holmes and Kirk Hazen (eds) *Research Methods in Sociolinguistics.* Oxford: Wiley Blackwell, 262–275.

Eckert, Penelope. 1989. *Jocks and Burnouts: Social Categories and Identity in the High School.* New York: Teachers College Press.

Eckert, Penelope. 2000. *Linguistic Variation as Social Practice.* Malden, MA: Blackwell.

Gardner-Chloros, Penelope. 1991. *Language Selection and Switching in Strasburg.* Oxford: Clarendon Press.

Holmes, Janet and Miriam Meyerhoff. 1999. The community of practice: Theories and methodologies in language and gender research. *Language in Society* 28: 173–183.

Labov, William. 1972. *Sociolinguistic Patterns.* Philadelphia, PA: University of Pennsylvania Press.

Labov, William. 1984. Research methods of the project on linguistic change and variation. In John Baugh and Joel Sherzer (eds) *Language in Use: Readings in Sociolinguistics.* Englewood Cliffs, NJ: Prentice Hall, 28–53.

Labov, William, Ingrid Rosenfelder and Josef Fruehwald. 2013. One hundred years of sound change in Philadelphia: Linear incrementation, reversal, and reanalysis. *Language* 89: 30–65.

Mackeigan, Terri and Stephen Q. Muth. 2006a. The structures of conceptual change. XXVI *International Sunbelt Social Network Conference*, Vancouver BC, April 2006.

Mackeigan, Terri and Stephen Q. Muth. 2006b. A grammatical network of Tzotzil Mayan colour terms. In Carole P. Biggam and Christian J. Kay (eds) *Progress in Colour Studies: Vol. 1 Language and Culture.* Amsterdam: John Benjamins, 25–36.

Mendoza-Denton, Norma. 2008. *Homegirls: Language and Cultural Practice among Latina Youth Gangs.* Malden, MA: Blackwell.

Milroy, Lesley. 1987. *Language and Social Networks.* 2nd edition. Oxford: Blackwell.

Milroy, Lesley and Matthew Gordon. 2003. *Sociolinguistics: Method and Interpretation.* Malden and Oxford: Blackwell.

Patrick, Peter. 2002. The speech community. In J.K. Chambers, Peter Trudgill and Natalie Schilling-Estes (eds) *The Handbook of Language Variation and Change.* Malden, MA: Blackwell, 573–597.

Schilling, Natalie. 2013. *Sociolinguistic Fieldwork.* Cambridge: Cambridge University Press.

Schleef, Erik, Miriam Meyerhoff and Lynn Clark. 2011. Teenagers' acquisition of variation: A comparison of locally-born and migrant teens' realisation of English (ing) in Edinburgh and London. *English World-Wide* 32: 206–236.

Tagliamonte, Sali A. 2006. *Analysing Sociolinguistic Variation.* Cambridge: Cambridge University Press.

Wenger, Etienne. 1998. *Communities of Practice.* Cambridge and New York: Cambridge University Press.

Further reading

Dodsworth, Robin. 2013. Speech communities, social networks, and communities of practice. In Janet Holmes and Kirk Hazen (eds) *Research Methods in Sociolinguistics.* Oxford: Wiley Blackwell, 262–275.

Eckert, Penelope. 1989. *Jocks and Burnouts: Social Categories and Identity in the High School.* New York: Teachers College Press.

Holmes, Janet and Miriam Meyerhoff. 1999. The community of practice: Theories and methodologies in language and gender research. *Language in Society* 28: 173–183.

Milroy, Lesley and Matthew Gordon. 2003. *Sociolinguistics: Method and Interpretation.* Malden and Oxford: Blackwell.

Schilling, Natalie. 2013. *Sociolinguistic Fieldwork.* Cambridge: Cambridge University Press.

5 Interviews as a source of data

In the last chapter, we introduced a few of the ways that you can structure your data collection and we also talked about how you can decide who you will record for your study. In this chapter, we look in detail at one of the methods that has become central to sociolinguistics over the years: the sociolinguistic interview. This is a semi-structured event; in Chapters 6 and 7, we will talk about working with unstructured events, such as naturally occurring spontaneous speech or data from the internet or in freely available corpora others have collected.

This chapter begins by asking a simple ontological question: why do we interview? Once that has been addressed, we explore in more detail what a sociolinguistic interview can consist of, and why you might want to guide it so that certain activities are covered. This is influenced by our own experience but also very much by Labov (1984). Anyone starting out in this field would be well-advised to read Labov's chapter – you may not want to sign on with all the goals and assumptions that he outlines there, but it is indispensible as an introduction to why certain methods have been so influential on the field of sociolinguistics. Even if you disagree with some of the premises underlying these methods, an informed critique needs to be thoroughly familiar with where the field has come from.

Finally in this chapter, we'll say a little bit about the mechanics of recording interviews, particularly insofar as the mechanics might impact on the success of your interview.

Why interview?

Interviews have been a favoured mode of data collection among sociolinguists for years. They are a very good, and quick, way to collect quite substantial amounts of talk and they are especially attractive because of the kind of speech that we collect in them. A skilled interviewer can collect substantial amounts of fluent and relatively natural speech from the people s/he is working with.

We set a target of obtaining natural speech because speakers sometimes (consciously or unconsciously) supress aspects of their vernacular in situations

where the focus seems to be on how they are talking rather than simply on what they are talking about. It is, of course, possible to take a completely hands-off approach to collecting speech, and methods of data collection that are informed by the anthropological notion of the participant-observer are discussed in the next chapter.

THE VERNACULAR

The notion of the vernacular is used in slightly different ways by different researchers. We do not use the term with any value judgements attached – by *vernacular* we simply mean the style of speech that people acquired naturally, at home and in talking with peers. One of the functions of formal education, of course, is to convey other norms and styles which we are encouraged to use in appropriate situations (e.g. when writing or speaking in highly formal contexts like a job interview).

It is in pursuit of the vernacular that sociolinguists actively seek out ethical means of obtaining recordings that are as close as possible to how people talk when a researcher isn't around or when someone doesn't feel like the situation is very formal. This is not to say that other forms of speech, like reading aloud, aren't also useful resources, and we'll say more about how they can all be used together shortly.

What is an interview?

> The sociolinguistic interview is considered a failure if the speaker does no more than answer questions.
>
> (Labov 1984: 38)

At its most minimal, an interview involves someone sitting down with a person who fits your target sample, posing them questions or suggesting topics for discussion and recording the questions and answers with good quality equipment. But as the quote above indicates, a good interview goes beyond this. A good interview is co-constructed; this means that the conversational topics are suggested and led by the interviewee as well as by the interviewer. You may start out with a conversation that has a clear question and answer tone to it but you should try and end up in a chat. You can achieve this by sounding natural, by showing interest, by volunteering experience and by responding to new issues and following subjects' interests. Just always remember that the interviewee should speak most of the time, not you.

Some preparation is important, both to make sure that the *ways* you introduce topics and the *kinds* of topics you introduce are likely to flow well for you and for the person you're interviewing. A lot of people prepare a series of topics or modules that experience has shown can be good prompts for narratives or very engaged speech. How kids are disciplined or given freedom now (compared to in the past) are often topics that people have a lot to say about – even so, it's a good idea to have follow-up questions. "Tell me about your family when you were growing up" may not elicit much personal or animated detail. But questions like "When you were a kid, do you remember ever being blamed for something you didn't do?" or "What kinds of games did you and your sister play together?" might be more fruitful.

Labov's interviews have become well-known for use of the so-called 'danger of death' question ("Can you tell me about a situation where you thought you were about to die?") which is used because it often elicits animated narratives. In some cases, the question does not generate the kind of engaged speech that is intended (e.g. if you are interviewing someone like a police officer who is trained to talk about this dispassionately). But this wasn't the only topic he recommended for getting people to speak at length. Other successful topics include things like "Have you ever had a dream that really scared you? A dream that ended up coming true?" or other questions about the supernatural (even sceptics who have no truck with the supernatural usually have quite a lot to say about it!). A set of some of Labov's interview modules are available on our companion website.

Interviews often include some direct questions about language in the community, but generally it's a good idea to leave this discussion to later in an interview so people don't end up focused on and thinking about how they talk. That would be counter-productive to the goal of obtaining speech as close to the vernacular as possible.

So to offer some generalisation: ask short, clear questions and start with general, impersonal questions but then move to more specific and personal questions, as the vernacular is more likely to be used here. Avoid questions that would only result in a *yes* or *no*. Avoid vague questions, leading questions and any topic that may be seen as too personal. So ask questions that make participants talk for long stretches of time. That may require you to learn more about local culture and to get an idea of a participant's point of view. Don't be afraid to ask for elaboration or examples, "what happened then?" It's normally a good idea for the interviewer to behave as naturally as possible, so give backchannelling signals, such as *uhum*, *yeah*, etc. However, you may want to use those sparingly if you are interested in conducting a phonetic analysis of speech later on or if you want to use stretches of speech to create stimuli for perception experiments. Those *uhums* can be a terrible nuisance.

One of the other ways that sociolinguistic interviews differ from recordings of unstructured conversation is that the interview may combine other activities with the conversational component. Understanding the rationale behind the different activities is helpful because it encourages you to think ahead and critique your own research plans.

For instance, you can certainly get a lot of quality data from just chatting with people. But some critical reflection will lead you to realise that not everyone will talk about the same things and you may end up with many tokens of one feature from Person A and very few from Person B. In addition, although you can find out a reasonable amount about the attitudes speakers have to language by asking them directly about language correctness and their awareness of variation in the community, non-linguists may be limited in how well they can articulate their attitudes (one of the things we're doing when we study linguistics is learning how to make explicit what we know). There are various means of ensuring that you get comparable data on production and perception from everyone you interview. Perhaps the most common is to ask people to undertake reading aloud tasks as well as free conversation or to listen to and comment on prepared stimuli.

SOME PRACTICAL ISSUES

Interviews normally take about an hour but they can also be much shorter or longer, depending on the kind of data you're after. Do make sure you collect demographic data about your participants and think carefully about where you conduct your recording session.

You want to get the best sound possible, so tell people where to sit and stay clear of any noisy machines and devices, such as televisions, radios, fans, fridges, clocks, etc. Outdoor noises can be a nuisance; so don't record outdoors or in public spaces, such as cafés. Normally, the best room in the house is the living room – if you can bring yourself to tell your participants to turn off that telly! The most important advice to give is: practice your recording techniques and your 'story' before you conduct your interviews.

Reading aloud

Since Labov's study of New York City English in 1966, the sociolinguistic interview has been associated with conversation and three reading aloud tasks. At one extreme, participants are asked to read a list of minimal pairs (and sometimes to comment on whether they sound the same or different, thereby combining production and perception data). Alternatively, they might be asked to read aloud a list of words in isolation (like a vocabulary list). The third reading aloud task might require them to read a short story or a passage of connected prose.

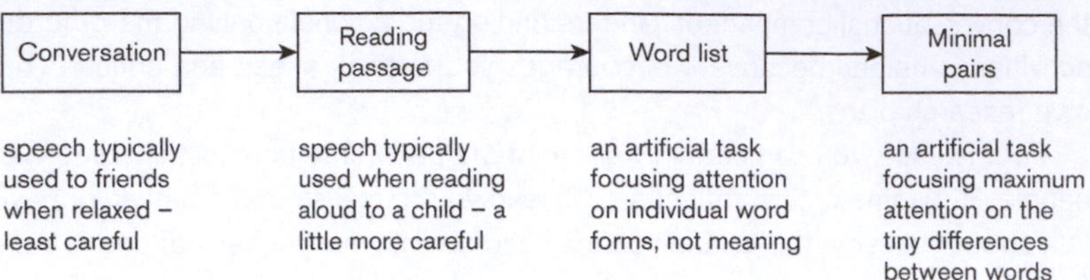

Figure 5.1 Progressively more careful (attention paid to) speech in the tasks of the classic sociolinguistic interview

If they are well-designed, all of these tasks can be invaluable complements to the unscripted conversation that makes up the bulk of the interview. The reading aloud tasks can be construed as constructing a continuum of progressively more careful speech (see Figure 5.1). As complements to conversational speech (especially if you are able to record someone talking not only to you but also to one of the friends or family members), these tasks give you a way of assessing the range of variants individuals are capable of drawing on, and they provide one way of starting to explore awareness of how different variants are deployed by individuals across the group. By treating these tasks as a continuum – along with the conversation – we hope to get a clearer idea of how speakers draw on different forms to create different styles of speech.

DATA AND STYLE

The format we have outlined here is associated most closely with analyses of style as being the speaker's fluctuating levels of attention to speech. Other approaches to analysing style are less inclined to use these kinds of structured tasks. Instead, they are more likely to draw on other forms of data, such as the close qualitative analysis of features in naturally occurring conversation (see Chapter 15 on combining approaches). For example, they might bring together data about how speakers perceive different forms or different ways of talking and the attributes they ascribe to users of those forms with data gained from the different variants speakers spontaneously produce when adopting different interactional stances or routines. For example, if someone often uses one set of forms when they are expressing an ironic demeanour *and* it turns out that listeners have strong associations between use of those forms and speakers who hold down high prestige jobs, and young male speakers, then as a researcher you might be inclined to interrogate in more detail how that community links individual attributes like 'being ironic' with larger social groupings like 'being young' or 'having social prestige'.

WHAT RECORDING MEDIUM TO USE

Traditionally, sociolinguists have been happy to have audio recordings – for many years that was the only feasible option – but increasingly researchers are using video as their basic record. This is essential, of course, if you are working with sign language, but it can also be tremendously helpful for multi-party speech events, or even for one-on-one interviews, since it gives you the option of perhaps looking at how speech, gesture and eye gaze combine to add meaning to a conversation. The extract from Skarabela et al. in Chapter 2 (Exercise 1), for instance, used eye gaze and other markers of joint attention to assess how and when pronouns were used in Inuktitut.

Video recorders are now so small and memory on computers is so cheap that the logistics and storage of recordings are less of an issue. In addition, some of the best software for transcribing also accommodates video (e.g. ELAN, see Chapter 10). What is still a challenge for video is people who are moving around a lot, as in some workplaces.

Researchers do not always follow the same ordering of activities in a sociolinguistic interview. A lot of people start with the most structured activities like reading aloud, then deliberately shift the frame of the interview to something more casual by saying something like "Now that the business side of things is over . . .". On the other hand, we know some people who ask speakers to do reading aloud tasks after the conversational component of the interview is over. Again, this sets the tasks off from the conversation.

In fact, talking about 'the' interview may be misleading and suggest you have one chance to record everything you might need from someone. Ideally, you want to record someone more than once, as this allows you to get to know each other. In that case, your growing relationship becomes a way of avoiding the observer's paradox. It also means you can gradually introduce some of the more structured tasks, and tailor them so they best suit the speakers you're working with.

THE OBSERVER'S PARADOX

Sociolinguists are particularly interested in vernacular, informal speech. Collecting such speech can be difficult as in the majority of cases a researcher is present during recordings. Sociolinguists, therefore, must find ways to reduce the impact of the researcher's presence, a fact which led Labov to formulate what is now widely known as the observer's paradox: "To obtain the data that is most important for linguistic theory, we have to observe how people speak when they are not being observed". (Labov 1972: 113)

EXERCISES

Exercise 1

In any community where you start fieldwork there will be some topics that are more relevant there than they would be elsewhere. When Miriam and her colleagues were working in Bequia, in the Caribbean, for instance, they included a section of the interview that asked people to talk about the worst storm or hurricane they had experienced. And they asked them to explain when they might use a local saying like "What you expect of a sperm whale head but a tank of oil?" (which is roughly equivalent to "Blood will out" in English).

Come up with two modules of your own that would be suitable in your home community or the community where you plan to do fieldwork.

Exercise 2

How you structure your contributions to the interview can be very important. In the following extract, translated (and edited, a bit) from Miriam's fieldwork in Vanuatu, you can see how a yes/no question can close an otherwise lively, co-constructed conversation down. Can you suggest ways that this could have been better phrased to make the person more likely to expand on the topic?

Janette: When they went to pay my bride price and they'd paid for me, Jehu's [her husband's] oldest brother went and gave money to my father. And he said he was paying compensation for my daughter. When he paid compensation, well my father cried and cried. He said "I don't want you to pay for her". And Jehu's brother said "No we have to do this because Uncle B** said so".

Maelin: Mhm.

Janette: He said, "I have to pay". My father cried and said he couldn't take it. He wouldn't budge and they said to him "You must take it. If you don't take it, when we get back home, people will talk about us because of it. They'll say we didn't pay proper compensation."

Maelin: Mhm

Miriam: Oh, because it's not right on Malo

Janette: No, it's not right on Malo. [pause]

Miriam: Why was your father crying? Was he ashamed?
Janette: He was sad, he didn't want –
Lolan: He didn't want them to make –
Janette: He didn't want them to pay him compensation for his granddaughter having been born at his own house . . . [Janette and Maelin continue on this topic for another five minutes]

Exercise 3

Figure 5.2 is from William Labov's 2001 paper where he summarised years of interview experience and organised the topics covered into ones that foster more or less careful ways of talking.

Imagine the way two interviews might progress if you wanted to balance your topics between the ones that foster *careful* and *casual* speech. How might you move from one topic to another?

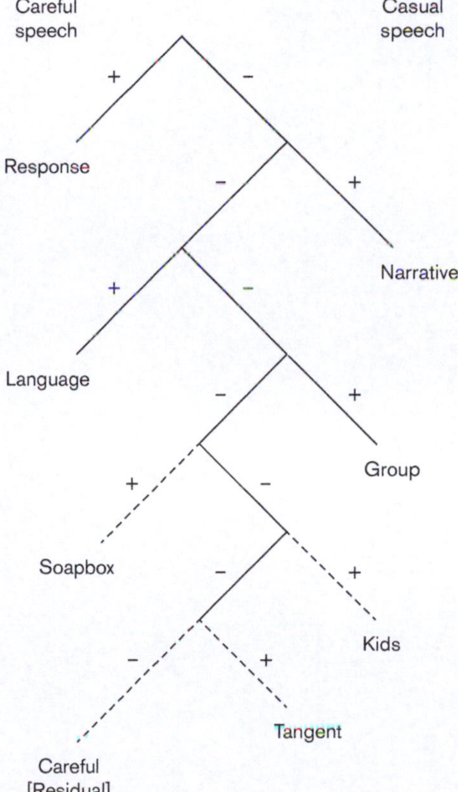

Figure 5.2 Decision tree for stylistic analysis of spontaneous speech in the sociolinguistic interview

Source: Labov (2001)

References

Labov, William. 1972. Some principles of linguistic methodology. *Language in Society* 1: 97–120.

Labov, William. 1984. Field methods of the project Linguistic Change and Variation. In John Baugh and Joel Scherzer (eds) *Language in Use: Readings in Sociolinguistics*. Englewood Cliffs, NJ: Prentice-Hall, 28–53.

Labov, William. 2001. The anatomy of style-shifting. In Penelope Eckert and John R. Rickford (eds) *Style and Sociolinguistic Variation*. Cambridge: Cambridge University Press, 85–108.

Further reading

Milroy, Lesley and Matthew Gordon. 2003. *Sociolinguistics: Method and Interpretation*. Malden and Oxford: Blackwell.

Schilling, Natalie. 2013. *Sociolinguistic Fieldwork*. Cambridge: Cambridge University Press.

Tagliamonte, Sali A. 2006. *Analysing Sociolinguistic Variation*. Cambridge: Cambridge University Press.

6 Naturally occurring, spontaneous speech as a source of data

A large proportion of variationist sociolinguistic work is based on interview speech. However, there has always been a concern that interview speech somehow isn't 'real', that it's highly asymmetrical in terms of the speakers' relative power, that it's contrived and unnatural – not how people really speak. This isn't quite the case. Interview speech is what it is: speech appropriate to an interview and those interviewed don't make up completely new linguistic strategies for the interview; they rely on those that they use in everyday life anyway. Nonetheless, we cannot exclusively rely on interview speech if we want to fully understand how language works.

In order to exclude interviewer effects and to explore everyday language, many linguists record naturally occurring, spontaneous speech: speech that, no matter whether you would have recorded it or not, would have occurred in a very similar form anyway. There are many features that occur rarely or not at all in interview speech. For example, very informal speech, structures bound up with speaker roles and power hierarchies (e.g. tag questions) and language restricted to a particular age group (e.g. *pure* as an intensifier) may occur infrequently in interviews. This chapter deals with how best to gather and explore speech where such features might more readily occur.

Recording spontaneous speech

In principle, all speech can be recorded if we have speakers' permission. However, some spontaneous speech is more suited for recording than others. For example, it is difficult to collect good data when people are walking around or when they are engaged in activities when they would not naturally speak much. Recording events when people routinely come together to talk are good sources of data. In their Belfast study, Milroy and Milroy (1985) found that recording extended visits between friends and relatives was a great source of data. Similarly, Ochs and Taylor (1995) found narratives told during dinnertime to be linguistically and socially very fruitful. You still play a role in the recording, e.g. by placing the recorder in a suitable position and turning it on, but you will not normally influence the flow of conversation.

It is certainly possible to take the researcher out of the recording situation completely and ask participants to self-record. In several studies, researchers have provided interviewees with audio-recorders and asked them to record all their conversations for a certain amount of time (e.g. a week), or during working hours at their job, during recess break at school or weekly social get-togethers. Be specific as to what is to be recorded if you do this. This specificity can later facilitate data analysis, because self-recording brings up several issues. First, the amount of speech you obtain from different people will vary. Second, if context is not specified, the recordings you receive may have been made in a very wide range of settings and may not allow direct comparison.

Self-recordings do not magically solve all problems in data collection. The research context will never completely disappear. For example, while you may not be present in person, you may still be there as an imagined audience. This may result in self-recordings that include speech which was intentionally produced and performed for you, the researcher. Consider the example from the Bequia corpus below. It was recorded by a local fieldworker while driving alone in his taxi and clearly had the researchers in mind as the primary audience:

> and [the] biggest thing for the locals actually is taking part in the politics and looking at the boat races and all of that. Uh for the party people there's too much music, just about everywhere for the whole weekend, so there's plenty to do, and tons of partying and and having a ball

Finally, because the researcher has no control over the recording situation, the quality of recordings can sometimes be rather poor, in terms of background noise, recording volume or even the type of speech recorded.

Some of these potential issues can be mitigated by not only being clear about the context where recording is to take place but also by giving clear instructions and, if appropriate, providing training. This could include points such as where to put the recorder, which groups of people to record and what recording techniques to use. You will want to provide the recording equipment yourself to ensure the recorders and microphones are of good quality. One study that has addressed these issues successfully is the Language in the Workplace Project (Victoria University of Wellington – Holmes, Marra and Vine 2011) and you can find out more about this project on their website.

Rather than merely aiming to record naturally occurring *language*, you could also follow a more ethnographic approach to data collection and extend your focus on language to a focus on the social embedding of language. On the next few pages, we will outline how you can collect naturally occurring speech ethnographically.

Ethnographic research

What is ethnography and what kind of data does it collect?

Duranti (1997: 85) defines ethnography as the study of the "social organisation, social activities, symbolic and material resources, and interpretive practices characteristic of a particular group of people". Where's the language in this? Language can be a social or symbolic, even material, resource. What makes ethnography most notably different from other data collection methods is that it normally involves participant observation: the researcher develops personal associations with members of a community and becomes a member of it. This allows us to develop an insider perspective, while at the same time preserving some outsider detachment. It also makes it possible for us to collect data about the cultural context of the group of speakers, which can be useful information when interpreting the data. Ethnographic research focuses not only on what is said, but also on how people orient to what is said and, in fact, what isn't said, as well as the effects that the participant-observer has on speakers and language use.

Although ethnography aims not to interfere with the normal course of events, apart from participant observation, ethnography also often involves individual or group interviews or even questionnaires. The collection and analysis of cultural artefacts also occurs frequently in ethnographic research. This may include material artefacts (such as signs or dress), images, audio and video recordings, texts (such as obituaries or love letters) or legal information. It may involve collecting background information about the community (e.g. in censuses), its social organisation, and of course about its language: what are the beliefs about language, what linguistic codes are there, what norms and common knowledge exist and how are they expressed? This information is noted in fieldnotes or diaries. This exceedingly rich data is one of the advantages of ethnographic research. It allows us to gain a well-grounded and multi-faceted view of a community. On the other hand, data collection can take a very long time and, due to its participant-observer nature, may also be very demanding.

Goals of ethnographic work

So a variety of different methods are used in order to get a multi-faceted view of a community. But why? What's the point, and, most importantly, what is the role of ethnography in sociolinguistics, a discipline that is often interested in macro categories, such as gender and class? Ethnographers go beyond these externally identifiable categories, because, often, different categories matter to speakers. Sociolinguists who make use of ethnography examine how certain linguistic forms are *locally* meaningful. Categories, thus, often emerge in the fieldwork and are based on what the researcher sees the community members orient to (consciously or unconsciously), such as a group of jocks or nerds, rather than on pre-formulated frameworks of analysis, such as social class. (This distinction between what are called emic and etic categories is discussed a bit more in Chapter 11.)

Often there is a need to refer to larger linguistic patterns in a speech community as participants may draw upon them to produce an exchange that has local meaning, for example, the social class system may be replicated at the local level through small groupings of people. Identifying systematic patterns of behaviour and explicating it in relation to some sort of external factor (such as a setting, or some sort of grouping that is relevant to participants) is the ultimate goal of ethnographic sociolinguistics.

Participant-observation is not the only way to find out about locally relevant social categories. Mathews (2005) used sorting tasks to discover the category labels relevant to the community she was working in. These could be based on pictures, name tags or lists, as long as they allow the researcher to find out what the social position of individuals is in a group of people.

How to do ethnographic research

Ethnographers have helpful advice on how to observe (e.g. see Saville-Troike 2003, Schilling 2013) and how to document data and plan ahead. The details of ethnographic research are difficult to plan because it is often driven by opportunities that arise serendipitously, and it is based on long-term interactions between the researcher and community members. It requires researchers to be prepared for the unexpected, set up a preliminary fieldwork plan and learn as much as possible about the community before entering it, yet remain adaptable throughout the fieldwork period. There are two group structures that have frequently served as the basis for ethnographic observation in sociolinguistic research: social networks and communities of practice (see Chapter 4), but there is absolutely no need to limit yourself to these. You can also explore the wider community.

Normally, you start with going into a community, observing it and then trying to become a member of the community. But entering a community involves a constant process of reflection. Schilling (2013: 117) notes that ethnographic work involves immersing yourself but then stepping outside of the community: you need to reflect on your observations and (re-)formulate hypotheses before you go back into the community to test them. And you may then also make use of other methods such as interviews, surveys and recordings. True ethnographic research is, thus, not a two-week stint of observation but a constant back and forth between insider and outsider status. As Besnier and Philips very forcefully say: "interviews of research participants with which the researcher is unlikely to interact before or after do not constitute ethnography, despite . . . claims to the contrary" (2014: 126).

Thorough and well-organised fieldnotes are central to good ethnographic research. You will need to take notes of as much as possible and write down your recollections as soon as possible in order to get that multi-faceted view of a community. This will ultimately allow you to identify systematic patterns of behaviour, and you will be able to explain these patterns in relation to some sort of external factor.

Develop a template that works for you, one that allows you to note down information as efficiently as possible and reminds you of what to look out for, e.g. the setting, the participants, clothing, who speaks, who is silent, etc. The reflexive quality of ethnography means ethnographers often return to the people they have previously recorded for debriefing, i.e. community members are shown/played recordings and then invited to comment on what they've heard/seen (Besnier and Philips 2014: 131).

What to observe

Hymes (1974) offers a useful mnemonic – SPEAKING – to remind us what ethnography pays attention to. If this is too abstract for you, you can focus on more tangible units and try to apply the SPEAKING features to these units. For example, Saville-Troike (2003) suggests observing activities and interactions (e.g. service encounters, classroom interactions), events (birthday parties, business meetings, religious ceremonies), social processes (e.g. naturalisation, socialisation), and other groups of people.

> **SPEAKING (Hymes 1974)**
>
> **S**ettings (physical and psychological, i.e. how participants view an interaction);
> **P**articipants (including those talked about);
> **E**nds (the goals and outcomes of an interaction);
> **A**ct sequence (message form, content, what is happening);
> **K**ey (the tone, manner or spirit, e.g. bragging, joking, formal speech);
> **I**nstrumentalities (channels, forms of speech: written/spoken, variety, register, practices, etc.);
> **N**orms; and
> **G**enres.

The difficult part now is relating your data to your research question and creating a coherent argument, ultimately in writing. Chapter 16 will give you some pointers as to how this can be done. It introduces you to the process of writing a research paper. However, note that, depending on precisely what your interest is, ethnographic work is sometimes more suited to be summarised in other genres, such as an essay or even a diary format.

After having read these chapters on data collection techniques, you may wonder which is the best one. Don't! Good sociolinguistic studies often utilise a mixture of techniques: interviews, participant-observation, sometimes experimental methods. Focusing on local as well as global categories and working quantitatively as well as qualitatively (see Chapter 15) is always a good idea. It can only enrich your analysis.

EXERCISES

Exercise 1

How would you conduct an ethnographic study of how people in your town buy coffee in a coffee shop? What methods would you use? What would you observe? Why do you think it might be important to do such a study?

Exercise 2

Smith, Durham and Fortune (2007) study the acquisition of variable forms in the Scottish dialect of Buckie (population 8,000). Buckie is a small fishing town situated on the northeast coast of Scotland. They target two linguistic variables in the speech of 11 children and their primary caregivers. They compare data from a caregiver/child corpus with that of an adult-to-adult corpus. Read the excerpt from their methods section below and consider the following questions:

1 Why did they choose to collect naturally occurring speech for the caregiver/child corpus?
2 How did they go about collecting the data?
3 Which issues discussed under "Recording spontaneous speech" are of relevance to their study and how did they address them?
4 To what extent are the caregiver/child corpus and the adult-to-adult corpus comparable?

Caregiver/child corpus

The caregiver/child corpus contains 24 dyads aged between 2;6 and 4;0 (Smith, 2003–2005). This age group was specifically targeted because it has been claimed that "the 3- to 4-year old level is a critical period for the acquisition of dialectal norms of the speech community" (Roberts & Labov, 1995:110). [. . .] In addition, children by these ages are at a stage where full clauses are used, allowing for the analysis of morphosyntactic variation, such as agreement phenomena, negation, and tense formation.

To control the sample as much as possible, the participant selection process was guided by the following criteria: (1) both parents must have been born and raised in the community, (2) there were no referrals for speech or language therapy, (3) the mother was the main caregiver (i.e., there was no substantial time with extended family, childminders, etc.), and (4) no child was in formal nursery education.

Data collection. Collection of naturalistic data from young children poses two major problems. The first is the amount of data required. For example, Roberts (2002:336) estimated that 8–14 hours of young children's speech is required to collect data comparable to that found in 1–2 hours of adult speech. The second problem is the elicitation of vernacular data. The Observer's Paradox (Labov, 1972) is exacerbated in the case of young children, where the presence of an outsider in the home can render the child literally "speechless." To mitigate these problems, the caregivers themselves were requested to undertake a series of recorded sessions with their child, in a variety of situations in which interaction takes place, such as mealtimes, trips in the car, walks, and even visits to the bathroom (!). Lightweight minidisc recorders (Sony MZ-R700) and lapel microphones (Sony ECM-T145) were provided to allow freedom of movement and to be as unintrusive as possible. [. . .] Recordings for each child/caregiver dyad amounted to ten hours of data, five hours of which are fully transcribed. The corpus currently stands at approximately 500,000 words. [. . .]

Adult-to-adult corpus

A fully transcribed corpus of adult-to-adult community speech is stratified by age and sex, and amounts to approximately 300,000 words. This corpus was collected using sociolinguistic interviews by the first author who comes from the community in question. The data is highly informal in nature, containing narratives from the past and local gossip (see detail in Smith, 2000a). [. . .]

These two data sets differ. The caregiver/child corpus represents a range of situational contexts, both formal and informal. The adult corpus, on the other hand, represents one context of use—an informal style as close to vernacular norms as can be possibly achieved within the sociolinguistic interview situation. In this case, the adult sample represents the norms of usage in everyday conversation from which caregiver/child interaction can be directly compared.

Source: Smith, Durham and Fortune (2007)

References

Besnier, Niko and Susan U. Philips. 2014. Ethnographic methods for language and gender research. In Susan Ehrlich, Miriam Meyerhoff and Janet Holmes (eds) *The Handbook of Language, Gender and Sexuality*. New York and Oxford: Wiley Blackwell, 123–140.

Duranti, Alessandro. 1997. *Linguistic Anthropology*. Cambridge: Cambridge University Press.

Holmes, Janet, Meredith Marra and Bernadette Vine. 2011. *Leadership, Discourse and Ethnicity*. Oxford: Oxford University Press.

Hymes, Dell. 1974. *Foundations in Sociolinguistics: An Ethnographic Approach*. Philadelphia, PA: University of Pennsylvania Press.

Mathews, Tanya. 2005. Discourses of intergroup distinctiveness among adolescent girls. Unpublished PhD dissertation, Cornell University.

Milroy, James and Lesley Milroy. 1985. Linguistic change, social network and speaker innovation. *Journal of Linguistics* 21: 339–384.

Ochs, Elinor and Carolyn Taylor. 1995. The "father knows best" dynamic in dinnertime narratives. In Kira Hall and Mary Bucholtz (eds) *Gender Articulated: Language and the Socially Constructed Self*. London and New York: Routledge, 97–120.

Saville-Troike, Muriel. 2003. *The Ethnography of Communication*. 3rd edition. Malden, MA: Blackwell.

Schilling, Natalie. 2013. *Sociolinguistic Fieldwork*. Cambridge: Cambridge University Press.

Smith, Jennifer, Mercedes Durham and Liane Fortune. 2007. "Mam, my trousers is fa' doon!": Community, caregiver, and child in the acquisition of variation in a Scottish dialect. *Language Variation and Change* 19: 63–99.

Further reading

Eckert, Penelope. 1989. *Jocks and Burnouts: Social Categories and Identity in the High School*. New York: Teachers College Press.

Hymes, Dell. 1974. *Foundations in Sociolinguistics: An Ethnographic Approach*. Philadelphia, PA: University of Pennsylvania Press.

Johnstone, Barbara. 2000. *Qualitative Methods in Sociolinguistics*. New York and Oxford: Oxford University Press.

Levon, Erez. 2013. Ethnographic fieldwork. In Christine Mallinson, Becky Childs and Gerard Van Herk (eds) *Data Collection in Sociolinguistics: Methods and Applications.* New York and London: Routledge, 69–79.

Milroy, Lesley and Matthew Gordon. 2003. *Sociolinguistics: Method and Interpretation.* Malden and Oxford: Blackwell.

Saville-Troike, Muriel. 2003. *The Ethnography of Communication.* 3rd edition. Malden, MA: Blackwell.

Schilling, Natalie. 2013. *Sociolinguistic Fieldwork.* Cambridge: Cambridge University Press.

7 Corpora as a source of data

While the face-to-face data collection techniques we've introduced in the previous two chapters are excellent ways to observe language, there are some cases in which they won't be sufficient. Imagine, for instance, that you have developed an interest in a variable that occurs fairly infrequently in speech, such as the alternation between *would have* and *woulda*. After an hour-long sociolinguistic interview, you may only have heard the target construction a handful of times. Or, imagine you wish to track the real-time development of the verb of quotation *be like*, or explore men's and women's language in the Early Modern English period. Without access to historical language data, you won't get very far. This chapter introduces you to data sources known as corpora that you can use to address these and other sorts of research topics.

What is a corpus?

Briefly, a corpus (plural: *corpora*, with stress on the first syllable) is a body of language that someone has collected for a particular purpose. A corpus is designed to be representative of the type of language it has been drawn from, despite constituting only a tiny slice of the whole. Corpora are also typically large: some well-known corpora number in the hundreds of millions of words. This means that corpora cannot usually be analysed by hand, but there are a range of computational tools available to allow you to work with them, which we'll discuss later on.

If you can think of a scenario in which language is used, there's probably a corpus to represent it. Corpora can be based on spoken language or written language (and some corpora provide some of each). Where spoken language is concerned, some corpora comprise only transcripts, while others contain both transcripts and audio, a goldmine for researchers interested in phonetic and phonological variation. Corpora of written language can contain newspaper and academic writings, correspondence, literature and online communications. Video corpora of signed languages are available too, as are many other non-English corpora, including multilingual corpora containing parallel translations of the same text. Even YouTube has been used as a corpus (e.g. Wrobel 2012, and the study of Victoria Beckham's language in Chapter 14).

Corpora can be used to investigate variation in register, both in speech and writing, as you can find corpora that represent formal language (like MiCASE, the Michigan Corpus of Academic Spoken English; or the academic writing subset of COCA, the Corpus of Contemporary American English) and corpora that represent informal language (like the Buckeye Speech Corpus, a collection of 40 sociolinguistic interviews; or the Enron Email Dataset, a corpus of public-domain emails sent between employees of the now-defunct American energy company Enron). Cheng (2012: 33–34) provides a list of major English-language corpora; you can find a few easy-to-use corpora listed below, and there are plenty of further lists online.

GET UP AND RUNNING WITH SOME ONLINE CORPORA

You can get started with corpora by exploring the following (search for them online):

Corpora of written language:

- The Corpus of Contemporary American English (COCA)
- The Corpus of Global Web-based English (GloWbE)
- The Corpus of Historical American English (COHA)
- Google Books Ngram Viewer

Corpora of spoken language:

- The Switchboard and Fisher corpora via LDC Online (NB: full access requires a subscription through your university)
- The Michigan Corpus of Academic Spoken English (MiCASE)

Why would I want to use a corpus?

By using a pre-existing corpus, it could be argued that you're surrendering control of the nature of your data. After all, you don't get any say in the topics that speakers discuss, or the demographics of your speaker sample, in the way that you do when you design an interview-based study. For many studies, though, the benefits of working with corpora can outweigh these drawbacks.

One such benefit is size: the Corpus of Contemporary American English contains 450 million words, and the Linguistic Data Consortium's Fisher corpus consists of 2,700 hours of transcribed audio. This can allow you to study lexical or syntactic variables that occur only infrequently in speech. For instance, Rickford et al. (1995) carried out a study of variation in *as far as* constructions, having noticed that people can alternate between, say, 'as far as the government is concerned', 'as far as the government goes' and 'as far as the government'. The authors and their colleagues jotted down each *as far as* construction they noticed in everyday use, and managed to come up with 650 examples – but this required the efforts of several researchers over the course of eight years. By contrast, a collection of spoken and written corpora gave them 500 tokens. If time is of the essence, corpora are your best bet with an infrequent variable.

Working with a corpus can also allow you to generalise over individuals to uncover broader trends about language. Data from a single speaker can tell us a lot about that one individual, but she may not be representative of the larger population of women, teenagers or Philadelphians. The more data we collect, though, the more certain we can be that the patterns we're observing are not a fluke. Working with corpus data has allowed researchers to determine that female users of Twitter are more likely to use emoticons than male users (Bamman, Eisenstein and Schnoebelen 2014), and to track changes in the Philadelphia vowel system over 110 years of apparent time (Labov, Rosenfelder and Fruehwald 2013). A quick check in a diachronic corpus can allow you to confirm whether a case of variation in the present day represents a change in progress. For instance, Laurel noticed people alternating between constructions like 'out the window' and 'out of the window'. Checking the ratio of these phrases in the Google Books Ngram Viewer corpus of digitised books (Michel et al. 2011) resulted in the graph in Figure 7.1, and a study of language change was born.

How do I use a corpus?

You'll first want to figure out what sort of corpus is appropriate to what you want to study. Are you working with a phonological variable, for which having audio is going to be essential? Or a syntactic variable, for which you're fine working just with written data? (If the latter, are you sure you can get away with not analysing sound? What if intonation might be relevant to the variation?) Also consider whether your corpus provides information on factors that might be conditioning the variation. If you're working with a corpus of child language data, for example, information on parents' level of education or occupational status could be useful.

The size of most corpora means that listening or reading through them in real time is an unrealistic means of gathering data. Instead, linguists use computational tools to help them get what they want. Depending on the nature of your linguistic variable and the corpus you select, collecting your data may be as easy as typing out some search queries, or it may require you to learn some basic

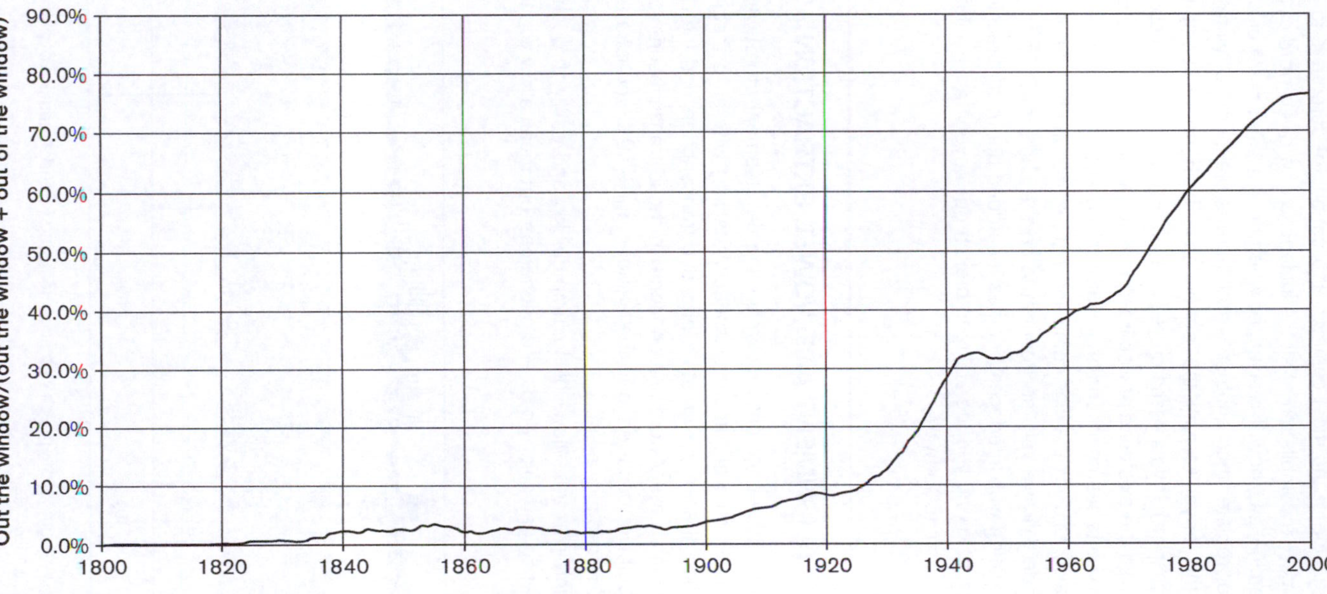

Figure 7.1 The rise of *out the window* in Google Books Ngram Viewer

programming. One of the most common applications of corpora is to generate a concordance – a compilation of all the instances of a given word or phrase in order to examine, say, how it is used, or whether it is used more or differently in one text or register than another – and there is plenty of software available that can do this for you (consult the references in the Further Reading list at the end of this chapter). If your research requires listening to words in context, you will benefit from the existence of web interfaces for audio corpora like BNCWeb, which allows you to search for and hear words and phrases in the British National Corpus as easily as using the Find command in a text document. Learning to write computer code will give you the freedom to do the same even in corpora that don't have existing web interfaces, and has the added bonus of 'teaching you to fish' – that is, of giving you the ability to branch out beyond any limitations you encounter in existing software.

FORCED ALIGNMENT AND VOWEL EXTRACTION

A recent advance in corpus research is the development of software for the automatic time-alignment of speech. Starting with an orthographic transcription, these tools create a phonetic transcription, and then automatically match every word and phoneme in these transcriptions to their precise point of occurrence in the audio. Figure 7.2 demonstrates the output of forced alignment.

Not only can this allow you to jump quickly and easily through your sound files to particular words and phonemes, but it can allow you to use

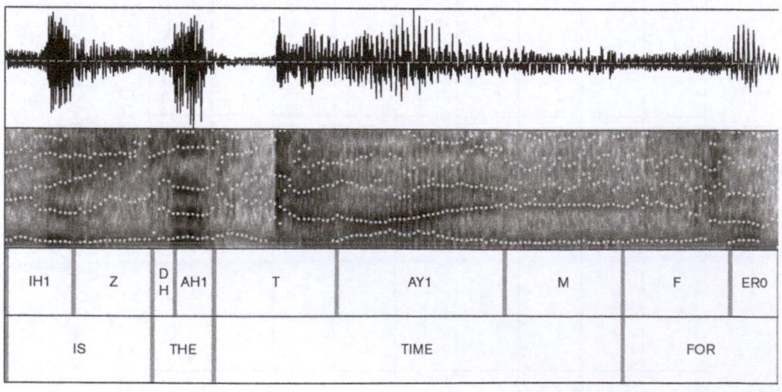

Figure 7.2 A segment of speech with accompanying forced alignment of phonemes and words

tools for vowel extraction: automatic measuring of the formant values of every vowel in a recording. Measuring vowels by hand is arduous, but, as long as you have a transcribed recording, these new techniques can provide thousands of vowel measurements in minutes. Search the web for *forced alignment* to see the kinds of software available.

Corpora differ in how much linguistic annotation they provide, meaning that your task of coding a variable may be easier with some corpora than others. The Buckeye Speech Corpus is unusual among audio corpora in having alongside its audio files not only orthographic transcriptions, but also narrow phonetic transcriptions. This takes all the work out of coding a phonological variable like *t/d*-deletion. If you wanted to study *t/d*-deletion in the Switchboard corpus, by contrast, you'd be signing yourself up for the somewhat tedious task of listening to hundreds of *t/d*-final words to collect your data. On the other hand, the transcriptions in Switchboard have been annotated for part of speech, and some of them have even been syntactically parsed. This comes in handy if you need to differentiate in your study between, say, *ring* as a noun versus *ring* as a verb, or *have* as an auxiliary verb versus *have* as a main verb.

Like any other source of data, corpora have advantages and disadvantages. Though we hope the benefits of having a large body of language at your fingertips are apparent, remember that the findings of a corpus-based study will only be as representative as the corpus they come from. As always, you will help yourself out if you clearly articulate the specific research question you are asking before you choose your source of data.

EXERCISES

Exercise 1

Consider the linguistic variables below. What sort of corpus would you need in order to study them? What sort of annotation would be useful?

1 The change in English third singular present marking from *-th* to *-s*
2 The genitive alternation (e.g. *the tree's roots* ~ *the roots of the tree*)
3 The fronting of the GOOSE vowel in American or British English
4 The alternation between *would have*, *would've* and *woulda*

Exercise 2

Contextual style is well known to affect sociolinguistic variation. How could we study contextual style in present-day corpora? How about historical corpora?

References

Bamman, David, Jacob Eisenstein and Tyler Schnoebelen. 2014. Gender identity and lexical variation in social media. *Journal of Sociolinguistics* 18: 135–160.

Cheng, Winnie. 2012. *Exploring Corpus Linguistics: Language in Action*. London: Routledge.

Google Books Ngram Viewer. http://ngrams.googlelabs.com (last accessed 7 November 2014).

Labov, William, Ingrid Rosenfelder and Josef Fruehwald. 2013. One hundred years of sound change in Philadelphia: linear incrementation, reversal, and reanalysis. *Language* 89: 30–65.

Michel, Jean-Baptiste, Yuan Kui Shen, Aviva Presser Aiden, Adrian Veres, Matthew K. Gray, The Google Books Team, Joseph P. Pickett, Dale Hoiberg, Dan Clancy, Peter Norvig, Jon Orwant, Steven Pinker, Martin A. Nowak and Erez Lieberman Aiden. 2011. Quantitative analysis of culture using millions of digitized books. *Science* 331: 176–182.

Rickford, John R., Thomas A. Wasow, Norma Mendoza-Denton and Juli Espinoza. 1995. Syntactic variation and change in progress: loss of the verbal coda in topic-restricting *as far as* constructions. *Language* 71: 102–131.

Wrobel, Emilia. 2012. What can you find on YouTube, that's sociolinguistically interesting? *Journal of Pidgin and Creole Languages* 27: 343–350.

Further reading

Baker, Paul. 2010. *Sociolinguistics and Corpus Linguistics*. Edinburgh: Edinburgh University Press.

Hoffmann, Sebastian, Stefan Evert, Nicholas Smith, David Lee and Ylva Berglund Prytz. 2008. *Corpus Linguistics with BNCweb–a Practical Guide*. Oxford: Peter Lang.

McEnery, Tony, Richard Xiao and Yukio Tono. 2006. *Corpus-Based Language Studies: An Advanced Resource Book*. London: Routledge.

8 Written surveys and questionnaires as a source of data

Sometimes it's just not possible to access a corpus or collect new, written or spoken language data. Surveys or questionnaires can be a big help here. They produce highly reliable data if used appropriately, and they may be especially good for accessing information on linguistic behaviour that is difficult to observe or record. Writing a good questionnaire is not easy. You have to put a lot of thought into its construction before you can use it for data collection, but one of the pay-offs is that the results can be quick to analyse. In this chapter, we outline (a) the different uses that questionnaires can be put to, (b) their limitations and advantages and (c) how to write good questions and develop, structure, test and administer a questionnaire.

Questionnaires in sociolinguistics

Written surveys and questionnaires allow you to explore how people behave in certain situations, but you can also find out a lot about their beliefs, knowledge, attitudes and their social characteristics. Questionnaires have been used to:

- find out who uses what language, who they use it with and when (e.g. Choi 2005).
- investigate the sociolinguistic profile of ethnic minorities in an urban area (e.g. Extra and Yagmur 2004).
- explore who uses different words and phrases in different contexts, e.g. swear words, loanwords or sexist vocabulary (e.g. Fuller 2005).
- explore attitudes towards dialects, accents, certain lexical items or pronunciations (see Chapter 9). Attitudes are also an important component of ethnolinguistic vitality (Bourhis, Giles and Rosenthal 1981).
- find out about discourse pragmatics in one or more cultures using discourse completion tests (see textbox on DCTs).

DISCOURSE COMPLETION TESTS (DCTs)

In DCTs, you give participants scenarios, which include the setting, the status of participants and the social distance between them, as well as incomplete scripted dialogue in a variety of different social situations. Then you ask respondents what they would say there. Here's an example from Blum-Kulka, House and Kasper (1989: 14), constructed to elicit a request (we've removed the questionnaire instructions here):

> Ann missed a lecture yesterday and would like to borrow Judith's notes.
>
> *Ann*: ____
>
> *Judith*: Sure, but let me have them back before the lecture next week.

Sometimes, multiple-choice options are given for the missing piece of dialogue, and sometimes respondents are only given a situation and some space for their response. DCTs are a frequently used method in cross-cultural pragmatics, and some interesting findings have been made. For example, how would you ask your roommate to clean up the kitchen, if they had left it in a mess the night before? Turns out that 74 per cent of Argentineans prefer direct bald-on strategies, as in "Hey, Fernanda, you have to clean the kitchen before you leave", in contrast to only 12 per cent of Australians (Blum-Kulka 1997: 56). Who knew?! But remember that what people tell you they do, may tell you what they would like to *think* they do, rather than what they actually *do* do (see Beebe and Clark Cummings 1996).

Questionnaires can also find out whether particular constructions are considered grammatical or not. Traditionally, linguists did this by asking people to report judgements in terms of categories such as *acceptable*, *marginally acceptable*, *unacceptable*, *good*, *terrible*, etc. This isn't ideal. Bard, Robertson and Sorace (1996) outline advantages and shortcomings of the traditional format, and they propose the method of magnitude estimation as a way to overcome these issues. Magnitude estimation allows graded acceptability to be measured, e.g. people can tell you that they think a sentence is four times more acceptable than another.

Written surveys are frequently used to investigate regional and social variation. Many traditional dialect surveys are based on a questionnaire, e.g. the *Linguistic Atlas of England* (Orton, Sanderson and Widdowson 1978). Search for Laurel MacKenzie's *Dialect Variation Maps* online for a modern example. You can also combine questionnaires with other data elicitation methods. Llamas (2007) developed a set of questionnaires, which she used in combination with an interview, to collect data on Teeside English.

There are some clever question formats that you can use when you investigate regional and social variation with a written survey.

1 You can elicit forms and features. You can find out whether someone is familiar with a particular form by asking directly, or indirectly, by prompting them to use a particular item. You could ask, "Are you familiar with the word *bairn*? If so, how often would you use it?" (the direct approach). Or you might ask, "What do they call a person who's not an adult around here?" (more indirect). Or you might give respondents a fill-in-the-blanks task.
2 You can collect judgements about structural constraints on a feature. This can be helpful if you want to find out if a particular variant can or cannot be used in certain tenses or with certain subjects, etc. Judgement or permutation tasks are outlined in Schilling (2013: 71–75).
3 And you may also want to find out whether a feature is the same or different from another one (see box below on phonological variables).

Some variables are more suited to use in written surveys than others. Many morphological, syntactic, lexical and semantic variables are easy to represent in writing and quite suited to use in a questionnaire if they are not affected by strong, overt social evaluation. Variable forms are often given in a list of options, asking participants to select a form that they would use in daily conversations, possibly with some space for alternatives not listed.

PHONOLOGICAL VARIABLES IN WRITTEN SURVEYS

It's difficult to design a written survey on phonetic variation, e.g. vowel shifts, as phonetic details cannot easily be transmitted to lay-people in writing. Variation at the phonemic level, on the other hand, can often be represented in conventional orthography, so mergers of phonemes can be studied relatively well with a questionnaire. You can give participants in your study minimal pairs and ask them whether the words sound the same or different or whether they rhyme. For example, Dollinger (2012: 93) asked respondents questions such as:

> Do the words ***cot*** and ***caught*** sound the same to you? Yes No
>
> Does the ending of AVENUE sound like ***you*** or ***oo***?

Alternatively, give respondents a pre-recorded list of word pairs and ask whether each of the pairs is the same or different words. A more indirect version of this task is the "communication test" (Labov 1994: 356ff). Whether or not someone can distinguish between members of minimal pairs is an indication of whether they merge the sounds under investigation or not. This method can reveal *near mergers*: sometimes people claim not to hear a difference but spectrographic analysis of their speech reveals that they produce the sounds differently.

But you may not be interested in mergers at all. Similar methods can be used if you just want to find out which phonemes occur in particular words. Boberg (2010: 140) asked respondents to classify words such as *soprano*, *Iraq*, *pasta* and *plaza* into one of two categories: whether their vowel is pronounced like the <a> sound as in *cat* or the <ah> sound as in *father*.

Limitations and opportunities

Questionnaires are a great resource; however, we must be aware of their limitations. They are not particularly suited to delve deeply into an issue, and what respondents claim they do may not match up with what they actually do, partly because they may find it difficult to assess their language behaviour. In addition, they may understand and talk about non-standard features in a way that limits what we can find out from them. People tend to equate grammaticality with standard language and although we can frame our questions avoiding terms such as *correct* and *grammatical* by asking "How would you say . . .?", "Can you say . . .?", "Which is more natural to you . . .?", standard forms often continue to influence assessment.

If our question is very direct, we effectively ask respondents to pay attention to how they speak, which we don't really want because it often results in irregular linguistic patterns and hypercorrection (Labov 1972: 134; see discussion of the observer's paradox in Chapter 5). Though direct questions often tell us more about people's opinions than how they use language, this is much truer for highly stereotyped, non-standard grammatical forms and obsolescent forms than less socially sensitive variables (Boberg 2013).

A further issue with questionnaires concerns ordering effects. This refers to the way a response may be influenced by previous ones. People can also misread questions or interpret questions differently to what you'd intended, or they may not be able to read and write at all. Dörnyei (2003) notes that people tend to agree rather than disagree, and they show a tendency to overgeneralise. So, when they like one aspect of a person or event, they overestimate *all* characteristics associated with that person or event. Long questionnaires may simply tire people out so they give incorrect answers or leave questions blank.

Many of these limitations can be minimised: you can randomise items, use indirect elicitations if possible, avoid the term *grammatical* and design the survey to be more like a game than a test. Most importantly, you can keep its length

manageable: four pages, 30 to 50 items, or 30 minutes of completion time are the maximum.

Having said all that, written questionnaires also have many advantages; they are cost-effective and collect a lot of data quickly. That's good news because confidence in the results of a study improves as the number of respondents increases. If the questionnaire was designed well, preparing the data for quantitative analysis will also be efficient.

Developing questionnaire items

Thorough preparation will make your questionnaire infinitely more useable. It should be as clear as possible and one way to achieve this is to develop a precise research question. You can then scaffold your knowledge or theory on this to build survey questions. Focus groups, interviews, a short open-ended pilot survey and a trawl of the existing literature may help you decide what further questions to include.

Questions in a questionnaire are sometimes called *items*. That's because they often don't look like a canonical question. There are two main types of questions/items: closed questions and open questions. Closed questions provide a closed set of possible answers, and because the answers are pre-defined, this type of question can be analysed quickly. A closed question typically has three clearly marked parts: (a) instructions, (b) a question or statement and (c) possible answers, as in the following example:

> Below are listed five questions about swearing. We would like to ask you to answer each one by circling the number that most closely matches your opinion.
>
> 1 How acceptable do you think swearing is?
>
> Not at all | | | | | Very
> ---|---|---|---|---|---
> 1 | 2 | 3 | 4 | 5 | 6

Be mindful of the hazards associated with biasing question options. If there is a neutral position, there should be the same number of response options on either side. There is no consensus as to whether the points on scales should be an even or an odd number. Sometimes researchers worry that people may drift to the mid-point in a series to weasel out of committing firmly to something, but sometimes the middle is precisely what respondents feel if they are undecided.

There are many different closed question formats. Sociolinguists most frequently use checklists, rankings, rating scales (as in the example above), true–false questions, multiple-choice questions and semantic differential questions (where people get polar adjectives and rank a speaker along a scale: e.g. rich↔poor). More detailed examples are in De Vaus (2005) and Schleef (2013).

Open-ended questions do not provide pre-formulated answers. You can ask specific open-ended questions, questions of clarification, sentence completion items and short-answer questions, which ask for one concept or one idea only. Open-ended questions give respondents some space to provide an answer themselves, and, thus, assume they can express themselves in writing (but remember if they are completing the questionnaire by hand, you may have to decipher what they express!). The idea here is to get more personal responses, but the downside is that you often get lots of blank spaces and a large number of individual answers that may be difficult to categorise and quantify (assuming that's the goal). Answering open-ended questions is also quite time-consuming, so they should be used sparingly and towards the end of the questionnaire.

SOME TIPS FOR WRITING GOOD ITEMS (BASED ON DÖRNYEI 2003)

- If you ask questions about behaviour that respondents may disapprove of, mitigate questions, e.g. by assuming it occurs and asking about detail, or by casualising it.
- Write short, simple and natural-sounding items.
- Do not put all negative terms on one side of the questionnaire and all positive ones on the other. Alternate them.
- *Don't know* or *Other* options may be appropriate when none of your options may apply, otherwise you are better not to include these.
- A well-tested method that reduces idiosyncratic interpretation of some questions is multi-item scaling: you use differently worded items that all focus on the same target, for example the perceived acceptability of swearing, and then you average out responses.

Avoid

- acronyms, abbreviations, technical terms, colloquialisms;
- questions that ask about two different things at once, while expecting only one answer;
- items containing negatives;
- unclear, unspecific terms, such as *frequently, sometimes, good*;
- potentially loaded or leading questions;
- sensitive questions – if that's not possible, renew the promise of confidentiality when you do;

- words that do not allow exceptions, such as all-inclusive or all-exclusive words (e.g. *all the time, nobody*), as they may result in a lack of variability in answers. They are fine as options on a continuum.

Questionnaire structure

Your questionnaire should consist of more than just a list of questions. A good questionnaire starts with an informative, reassuring and polite introduction, and it ends with a conclusion. The introduction should include: (1) the questionnaire title; (2) a very brief outline of what the research is about and who is responsible for conducting the study; (3) a friendly request to fill in the questionnaire fully and honestly; (4) a brief overview of what will be asked in the questionnaire and, roughly, how long its completion will take; (5) a clear statement saying that responses will be treated with absolute confidentiality and that respondents will remain anonymous; (6) the researcher's name, institution and (7) a thank you for participating in the study.

Next follows the main text, which should be logically ordered. Make the first questions ones that keep the reader interested and involved and vary the question formats. You don't want to bore, or put off people at the start. This is also why you might want to put open-ended, personal or more demanding items towards the end of the questionnaire. If your questionnaire consists of different subsections, you can use headings to help people through. It also helps readers when you emphasise instructions clearly. A good questionnaire is attractive, looks professional and is error-free.

You end the questionnaire by thanking respondents once again and leaving them your contact details. Additionally, you could renew the promise of anonymity and provide further information you consider vital for respondents or your study, e.g. ask respondents to make sure no questions are blank, tell them how questionnaires can be returned and where they can view the survey results.

Testing, administering and processing questionnaires

Before you distribute your questionnaire, make sure to test it. One strategy is to ask a few friends to read it (without completing it) and tell you what they think as they read it. You might also want to ask people to answer the survey questions and think aloud, explaining their reasoning as they go (Willis 2005). This allows you to check whether questions are worded clearly. You may also want to consider piloting your questionnaire in a small group of people and then have a good look at the answers. Are some questions left blank? Are some questions open to misunderstanding? Is the questionnaire too long? Will you be able to process the responses?

Once all this is done, you can finally distribute the questionnaire! For your sample to be roughly representative, you want to collect data from more than 30 people per subgroup (i.e. per category investigated, for example at least 30 per age group, per speaker sex, etc.). That's because your sample will likely have a normal distribution with more than 30 people (Hatch and Lazaraton 1991). This is different from the minimum of five or six speakers per cell we recommend in Chapter 2. It makes sense, though. Think about it. You will get only one questionnaire per person. However, you normally get many, many tokens of a single variable per speaker in a study that's based on speech recordings. Thirty may be more than you can handle in a small student project, so if that's not feasible, try to get as many responses per subgroup as you can – definitely more than ten per group – but keep in mind that results may change radically with more data.

You can administer written surveys and questionnaires face-to-face (with the researcher noting down answers) or long-distance (with the respondent writing all answers without the researcher being present). Both have advantages and disadvantages. Have a look at De Vaus (2005: 126ff) for a comparison of distribution methods, including expected response rates. Dörnyei (2003: 83ff) outlines some tips to ensure many respondents spend sufficient time and effort completing the questionnaire.

LONG-DISTANCE DISTRIBUTION AND CROWD-SOURCING

Long-distance surveys can be sent by e-mail, post, or they can be distributed by hand or on the internet. Telephone, computer or internet surveys make it possible to play recordings even to participants who are miles away. Online surveys also allow you to make use of crowd-sourcing tools such as Amazon Mechanical Turk. At the time of writing, its main limitation is that you need to have an American address to use it. You could also advertise your survey on various social media sites.

Once all questionnaires are collected, you process the data. Assign each questionnaire a number and enter the data into a spreadsheet, using codes that you've made clear notes on for future reference (your coding guide). Now check for potential inaccuracies and mistakes in the database and, if appropriate, reverse the scores of negatively worded items. For example, you may want to make sure all positive items have a high or positive number code and negative items have a low one. If data is missing, you'll have to consider removing participants or certain questions from the survey. Dörnyei (2003) talks about ways to evaluate questionnaires for validity and reliability.

If space allows, all decisions about questionnaire structure, items and data exclusion should briefly be mentioned in the methods section of your report. When presenting your results, consider who may have filled in your questionnaire. Was it based on self-selection? A particular medium? This may bias your findings.

Now you can finally analyse the data. You can jump to Chapters 12 to 14 for help on how to do this or to Chapter 15 for some thoughts about complementing questionnaire data with qualitative analysis. This can be a valuable reminder about the people behind your numbers.

EXERCISES

Exercise 1

What are the advantages and disadvantages of administering questionnaires face-to-face and by distance, especially online?

Exercise 2

Consider Figure 8.1 from Campbell-Kibler (2011: 441). This is *part* of a written survey which aims to find out what social attributes speakers associate with the variants of (ing). Respondents listened to audio recordings of eight speakers. For every one of these speakers, several naturally produced sentences had been digitally altered to create triplets: one had an [ɪŋ], one an [ɪn] and one was a neutral guise with no audible (ing) token. A survey page for one speaker is shown over the page.

As mentioned above, questionnaire length must be limited. Campbell-Kibler has limited the number of recordings each participant would hear to eight and she managed to keep the survey page for each of the eight voices quite short and to the point.

What decisions did she have to make to do this? What kind of question types does she use and which ones could she have used – with and without increasing questionnaire length? How does question type influence the kind of analysis you can conduct? Think about the type of answer you get from different questions and consult Chapter 12, if you need help.

Exercise 3

Dollinger (2012: 95ff) compares data collected using written questionnaires with interview data. Consider the results for the three examples of the low-back vowel merger in Canadian English (Table 8.1). Dollinger analysed interview data to find out whether ten people have the merger (or not) and then compared these results with what they claimed to do in a written questionnaire. The 'Merge/Nonmerge'

Survey

Speaker 1 of 8.

This is Bonnie:

Press the play button to hear the recording. You can play it as many times as you like. After listening to her, tell me as much as you can about Bonnie, based on what you hear.

She sounds:

Casual	O	O	O	O	O	O	Formal
Very Intelligent	O	O	O	O	O	O	Not at all Intelligent
Very Educated	O	O	O	O	O	O	Not at all Educated
Very Accented	O	O	O	O	O	O	Not at all Accented
Very Friendly	O	O	O	O	O	O	Not at all Friendly
Very Feminine	O	O	O	O	O	O	Not at all Feminine

Would you want to be friends with Bonnie?

Not at all O O O O O O Very Much

Would you want to be neighbours with Bonnie?

Not at all O O O O O O Very Much

How old does Bonnie sound (check all that apply, must choose at least one)?

☐ A Teenager ☐ College Age ☐ Under 30 ☐ In her 30's ☐ Over 40

From what you heard, does Bonnie sound like she might be (check all that apply):

☐ Lazy ☐ Hardworking ☐ Laidback ☐ Compassionate ☐ Condescending ☐ Confident
☐ Articulate ☐ Religious ☐ Annoying ☐ Family-oriented ☐ Funny ☐ Reliable
☐ Gay ☐ Hip/Trendy

☐ A Stoner ☐ A Metrosexual ☐ A Jock ☐ A Redneck ☐ A Nerd ☐ A Farmer
☐ A Student ☐ An Artist ☐ A Mother ☐ An Activist ☐ A Teacher
☐ Other:

Any other thoughts about Bonnie?

Continue

Figure 8.1 Sample from an online survey

Source: Campbell-Kibler (2011: 441)

columns show what the participants claim they do. If the questionnaire data matched the data in the interview there is a 'Yes' in the column 'Match'.

How reliable is the written questionnaire? What factors seem to influence reliability?

Table 8.1 Match between self-reporting and acoustic analysis

	cot/caught			*Don/Dawn*			*sorry/sari*		
	Merge	*Nonmerge*	*Match*	*Merge*	*Nonmerge*	*Match*	*Merge*	*Nonmerge*	*Match*
Anton	X		No	X		Yes		X	No
Mario	X		Yes	X		Yes		X	Yes
Gustave	X		Yes		X	No		X	Yes
Lola	X		Yes	X		Yes		X	Yes
Kelsey	X		Yes	X		Yes		X	Yes
Ella		X	No		X	Yes		X	Yes
Chad	X		Yes	X		Yes		X	Yes
Nancy	X		No?	X		Yes		X	Yes
Carl	X		Yes	X		Yes		X	Yes
Carla	X		Yes	X		Yes		X	Yes
			7/10			9/10			9/10

Source: Dollinger (2012: 95)

References

Bard, Ellen Gurman, Dan Robertson and Antonella Sorace. 1996. Magnitude estimation of linguistic acceptability. *Language* 72: 32–68.

Beebe, Leslie M. and Martha Clark Cummings. 1996. Natural speech act data versus written questionnaire data: How data collection method affects speech act performance. In Susan Gass and Joyce Neu (eds) *Speech Acts across Cultures: Challenges to Communication in a Second Language*. Berlin and New York: Mouton de Gruyter, 65–86.

Blum-Kulka, Shoshana. 1997. Discourse pragmatics. In Teun A. van Dijk (ed.) *Discourse as Social Interaction*. London: Sage, 38–63.

Blum-Kulka, Shoshana, Juliane House and Gabriele Kasper. 1989. *Cross-Cultural Pragmatics: Requests and Apologies*. Norwood, NJ: Ablex.

Boberg, Charles. 2010. *The English Language in Canada: Status, History and Comparative Analysis*. Cambridge: Cambridge University Press.

Boberg, Charles. 2013. The use of written questionnaires in sociolinguistics. In Christine Mallinson, Becky Childs and Gerard Van Herk (eds) *Data Collection in Sociolinguistics: Methods and Applications*. New York and London: Routledge, 131–141.

Bourhis, Richard Y., Howard Giles and Doreen Rosenthal. 1981. Notes on the construction of a 'subjective vitality questionnaire' for ethnolinguistic groups. *Journal of Multilingual and Multicultural Development* 2: 145–155.

Campbell-Kibler, Kathryn. 2011. The sociolinguistic variant as a carrier of social meaning. *Language Variation and Change* 22: 423–441.

Choi, Jinny K. 2005. Bilingualism in Paraguay: Forty years after Rubin's study. *Journal of Multilingual and Multicultural Development* 26: 233–248.

De Vaus, David. 2005. *Surveys in Social Research.* 5th edition. London and New York: Routledge.

Dollinger, Stefan. 2012. The written questionnaire as a sociolinguistic data gathering tool: Testing its validity. *Journal of English Linguistics* 40: 74–110.

Dörnyei, Zoltán. 2003. *Questionnaires in Second Language Research: Construction, Administration and Processing.* Mahwah, NJ: Lawrence Erlbaum.

Extra, Guus and Kutlay Yagmur. 2004. *Urban Multilingualism in Europe.* Clevedon: Multilingual Matters.

Fuller, Janet M. 2005. The uses and meanings of the female title Ms. *American Speech* 80: 180–206.

Hatch, Evelyn and Anne Lazaraton. 1991. *The Research Manual.* New York: Newbury House.

Labov, William. 1972. *Sociolinguistic Patterns.* Philadelphia, PA: University of Pennsylvania Press.

Labov, William. 1994. *Principles of Linguistic Change Volume I: Internal Factors.* Malden and Oxford: Wiley-Blackwell.

Llamas, Carmen. 2007. A new methodology: Data elicitation for regional and social language variation studies. *York Papers in Linguistics* 8: 138–163.

Schilling, Natalie. 2013. *Sociolinguistic Fieldwork.* Cambridge: Cambridge University Press.

Schleef, Erik. 2013. Written surveys and questionnaires. In Janet Holmes and Kirk Hazen (eds) *Research Methods in Sociolinguistics.* Oxford: Wiley-Blackwell, 42–57.

Orton, Harold, Stewart Sanderson and John Widdowson. 1978. *The Linguistic Atlas of England.* London: Croom Helm.

Willis, Gordon B. 2005. *Cognitive Interviewing: A Tool for Improving Questionnaire Design.* Thousand Oaks, CA: Sage.

Further reading

Boberg, Charles. 2013. The use of written questionnaires in sociolinguistics. In Christine Mallinson, Becky Childs and Gerard Van Herk (eds) *Data Collection in Sociolinguistics: Methods and Applications.* New York and London: Routledge, 131–141.

Brown, James Dean. 2001. *Using Surveys in Language Programs.* Cambridge: Cambridge University Press.

De Vaus, David. 2005. *Surveys in Social Research.* 5th edition. London and New York: Routledge.

Dollinger, Stefan. 2015. *The Written Questionnaire in Social Dialectology: History, Theory, Practice.* Amsterdam: John Benjamins.

Dörnyei, Zoltán. 2003. *Questionnaires in Second Language Research: Construction, Administration and Processing.* Mahwah, NJ: Lawrence Erlbaum.

Gillham, Bill. 2007. *Developing a Questionnaire.* 2nd edition. London and New York: Continuum.

Schleef, Erik. 2013. Written surveys and questionnaires. In Janet Holmes and Kirk Hazen (eds) *Research Methods in Sociolinguistics.* Oxford: Wiley-Blackwell, 42–57.

9 Studying perceptions and attitudes

Finding out what people think or believe about language is a very exciting area of research, and it is crucial for sociolinguistics because language attitudes influence language use. We'll tell you about three methods of data collection in this chapter: direct methods, indirect methods and the collection of pre-existing speech or text for further analysis of the social meaning of language. In keeping with the spirit of this book, we'll point you to some key readings that will help kick-start your own investigation. Our examples will mostly be about the social evaluation of speech, and Garrett (2010) is a particularly useful resource in this area, but we'll also consider social identification, speech perception and perceptual dialectology.

Direct methods

You might think the easiest way to find out about attitudes is to ask people. But for various reasons, people aren't always good sources of direct information on their attitudes. They may fudge (or even lie) if they think their answer might be interpreted negatively, or they may lack the necessary degree of introspection to answer your questions well. So be careful when analysing data based on this approach.

You can use a variety of different methods to find out about attitudes directly: interviews, rapid and anonymous surveys, questionnaires, etc. In the last few chapters, we offered advice on these methods and you could also look at a few studies that use direct methods: Hickey (2009) who explored language attitudes towards Irish and English in Ireland, or Sharp et al. (1973) who investigated attitudes to Welsh. Sharp et al. studied 12,000 children and, as you can see right at the start of their survey, they made no attempt to hide their interest in language: "The following exercise is designed to find out what kind of idea you have of the Welsh language" (Sharp et al. 1973: 167). Once the data is collected, it is often analysed by identifying the main emerging themes.

Indirect methods

Indirect methods use subtler ways to elicit attitudes, and the results based on indirect methods often differ from those based on direct methods (Garrett 2010: 42–43). In speaker evaluation studies, participants listen to a number of short recordings of different voices, and they are asked to evaluate these voices. See for example Giles (1977) for an early overview and Giles and Billings (2004) for a more recent overview of this approach.

In these studies, listeners are presented with recordings of speech, either from different speakers or the same speaker. We refer to the former as verbal guise (Cooper 1975) and to the latter as matched guise techniques (Lambert et al. 1960). For example, when investigating regional accent variation, one speaker (or several different speakers) will be heard saying the same thing with different regional accents, while other features (e.g. speech rate, hesitation, what is said) are held constant. People doing the study are told that they will hear different speakers – regardless of whether they will or not. You don't want to let them know they may hear the same person twice because you're trying to find out whether speakers of different linguistic varieties are evaluated differently on the basis of their speech alone. Speakers of stigmatised varieties are usually evaluated as less educated, less articulate and less wealthy than speakers of the standard. Conversely, speakers of non-standard varieties may be evaluated positively on other scales: they may be rated as being more down-to earth, more friendly or more trustworthy than the standard speakers. One of the interesting questions you can ask with this kind of study is whether the positive evaluation of non-standard voices is limited to members of one's ingroup (Lambert et al. 1960) or whether it applies more widely (Gallois, Callan and Johnstone 1984).

How it's done

The following steps are normally taken in a matched- or verbal-guise study:

1 Choose a contextual frame for your evaluation study: guidelines that contextualise your recordings and that clarify for participants what will happen.
2 Make your recordings.
3 Test the recordings. We often do this in focus groups in order to find out (a) whether they sound natural and (b) what social meanings participants associate with different varieties or linguistic features. We would ask general, open-ended questions, such as "What kind of person do you think this speaker is?"
4 Choose the social attributes for your survey. Speech evaluation often relates to scales of superiority, attractiveness and dynamism (Zahn and Hopper 1985). This is a good starting point, but whatever you choose needs to

have meaning to the listeners whose evaluation you are interested in. You may want to select some labels from previous research and supplement them with attributes that came out of your focus group or pilot, because you know they will make sense and be relevant to the people participating in the research. Consider including multi-item scales (see Chapter 8) and a question about where respondents think the speaker comes from (see perceptual dialectology, later in this chapter).

5 Create your written survey, bearing in mind our advice in Chapter 8. You may decide to include distractors and it's always a good idea to randomise or counterbalance stimuli and evaluation scales in order to avoid order effects (Clopper 2013: 158). Most experimental or survey software will be able to do this for you (e.g. search: *SurveyMonkey*, *SurveyGizmo*, *FluidSurveys* or *LimeSurvey*).

6 Run the survey. Perception studies are often done by university students. But remember that university students are not representative of the general population, particularly in respect to education, IT skills, literacy, life experience and social origin. Nowadays, web and field tools allow you to do these kinds of tests in a wide range of places and reach varied people. If you run surveys outside of the lab environment and you investigate the perception of fine phonetic detail, make sure you find a way to control the audio quality of recordings, for example by testing the degree to which participants can hear the stimuli. You may have to dismiss unsuitable responses.

7 Collect data in a spreadsheet and run your statistical tests (Chapters 12–14). Once data has been collected, evaluations are analysed statistically and taken to represent respondents' attitudes towards the varieties/features the speakers used – rather than the individual speakers themselves – since you have held other factors constant.

Have a look at Agheyisi and Fishman (1970) or Lee (1971) if you want to find out about some issues with these methods. We'll mention a few here. Indirect tasks are, of course, unnatural, and this will have repercussions for the attitudes we elicit. You could try and make these tasks more natural to respondents by designing an experiment that slots neatly into a natural context; but this really only works when the response you are interested in is relatively straightforward. For example, Bourhis and Giles (1976) report a study in which different audiences in a theatre in Wales heard public service announcements spoken in several language varieties. After the show, they were asked to fill in a questionnaire related to the content of the announcement. Positive evaluation of a variety was measured by the number of people who had filled in the questionnaire.

Also always remember that when you design a perception study, it is important that you try and hold as many things constant as possible, e.g. speech rate, frequency, content and placement of hesitations, etc. in order to put the focus of

We would like you to help in the rating of people who are studying to be news broadcasters on a national network. You will hear a person reading the same passage at different stages of training. We'd like you to register your overall judgment of her success as a broadcaster. Please rate each of the trials by moving the slide right towards "Perfectly professional" or left towards "Try some other line of work".

As you listen, keep the mouse on the slider and move it to indicate any changes in your overall judgment.

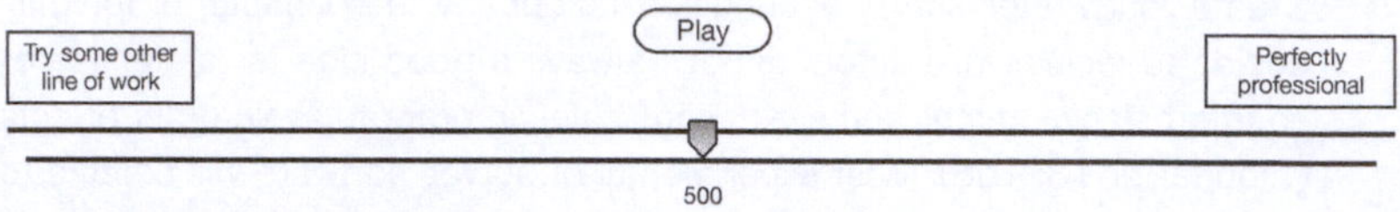

Figure 9.1 Newscast experiment

Source: Labov et al. (2011: 444)

investigation precisely on what you're interested in. Previous research has shown that people are influenced by a surprising range of things, not just their experience and knowledge, but also where a variety is used, e.g. at home or at school (Creber and Giles 1983), what is being said (Cargile and Giles 1998) and the experimenter's accent (Hay, Drager and Warren 2010).

It's awfully difficult to design a perception study 'without context' because people will naturally try and imagine one, and this may differ from person to person. It makes more sense to provide a scenario or a task for people taking part in your study. Labov et al. (2011) contextualised their study by saying that the speaker has been going through training as a newscaster and listeners are hearing this person at different phases of the training. What people aren't told is that in each repetition, the number and distribution of non-standard (ing) forms varied (Figure 9.1).

Of course, message content is an important contextual cue that listeners use to evaluate speakers. It's tricky to deal with. You can have each speaker read the same text, however, that means people are evaluating read – not spontaneous – speech. Labov et al. (2011) do a very good job of justifying the use of read speech in their study, but this may not always be possible. If you want to make claims about spontaneous speech, you need to use spontaneous speech but this will inevitably result in different speakers talking about different things. You can control for this a bit by asking people to speak on the same topic. We have summarised these and similar issues as well as potential solutions in a document entitled 'How to create good stimuli' on our companion website.

Manipulation of variables

Matched and verbal guise tests have been widely used to elicit information on how a speaker of a given *variety* is perceived. Recently, more complex questions have emerged, for example, what associations do specific variants, or combinations of variants, trigger and under what conditions do they do this? This is an exciting research area, and these questions are answered using similar methods to the ones outlined above. When you investigate lexical or syntactic variables, text-based guises can be used (e.g. Buchstaller 2006). When the focus is on accent features, properties of recorded speech are often manipulated to elicit attitudes to individual features. This results in resynthesised speech (e.g. Plichta and Preston 2005) or stimuli in which one sound was deleted in the original and different variants were cross-spliced into its place, creating multiple copies that only differ in a single cue (e.g. Labov et al. 2011; Campbell-Kibler 2011).

If you're interested in this, you can just focus on how a feature is evaluated, but you could also explore more complex questions (see textboxes on speech perception and social identification). How we evaluate someone's speech seems to be influenced by the social characteristics of survey respondents (Schleef and Flynn 2015) and by what we perceive speakers' social characteristics to be (Niedzielski 1999; Campbell-Kibler 2009); and you can manipulate these in your attitudes survey. So there's a lot to explore! These studies show that variables don't have fixed social meanings. They can be associated with indexical fields of ideologically related meanings (Eckert 2008). So be cautious about averaging out all the responses you get. If some people are telling you different things, that may be an important finding.

SOCIAL INFORMATION AND SPEECH PERCEPTION

Research in this tradition investigates how the social information available to speakers and listeners is used to make sense of speech or specific linguistic features. For example, Strand's (1999) study of listeners' beliefs about the gender of the speaker showed that whether listeners hear [s] or [ʃ] depends on whether the speaker looks prototypically masculine or feminine. It influences the perception of the phonemic boundary between /s/ and /ʃ/. In other words, listener perception is influenced by the social information received. If you are interested in this area and want to find out more, Thomas (2002), Drager (2010) and Foulkes, Scobbie and Watt (2010) are good places to start.

SOCIAL IDENTIFICATION

This research strand focuses on what linguistic features listeners use to extract social information from speech. Several studies of 'linguistic profiling' have shown that the social identification of individuals sometimes triggers discriminatory behaviour. Baugh (1996) showed such discrimination to occur during phone calls in which callers use different accents that index race. Other areas in which this line of research features include the perception of sexual orientation (Levon 2007; Smyth, Jacobs and Rogers 2003), the identification of regional origin, social stances and emotion (Nygaard and Queen 2008), as well as testing possible interventions to prevent discrimination, for example of non-standard speakers (Hansen, Rakić and Steffens 2014).

Perceptual dialectology

It has widely been assumed that the evaluation of a variety is a fallout of its association with particular social groups. This need not necessarily be the case; Preston (2013) argues that listeners may not know which variety they are evaluating. That means that even though group-based evaluation may be true for some varieties or features, other features may simply be regarded as bad or good without reference to a group. Gaining a better understanding of what language users think about language and what their beliefs, perceptions and evaluative paradigms are is at the heart of perceptual dialectology. It also investigates people's beliefs about where dialect areas are, their "mental maps of regional speech areas" (Preston 2013: 168). Preston (1999) and Niedzielski and Preston (2003) are excellent comprehensive accounts of this area. Montgomery and Beal (2011) and Preston (2013) give shorter overviews of the concerns and the methods of perceptual dialectology, and we suggest you read at least these last two if you would like to work in this area. Preston (1999: xxxiv) outlines the "Five Graces" of perceptual dialectology:

1. Map tasks: respondents are asked to draw boundaries of regional speech zones on a blank map or one with only minimal details. A composite map is created out of all these individual maps later on, resulting in "perceptual isoglosses" (Preston 1999: 361).
2. Difference tasks: respondents are asked to rank regions according to how different they perceive them to be from their home area.
3. Evaluation tasks: respondents are asked to rank regions for pleasantness and correctness of speech.

4 Identification tasks: respondents listen to a randomised set of recordings, which can be arranged into a dialect continuum, and are asked to assign each voice to an area.
5 Conversations: respondents are questioned about the tasks and language in general.

As you can see, this not only provides data on how different individuals view dialect space and how they perceive variation, it also tells us how good people are at actually identifying the varieties they have heard, and it allows us to link their responses to their mental maps of the world around them. For example, it turns out that respondents from different parts of the US have internalised different dialect boundaries, and their evaluation systems may differ as well.

Recent additions to the perceptual dialectology toolkit allow different kinds of visualisation (Montgomery 2011). Some of these make it easier to demonstrate the relationship between perceived provenance and actual provenance of a voice sample. This makes factors that influence dialect perception, such as cultural prominence of a place and the closeness of the respondent's area to the area from which the voice sample originates, very apparent.

Collecting pre-existing speech or text

It's not always necessary to go out and elicit original data yourself in order to ask interesting sociolinguistic questions. This is true for questions about perceptions and attitudes too. Many Letters to the Editor or comments sections on newspaper websites will throw up interesting views on language use. Relevant pre-existing speech or text can be collected quite easily and you can analyse it with a view to the social meaning of language. This involves assigning opinions to a set of categories that you found in your text, and inferring attitudes from these text sources. For example, in order to uncover attitudes towards English in a variety of African contexts, Schmied (1991) investigated, among other things, Letters to the Editor of African newspapers. He assigned evaluative material to one of five principal categories: communicative, national, personal, educational and cognitive arguments in favour of English or an African language. There is plenty of exciting material all around you that provides very rich sources of information on language attitudes, including advertisements (Cheshire and Moser 1994), cartoons (Kramer 1974) and Disney films (Lippi-Green 2012).

ANALYSING CONTENT

Assigning text to categories can be crucial when deriving attitudes from pre-existing speech or text. We provide a very quick guide on how you can go about categorising content on our companion website. This will make data analysis much easier, and once this is done, your data is ready for systematic analysis in whichever framework you like. If you are looking for a more theoretically informed way to do this, check out Content Analysis, but this may be much more than you need to know for your study. It's a useful method that helps you break down text into manageable units and assign them to categories based on an objective coding scheme that you have previously generated. Berg (2001: chapter 11) and Mayring (2000) are good introductions to Content Analysis.

Historical records, too, provide information about perceptions and beliefs about language. In historical sociolinguistics, the term *normative linguistics* is frequently applied to this strand of research (Tieken-Boon van Ostade 2000; Yáñez-Bouza forthcoming). Its focus is often on a specific genre where we know evaluative comments occur: normative writings such as grammar books, elocution guides and pronunciation dictionaries. For example, Yáñez-Bouza (2008) explores the evaluation of preposition stranding – e.g. who'd you give the book *to*? – in eighteenth-century grammar books. Turns out prescriptive opinions were actually quite varied back then.

NORMATIVE LINGUISTICS AND LANGUAGE CHANGE

This research strand also explores how normative writing may have influenced language use. First, you categorise comments on linguistic features mentioned in normative writing. Then, you compare these comments with relevant features in usage corpora (i.e. actual language used, for example, in letters and literary works) before, during and after the period from which the comments originate. Yáñez-Bouza (forthcoming) includes a list of normative sources, and she also summarises the methodological steps in detail. A good example of an online usage corpus is the ARCHER corpus: A Representative Corpus of Historical English Registers, but your library may also subscribe to other potential sources such as the Eighteenth Century Collections Online or American Periodicals.

If you do start delving into historical datasets, or data from any other culture for that matter, be mindful of the hazards associated with importing your own contemporary attitudes into the interpretation of different belief systems. As you can see, the study of attitudes and perceptions is a highly varied area with plenty of opportunities to apply your findings to real-world problems. One first important step to take is to recognise that not only linguistic forms vary, attitudes do too.

EXERCISES

Exercise 1

Consider this comment in a nineteenth-century grammar book describing dialect features in England. How does the writer conceptualise language variation, and what difficulties would emerge if one wanted to study the (ing) ending in historical texts?

> In the West, people often cut off the g from *nothing*, &c.; in London, they add a *k*: the former say, *nothin*, and the latter *nothink* · the latter specimen is barbarous. The Yorkshire and Lancashire dialects have also nearly the latter defect; the *ing* should have a *ringing* sound.
>
> Source: Cobbin (1864 [1828])

Exercise 2

Consider the composite New Zealand map of a perceptual dialectology study conducted at the University of Auckland (Duhamel and Meyerhoff 2014). Survey participants were given an unlabelled map of New Zealand. The enlarged section of the map showing Auckland in more detail was minimally labelled. They received the following instructions:

> Below is a map of New Zealand with an enlarged section for Auckland. Draw lines on the map where you think there are differences in how people talk. Label the different areas that you have drawn on the map. What do you think of how people talk in these areas? How would you describe people from these areas? Write these thoughts on the map.

Respondents could write as much and as little as they wanted, and the task was not combined with accent recordings of any kind. Figure 9.2 shows the main dialect areas in New Zealand identified as having a distinctive speaking style. It is based on data from 247 respondents.

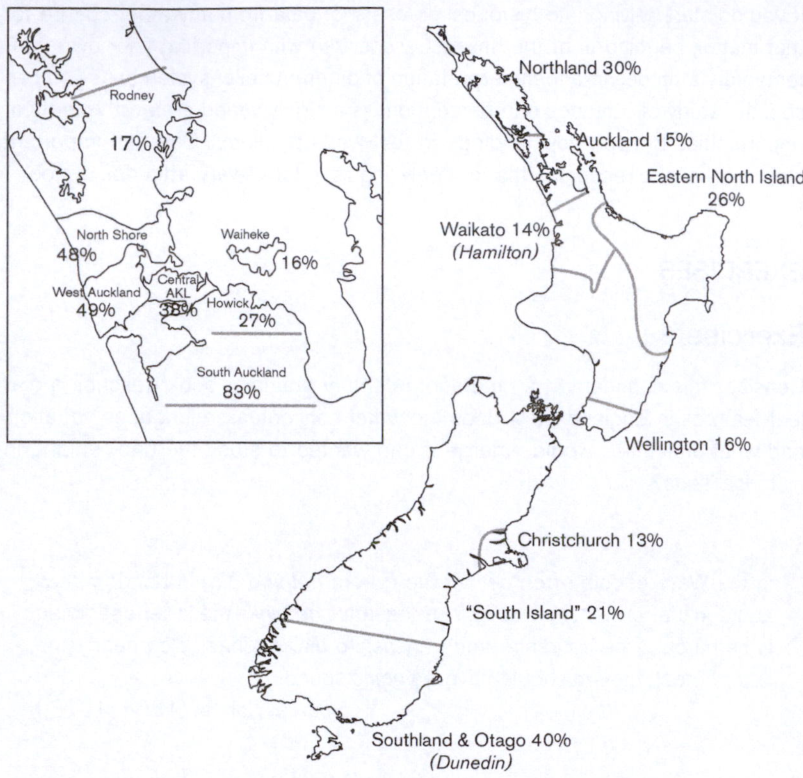

Figure 9.2 Main dialect areas in New Zealand identified by 247 respondents
Source: Duhamel and Meyerhoff (2014)

Applying the concerns of perceptual dialectology, how would you continue this study in order to find out whether these perceived maps are supported by acoustic evidence, i.e. whether these maps are mainly ideological constructs or whether there is actual perceptual evidence for them? What other steps would you be interested in taking and why? What locations would you choose for further study?

References

Agheyisi, Rebecca and Joshua A. Fishman. 1970. Language attitude studies: A brief survey of methodological approaches. *Anthropological Linguistics* 12: 137–157.

Baugh, John. 1996. Perceptions within a variable paradigm: Black and White racial detection and identification based on speech. In Edgar W. Schneider (ed.) *Focus on the USA*. Philadelphia, PA: John Benjamins, 169–182.

Berg, Bruce L. 2001. *Qualitative Research Methods for the Social Sciences*. 4th edition. Boston, MA: Allyn and Bacon.

Bourhis, Richard Y. and Howard Giles. 1976. The language of cooperation in Wales: A field study. *Language Sciences* 42: 13–16.

Buchstaller, Isabelle. 2006. Social stereotypes, personality traits and regional perceptions displaced: Attitudes towards the new quotative in the UK. *Journal of Sociolinguistics* 10: 362–381.

Campbell-Kibler, Kathryn. 2009. The nature of sociolinguistic perception. *Language Variation and Change* 21: 135–156.

Campbell-Kibler, Kathryn. 2011. The sociolinguistic variant as a carrier of social meaning. *Language Variation and Change* 22: 423–441.

Cargile, Aaron Castelan and Howard Giles. 1998. Language attitudes toward varieties of English: An American-Japanese context. *Journal of Applied Communication Research* 26: 338–356.

Cheshire, Jenny and Lise-Marie Moser. 1994. English as a cultural symbol. *Journal of Multilingual and Multicultural Development* 15: 451–469.

Clopper, Cynthia. 2013. Experiments. In Christine Mallinson, Becky Childs and Gerard Van Herk (eds) *Data Collection in Sociolinguistics: Methods and Applications*. New York and London: Routledge, 151–161.

Cobbin, Ingram. 1864 [1828]. *Elements of English Grammar: Expressly Designed for the Juvenile Student, either at Home or in Preparatory Schools*. Illustrated, 33rd edition. London: William Tegg.

Cooper, Robert L. 1975. Introduction to language attitudes II. *International Journal of the Sociology of Language* 6: 5–9.

Creber, Clare and Howard Giles. 1983. Social context and language attitudes: The role of formality-informality of the setting. *Language Sciences* 5: 155–183.

Drager, Katie. 2010. Sociophonetic variation in speech perception. *Language and Linguistics Compass* 4: 473–480.

Duhamel, Marie-France and Miriam Meyerhoff. 2014. An end of egalitarianism? Social evaluations of language difference in New Zealand. *Linguistic Vanguard* 1 December 2014. DOI: 10.1515/lingvan-2014-1005.

Eckert, Penelope. 2008. Variation and the indexical field. *Journal of Sociolinguistics* 12: 453–476.

Foulkes, Paul, James M. Scobbie and Dominic Watt. 2010. Sociophonetics. In William J. Hardcastle, John Laver and Fiona E. Gibbon (eds) *Handbook of Phonetic Sciences*. 2nd edition. Oxford: Blackwell, 703–754.

Gallois, Cynthia, Victor J. Callan and Michael Johnstone. 1984. Personality judgments of Australian Aborigine and white speakers: Ethnicity, sex, and context. *Journal of Language and Social Psychology* 3: 39–58.

Garrett, Peter. 2010. *Attitudes to Language*. Cambridge: Cambridge University Press.

Giles, Howard. 1977. Social psychology and applied linguistics: Towards an integrative approach. *I.T.L. Review of Applied Linguistics* 35: 27–42.

Giles, Howard and Andrew C. Billings. 2004. Assessing language attitudes: Speaker evaluation studies. In Alan Davies and Catherine Elder (eds) *The Handbook of Applied Linguistics*. Malden, MA: Blackwell, 187–209.

Hansen, Karolina, Tamara Rakić and Melanie C. Steffens. 2014. When actions speak louder than words: Preventing discrimination of nonstandard speakers. *Journal of Language and Social Psychology* 33: 68–77.

Hay, Jennifer, Katie Drager and Paul Warren. 2010. Short-term exposure to one dialect affects processing of another. *Language and Speech* 53: 447–471.

Hickey, Raymond. 2009. Language use and attitudes in Ireland: A preliminary evaluation of survey results. In Brian Ó Catháin (ed.) *Sochtheangeolaíocht na Gaeilge.* Léachtaí Cholm Cille 39: 62–89.

Kramer, Cheris. 1974. Stereotypes of women's speech: The word from cartoons. *Journal of Popular Culture* 8: 622–638.

Labov, William, Sharon Ash, Maya Ravindranath, Tracey Weldon, Maciej Baranowski and Naomi Nagy. 2011. Properties of the sociolinguistic monitor. *Journal of Sociolinguistics* 15: 431–463.

Lambert, Wallace E., Richard C. Hodgson, Robert C. Gardner and Samuel Fillenbaum. 1960. Evaluational reactions to spoken language. *Journal of Abnormal and Social Psychology* 60: 44–51.

Lee, Richard R. 1971. Dialect perception: A critical review and re-evaluation. *Quarterly Journal of Speech* 57: 410–417.

Levon, Erez. 2007. Sexuality in context: Variation and the sociolinguistic perception of identity. *Language in Society* 36: 533–554.

Lippi-Green, Rosina. 2012. *English with an Accent: Language, Ideology, and Discrimination in the United States.* Abingdon: Routledge.

Mayring, Philipp. 2000. Qualitative content analysis. *Forum Qualitative Sozialforschung / Forum: Qualitative Social Research* [On-line Journal], 1(2). Available at www.utsc.utoronto.ca/~kmacd/IDSC10/Readings/text%20analysis/CA.pdf (last accessed 12 June 2014).

Montgomery, Chris. 2011. Starburst charts: Methods for investigating the geographical perception of and attitudes towards speech samples. *Studies in Variation, Contacts and Change in English* 7. Available at www.helsinki.fi/varieng/journal/volumes/07/montgomery/index.html (last accessed 9 June 2014).

Montgomery, Chris and Joan Beal. 2011. Perceptual dialectology. In Warren Maguire and April McMahon (eds) *Analysing Variation in English.* Cambridge: Cambridge University Press, 121–148.

Niedzielski, Nancy. 1999. The effect of social information on the perception of sociolinguistic variables. *Journal of Language and Social Psychology* 18: 62–85.

Niedzielski, Nancy A. and Dennis R. Preston. 2003. *Folk Linguistics.* Berlin: Mouton de Gruyter.

Nygaard, Lynne C. and Jennifer S. Queen. 2008. Communicating emotion: Linking affective prosody and word meaning. *Journal of Experimental Psychology* 34: 1017–1030.

Plichta, Bartek and Dennis R. Preston. 2005. The /ay/s have it: The perception of /ay/ as a North-South stereotype in US English. *Acta Linguistica Hafniensia* 37: 243–285.

Preston, Dennis R. 1999. *Handbook of Perceptual Dialectology.* Volume 1. Amsterdam: John Benjamins.

Preston, Dennis R. 2013. Language with an attitude. In J.K. Chambers and Natalie Schilling (eds) *The Handbook of Language Variation and Change.* 2nd edition. Oxford: Wiley-Blackwell, 157–182.

Schleef, Erik and Nicholas Flynn. 2015. Ageing meanings of (ing) in Manchester, England. *English World-Wide* 36: 48–90.

Schmied, Josef J. 1991. *English in Africa.* London: Longman.

Sharp, Derrick, Beryl Thomas, Eurwen Price, Gareth Francis and Iwan Davies. 1973. *Attitudes to Welsh and English in the Schools of Wales.* Basingstoke: Macmillan.

Smyth, Ron, Greg Jacobs and Henry Rogers. 2003. Male voices and perceived sexual orientation: An experimental and theoretical approach. *Language in Society* 32: 329–350.

Strand, Elizabeth A. 1999. Uncovering the roles of gender stereotypes in speech perception. *Journal of Language and Social Psychology* 18: 86–99.

Thomas, Erik. 2002. Sociophonetic approaches of speech perception experiments. *American Speech* 77: 115–147.

Tieken-Boon van Ostade, Ingrid. 2000. Normative studies in England. In Sylvain Auroux, E.F. Konrad Koerner, Hans-Josef Niederehe and Kees Versteegh (eds) *History of the Language Sciences.* Vol. 1. Berlin and New York: Walter de Gruyter, 876–887.

Yáñez-Bouza, Nuria. 2008. Preposition stranding in the eighteenth century: Something to talk about. In Ingrid Tieken-Boon van Ostade (ed.) *Grammars, Grammarians and Grammar-Writing in Eighteenth-Century England.* Berlin and New York: Mouton de Gruyter, 251–277.

Yáñez-Bouza, Nuria. Forthcoming. Early and late modern English grammars as evidence in English historical linguistics. In Merja Kytö and Päivi Pahta (eds) *The Cambridge Handbook of English Historical Linguistics.* Cambridge: Cambridge University Press.

Zahn, Christopher J. and Robert Hopper. 1985. Measuring language attitudes: The speech evaluation instrument. *Journal of Language and Social Psychology* 4: 113–123.

Further reading

Campbell-Kibler, Kathryn. 2010. Sociolinguistics and perception. *Language and Linguistics Compass* 4: 377–389.

Garrett, Peter. 2010. *Attitudes to Language.* Cambridge: Cambridge University Press.

Giles, Howard. 1977. Social psychology and applied linguistics: Towards an integrative approach. *I.T.L. Review of Applied Linguistics* 35: 27–42.

Giles, Howard and Andrew C. Billings. 2004. Assessing language attitudes: Speaker evaluation studies. In Alan Davies and Catherine Elder (eds) *The Handbook of Applied Linguistics.* Malden, MA: Blackwell, 187–209.

Long, Daniel and Dennis Preston. 2002. *Handbook of Perceptual Dialectology.* Vol. 2. Amsterdam: John Benjamins.

Montgomery, Chris and Joan Beal. 2011. Perceptual dialectology. In Warren Maguire and April McMahon (eds) *Analysing Variation in English.* Cambridge: Cambridge University Press.

Niedzielski, Nancy A. and Dennis R. Preston. 2003. *Folk Linguistics.* Berlin: Mouton de Gruyter.

Preston, Dennis R. 1999. *Handbook of Perceptual Dialectology.* Vol. 1. Amsterdam: John Benjamins.

Preston, Dennis R. 2013. Language with an attitude. In Chambers, J.K and Natalie Schilling-Estes (eds) *The Handbook of Language Variation and Change.* Oxford: Wiley-Blackwell, 157–182.

Part II
Data analysis

10 Transcription

Your transcription is probably the first really serious step in your analysis. What you decide to include or exclude when you transcribe your data is necessarily shaped by what you plan to analyse. Mondada puts it quite nicely: transcriptions are "irremediably . . . tied to the context of their production and to the practical purpose of their accomplishment" (2007: 810). In other words, why did you decide to do this and what are you doing it for? This means that transcripts intended for discourse or conversation analysis look rather different to those destined for the quantitative analysis of specific features of variation.

In this chapter, we will talk you through several transcription examples, and using them, we will try to show you how the end goal of your transcription affects your transcription practices, how important good guidelines are and how your transcription can be subject to the law of unintended consequences.

End goals: What are you transcribing for?

The amount of detail that you can include in a transcript differs depending on what kind of analysis you are planning to do. We begin by considering the pros and cons of standard orthography and punctuation, issues with transcribing pauses and other non-linguistic information and whether to transcribe linguistic detail from the start.

Orthography and punctuation

Using standard orthography and punctuation makes for a very readable transcription and also one that allows you to search it easily. If you start trying to represent differences in the way people pronounce words, or the ways speakers run words together in fast speech, you can end up with a lot of respellings that are idiosyncratic and these will make it hard to isolate particular words or features you might be interested in. However, if you are doing sociolinguistic research that is less concerned with finding all and every instance of a particular word and instead is more concerned with how speakers express themselves at a moment in time, then respellings might appeal to you as a way of capturing the flavour of real speech (respelling is discussed further later in this chapter).

The style of spelling and use of punctuation is one of the main ways that transcription for conversation analysis (CA), discourse analysis (DA) and variationist sociolinguistics (VSLX) differ. As a rule of thumb, CA aspires to the most detailed transcription, while DA and VSLX can get by with something much more like the way speech is transcribed in a play or novel. Compare the CA transcription by John Heritage in (1) below, with the way we would be more inclined to transcribe it if we were planning an analysis of variation (1').

(1) Sample of CA transcription style (from Heritage 2012: 9)

```
5    Nan:        Well of course all the kids in this: p'tilar class yih
6                know,h are eether full time stud'nts or they work during
7                th'day en go tuh school et ni:ght,
8    Emm:        °M[m h m, ° ]
9    Nan:          [Lot'v'm w]ork par'time u- [a:nd
10   Emm:                                     [°Mm h[m, °
11   Nan:                                           [go: part day en part
12               ni:ght? .hhhhh uh::m
13   Emm:  ->    They're not real kookie then. =
14   Nan:        =Sev'ral of th'm are married,h Oh no:.h
```

(1') Heritage's transcription rendered in less detail

1	Nan:	Well of course all the kids in this particular class you know are either full time students or they work during the day and go to school at night.
2	Emm:	Mhm.
3	Nan:	Lot of them work part-time
4	Emm:	Mhm
5	Nan:	and go part day and part night.
6	Emm:	They're not real kookie then?
7	Nan:	Several of them are married, oh no.

As you can see, (1') loses information about where overlaps occurred (speech marked visually by aligning square brackets in (1)) and where one speaker follows on seamlessly from the other (shown with = in (1)), as well as information about speakers' breathing (marked with *.hhhhhh*) and drawn out segments (marked with a colon). In CA transcripts, the length of pauses will also be marked, often down to 0.2 second in length.

The transcription in (1) is less accessible than (1') (we are not 100 per cent sure that *p'tilar* in line 5 is 'particular' but that seems to make the most sense) and also takes a lot more time to undertake. On the other hand, most people would agree that pauses and overlaps contain a lot of potentially important information about how the interlocutors are orienting to each other and what they are (not) saying. Lots of overlaps, for instance, indicate a high level of engagement (whether supportive or antagonistic). And for the variationist, it is worth remembering that pauses may be important, even if their duration is not. Guy (1980) famously showed that two East Coast dialects differed in their rule for (t, d) deletion – New York City speakers treat following pauses more like a following consonant while Philadelphia speakers treat them more like following vowels.

TO TRANSCRIBE OR NOT TO TRANSCRIBE?

We strongly recommend you transcribe all your data. Having access to transcriptions will make data analysis so much easier. However, this may not always be possible as time or funding constraints may not allow you to have all data transcribed before your deadline. You will need about an hour to transcribe ten minutes of recorded speech, depending on the recordings. This comes to *at least* six hours for every hour of recorded speech (roughly the length of one sociolinguistic interview). If you've got 20 of those, do the maths . . .

If this is beyond your resources, you may resort to partial transcription or no transcription at all. However, you should know that this is only appropriate if you know exactly what feature(s) and sociolinguistic factors you want to explore and if you have no further plans to work with the data in the future. Let's say you're interested in the variable (ing). For a partial transcription, you only transcribe those sections in which your variable occurs. You also note down the speaker and the time point at which your variable occurred. In the case of (ing), this may just be a sentence or intonation phrase; it may be a thematically united discourse unit in the case of discourse or syntactic features, as topic and discourse function may influence the use of your variable. You will have to make sure to transcribe what preceded and followed your variable, as preceding and following context may influence productive variability. Partial transcription limits your analysis to what you have transcribed. For example, if you have only transcribed the intonation units in which (ing) occurs, it is unlikely that you will be able to explore how topic influences the variability of (ing).

These problems are multiplied if you do not transcribe at all. In this scenario, you only note down how certain variables are realised. In the case of (ing), you listen to the recordings and every time an (ing) occurs in unstressed position you note down whether you hear [ɪn], [ɪŋ], whatever other variants exist in the variety you're investigating or whether the pronunciation is unclear. As an absolute minimum, you should also note the word in which (ing) occurred, the following and preceding context, the time point at which it occurred and the speaker (easily done in ELAN, see textbox).

Variationists may find it expedient to include some detail in their transcription, especially if they know they plan to look in detail at certain features when they begin their analysis. Poplack, Walker and Malcolmson (2006), for instance, transcribed the word *like* in two different ways (*like* and *lyke*) in a corpus of Canadian English. *Lyke* was assigned as the distinctive spelling of the lexeme LIKE when it functioned as a discourse marker. Similarly, we have sometimes inserted zeroes to mark the place where the argument of a verb or preposition is missing in a stretch of discourse. The example in (2) shows how Miriam coded a corpus of Bislama (the creole spoken in Vanuatu) so that she could later search easily for structural features such as unexpressed arguments, or moved/fronted constituents. These are highlighted in bold in (2) (the other codes are fairly standard parts of speech).

(2) Vosale on the merits of selling fresh produce at market

1 Vs: [CNJ be **[FO kopra]**]
2 [CNJ sapos [SBJ yumi [VP katem [DO kopra]]]]
3 [SBJ yumi [VP smokem **[DO 0]**] [PP long hotea]]
4 [CNJ sapos **[SBJ 0** [VP i kasem [DO tu bag]]]]
5 [ADV maet] **[SBJ 0** [VP i [NEG no] save kasem [DO fo tausen]]]

Vosale: But **copra**, if we cut copra and then smoke **it** over hot air, say **there** are two bags, **they** might not even fetch four thousand Vatu.

This level of detail was very helpful for later analysis because it enables the corpus to be searched for things *that aren't there*. But it takes extra time to do this kind of transcription because it requires the transcriber to undertake a full analysis of each utterance.

TRANSCRIPTION SYMBOLS

Here are some examples of transcription symbols frequently used in VSLX and DA research:

.	Falling pitch at the end of an intonation unit
,	Level pitch at the end of an intonation unit
?	Rising pitch at the end of an intonation unit
(.), (..), (...)	Short pauses of up to one second
(2.0)	Longer pauses (of more than one second) are often timed with a stopwatch or computer. In this case, the symbol refers to a pause of two seconds.
underlined	Stressed syllable or word
:	Lengthening of sound
[ ]	Beginning and end of overlap. Overlapping speech of speakers is included in brackets. This also includes backchanneling phenomena and overlapping speech that may be heard as an interruption.
=	Latched utterance, i.e. one speaker starts talking exactly when the other one stops
(xxx)	Uncertain transcription or incomprehensible speech. Put what you think you hear in brackets.
< >	Contextual events, e.g. <laughing>

If you need more, you might want to draw them from a commonly used system, such as Gail Jefferson's, which is widely used in conversation analysis (most accessibly summarised in Atkinson and Heritage 1999). Just always remember that there is no need to use all existing transcription conventions and to be detailed in all respects. Transcribe what you think you need and make sure to list your transcription conventions in the methods section of your paper or in the appendix, similar to how Holmes and Schnurr (2006) and Bucholtz (1999) have done (see exercises). VSLX especially relies mostly on normal orthography without many special symbols.

Try to use the same spelling for the same words, including dialect words and colloquialisms (e.g. *wanna*). Use the same hyphenation rules and contracted and fused words throughout. Only include phonetic detail (e.g. vowel reduction or t/d-deletion) if it is meaningful to your discourse analysis. If you look at these phenomena from a VSLX perspective, you will code them in an additional step (Chapter 11), rather than marking these phenomena in your transcript. If you present discourse extracts in your paper, try to use (anonymised) names, rather than numbers. Number the lines and use left-hand side arrows to highlight phenomena important to your analysis (e.g. the excerpt on p. 100).

Transcribing gesture and eye gaze

Researchers working on sign languages will take it for granted that video is the basic medium and that any transcription needs to cover manual and facial gestures, and the field has a well-established set of standards for the kinds of features (e.g. hand shape, movement) that need to be annotated in the transcription. For sign language research, recent software developments have streamlined the transcription process considerably. Many sign language researchers have adopted ELAN (2014) which allows transcriptions to remain linked directly to the sound or video file that they originally came from (see Mondada 2007 for various other options). Lausberg and Sloetjes (2009) provide a useful decision tree for other researchers to use when deciding how much gesture to transcribe and at what level of detail.

ELAN

The format of ELAN (ELAN 2014) is particularly well suited to sociolinguistic work as it allows the researcher to time-align transcription and recording and make numerous dependent and independent annotations on any word, utterance or even eye flash. Have a look at the screen shot in Figure 10.1. Different speakers are transcribed on different tiers and you can also add several coding tiers. We're showing an example of (ing)-coding. ELAN needs .wav file input, so if you plan to use it, you should record interviews and conversations as .wav files.

Shifting old transcriptions into ELAN is a slightly cumbersome process (Nagy and Meyerhoff 2015), but it's not clear why anyone starting from scratch would not use this system, or an equivalent one. ELAN also allows you to work from video.

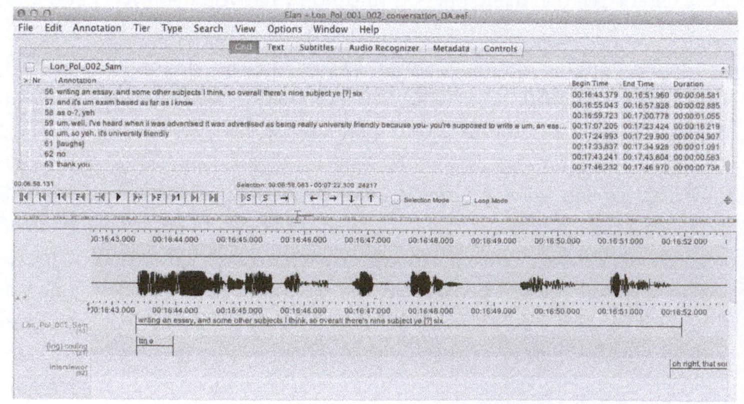

Figure 10.1 ELAN screen shot

Good guidelines: Systematising your transcription

Whatever transcription system you adopt, and whatever level of detail you decide to use, it is important to have a thorough set of guidelines. Very often more than one person will contribute to the transcription of a large corpus, and even if you are working on your own, it is good to have a checklist you can refer to for non-standard sounds or dialect words. This is also very helpful when you come to write up your study because you can use it as the basis of a guide for your readers explaining what you have decided to mark and how.

Dodging 'blowback': How your transcript will be read

A final factor to consider is how your transcript is going to be read. We mean 'read' in terms of comprehensibility but also in the political sense: what messages your transcription choices will send about the (speech of the) person you've transcribed. For a VSLX and CA/DA analysis, you probably won't 'clean up' your transcripts, i.e. you will consistently represent the messiness of your data, such as false starts, repetitions, overlaps, odd word choice and unfinished sentences, because these may influence your data analysis. And it's fine to do this as long as you're consistent and do it for every speaker. The situation becomes slightly more complicated when it comes to orthography. We've said above that standard orthography will facilitate data searches. On the other hand, the consistent use of dialect words can maintain the authenticity of the data, as the Scottish words for *own* and *yes* do in (3) (from the Edinburgh component of the Sociolinguistics and Immigration Corpus):

> (3) Spellings of meaningful and iconic Scottish words
>
> But they try and speak Scottish it's stupid, it's like go and talk your *ain* language.
> So she was like, *aye*, it looks like cellulitis.

However, when it comes to other orthographic conventions and different types of respellings, you might want to think about possible repercussions. Reputedly, the CIA talk about 'blowback' – unintended negative effects that follow on from their covert activities. Because our transcription decisions are usually only partly overt to our readers, we can talk about the unintended consequences of respellings as being 'sociolinguistic blowback'. So how can we be mindful of how our work might be read?

Preston (1985) usefully differentiates between three types of respellings: allegro speech forms, dialect respellings and eye dialect. The term *allegro speech forms* refers to non-standard spellings that capture casual or relaxed speech, e.g. *gettin'*, *'cause* and *an'* (for *and*). The term also covers reduction phenomena that occur frequently in spoken language, even among speakers that are considered articulate and refined. For example, final consonants are often reduced in function words such as *and* and *but* by all speakers, particularly when they are followed by another consonant. *Dialect respellings* are slightly different since they attempt to capture regional or social features of pronunciation. Although they may often be phonetically inaccurate or inconsistent, they are nonetheless attempts to represent a difference between standard and non-standard pronunciation, e.g. *wint* for *went* (in a dialect with a merger of [ɛ] and [ɪ]), or *dis* for *this.*

Eye dialect, on the other hand, refers to forms which seem to represent a phonological difference between standard and non-standard counterparts that doesn't actually exist, e.g. *sez* and *wuz* for *says* and *was*; *wot* for *what.* Preston (1985: 328) objects particularly to eye dialect forms, as they "serve mainly to denigrate the speaker so represented by making him or her appear boorish, uneducated, rustic, gangsterish, and so on". However, all forms of respellings evoke social meanings that transcribers should be aware of. They may characterise a speaker in terms of social status, character and linguistic abilities. Preston (1985) has demonstrated this in a controlled experiment. For this reason, some projects stick to standard orthography and use the subsequent detailed analysis (e.g. Chapter 11) to mark relevant pronunciation reductions.

Hence, although respellings may have several advantages – they're a useful short-hand for indexing characters, injecting narrative colour and representing spoken language – they also have disadvantages. Respellings may be seen as discriminatory. They may perpetuate stereotypes. They are often used inconsistently for a speaker, or even worse, they are used for only some speakers, particularly those from marginal groups.

It's worth noting that respellings do not only characterise socially marginal groups of speakers. In general, they characterise certain speakers as different, or as speakers that the writer has strong feelings about. For example, Steve Bell, a famously left-wing cartoonist in the UK, likes to represent the Queen's English as in Figure 10.2.

While at times respellings may be highly instrumental, especially if they are used consistently, you might want to ask yourself whether – if you really need a lot of phonetic detail – you might better use the IPA for words or sounds that are of interest. Also keep in mind that non-standard forms may not always be the most relevant ones; standard speech or hyper-articulation may be relevant too, and this may have to be clearly transcribed if it's relevant to the conversation or your analysis. However, you need not necessarily make these specific decisions during your first run of transcriptions. More often, what happens is that researchers transcribe recordings and once specific questions emerge, they re-transcribe the relevant portions. There is a considerable literature on transcription and if you find yourself drawn into the intellectual and practical challenges that transcribing poses, you will find the Further Reading at the end of this chapter rewarding.

Figure 10.2 Comic strip

Source: Bell (1985: 71)

EXERCISES

Exercise 1

The following extract is taken from Zadie Smith's novel *White Teeth*. It comes from a speech made by an elderly woman from the Caribbean.

> "I came into dis world in an eart-quake at de very beginning and I shall see the hevil and sinful pollution be herased in a mighty rumbling eart-quake once more. Praise de Lord! . . . My grandmudder live to see one hundered-and-tree an de woman could skip rope till de day she keel over and drop col'. Me gwan make it. I make it dis far. . . . And tanks to you, Lord, I'm gwan a feel a rumble at both ends."
>
> Smith (2000: 410–411)

Create a table with the following headings: tokens; substitution of . . .; for Standard English; exceptions? Then answer the questions below based on the data in the extract on p. 107.

1 How does Smith make use of respellings?
2 What dialect features does she mark? Is she consistent?
3 Are they the features *you* would mark if you were trying to represent Jamaican Patois?
4 Does she only mark features that are particular to Patois?
5 What is the effect of the internal consistencies and inconsistencies in her use of respellings? Does it suggest anything to you about the character of the speaker, or about the attitude of the writer to the character she is representing?

Moving beyond this example:

6 Are there some varieties that you think can *not* be represented in standard spelling (e.g. hip-hop language)?
7 Are the conventional IM (Instant Messaging) and texting abbreviations the same as *eye dialect*? How are they the same and how do they differ?
8 Gail Jefferson argues that using standard spelling in transcriptions "obscure[s] the very data upon which [linguistic] theories should be based" (1983: 11). Do you agree with her? Why?

Exercise 2

Consider the transcription conventions from Holmes and Schnurr (2006) and Bucholtz (1999). How are they similar and how are they different? Could confusion arise if conventions are not made clear to readers in the methods section or in the appendix?

Transcription conventions from Holmes and Schnurr (2006: 51)

<u>yes</u>	Underlining indicates emphatic stress
[laughs]::	Paralinguistic features in square brackets, colons indicate start/ finish
+	Pause of up to one second
(3)	Pause of specified number of seconds
. . ./. . . . . .\ . . . . . ./. . . . . .\ . . .	Simultaneous speech
(hello)	Transcriber's best guess at an unclear utterance
?	Rising or question intonation

- Incomplete or cut-off utterance
...... Section of transcript omitted
= Speaker's turn continues
[*edit*] Editorial comments italicized in square brackets

All names used in examples are pseudonyms.

Transcription conventions from Bucholtz (1999: 221f)

Symbol	Meaning
.	end of intonation unit; falling intonation
,	end of intonation unit; fall-rise intonation
?	end of intonation unit; rising intonation
–	self-interruption
:	length
underline	emphatic stress or increased amplitude
(.)	pause of 0.5 seconds or less
(n.n)	pause of greater than 0.5 seconds, measured by a stopwatch
h	exhalation (e.g. laughter, sigh); each token marks one pulse
( )	uncertain transcription
⟨ ⟩	transcriber comment; nonvocal noise
{ }	stretch of talk over which a transcriber comment applies
[ ]	overlap beginning and end
/	latching (no pause between speaker turns)
=	no pause between intonation units

References

Atkinson, J. Maxwell and John Heritage. 1999. Jefferson's transcript notation. In Adam Jaworski and Nikolas Coupland (eds) *The Discourse Reader*. London and New York: Routledge, 158–166.

Bell, Steve. 1985. *The Unrepeatable If*. . . London: Methuen.

Bucholtz, Mary. 1999. "Why be normal?" Language and identity practice in a community of nerd girls. *Language in Society* 28: 203–223.

ELAN: Language archiving technology, version 4.6.2. 2014. www.lat-mpi.eu/tools/elan/. Max Planck Institute for Psycholinguistics, The Language Archive, Nijmegen, The Netherlands.

Guy, Gregory R. 1980. Variation in the group and the individual: The case of final stop deletion. In William Labov (ed.) *Locating Language in Time and Space*. New York: Academic Press, 1–36.

Heritage, John. 2012. Epistemics in action: Action formation and territories of knowledge. *Research on Language and Social Interaction* 45: 1–29.

Holmes, Janet and Stephanie Schnurr. 2006. "Doing femininity" at work: More than just relational practice. *Journal of Sociolinguistics* 10: 31–51.

Jefferson, Gail. 1983. Issues in the transcription of naturally-occurring talk: Caricature versus capturing pronunciational particulars. *Tilburg Papers in Langue and Literature* 34: 1–12. Tilburg: Tilburg University.

Lausberg, Hedda and Han Sloetjes. 2009. Coding gestural behavior with the NEUROGES-ELAN system. *Behavior Research Methods* 41: 841–849.

Mondada, Lorenza. 2007. Commentary: Transcript variations and the indexicality of transcribing practices. *Discourse Studies* 9: 809–821.

Nagy, Naomi and Miriam Meyerhoff. 2015. Extending ELAN into variationist sociolinguistics. MS, The University of Toronto/Victoria University of Wellington. www.individual.utoronto.ca/ngn/Resources/resources.htm.

Poplack, Shana, James A. Walker and Rebecca Malcolmson. 2006. An English "like no other"? Language contact and change in Quebec. *Canadian Journal of Linguistics* 51: 185–213.

Preston, Dennis. 1985. The Li'l Abner syndrome: Written representations of speech. *American Speech* 60: 328–336.

Smith, Zadie. 2000. *White Teeth*. London: Penguin.

Further reading

Antaki, Charles. 2011. An introduction to conversation analysis. Available at http://homepages.lboro.ac.uk/~ssca1/sitemenu.htm (last accessed 17 February 2014).

Bucholtz, Mary. 2000. The politics of transcription. *Journal of Pragmatics* 32: 1439–1465.

Cameron, Deborah. 2001. *Working with Spoken Discourse*. London: Sage.

D'Arcy, Alexandra. 2013. Advances in sociolinguistic transcription methods. In Christine Mallinson, Becky Childs and Gerard Van Herk (eds) *Data Collection in Sociolinguistics: Methods and Applications*. New York and London: Routledge, 187–190.

Mondada, Lorenza. 2007. Commentary: Transcript variations and the indexicality of transcribing practices. *Discourse Studies* 9: 809–821.

Ochs, Elinor. 1979. Transcription as theory. In Elinor Ochs and Bambi Schieffelin (eds) *Developmental Pragmatics*. New York: Academic Press, 43–72.

The exchange of papers in the journal *Discourse Studies*, December 2007.

11 Identifying, coding and summarising your data

If transcribing is the first stage in your analysis, then identifying examples of the things you want to look at and isolating them for more detailed investigation is the second. We are going to focus on the steps needed to prepare data for quantitative analysis, but some of the general steps apply to qualitative studies as well. One of the major points of difference between quantitative and qualitative analysis at this stage in a study lies in the application of the principle of accountability, i.e. the need for a quantitative study to identify *all* the places where the form you're interested in could possibly appear, and account for even the places where it fails to appear. Qualitative studies may analyse a few examples that the researcher believes are (proto)typical or extreme instances of the general pattern.

The potential for snowballing errors is perhaps greater for quantitative analysis, so getting the early stages of isolating and coding the data right is really important. In the remainder of this chapter, we'll talk through the workflow we follow in our studies.

The hunting of the variable

> What I tell you three times is true
>
> (Carroll 1876: 3)

If you have taken our (thrice?) repeated advice to transcribe in ELAN (Chapter 10), the best and most efficient place to isolate the individual tokens of your variables and to start annotating each token in relation to each of the independent/predictor variables is also in ELAN. This annotation process is what variationists refer to as 'coding'. Nagy and Meyerhoff (2015) give a detailed step-by-step guide to doing this in ELAN and most people who have tried it become firm converts. Its principal advantage is that it allows you to retain a direct link between the place in the audio or video recording where each token occurs and your coding for all the features that you think may influence its distribution. That means it is much easier to check previous work and add more detail later than it is if you literally 'extract' tokens from their source file and move them somewhere else. In fact, this chapter will work on an extractive model – we'll show you how to identify tokens in context, isolate them for further annotation and code them for different possible predictors.

If you haven't yet had a chance to work with ELAN or a similarly flexible transcribing system, you will probably be working (in the traditional manner) with a transcription in something like a Word file. Here, you will identify or isolate the examples of the variable that you're interested in, and you will need either to rely on your detailed transcription, or go back to the audio of your recording, to describe where the token you have found occurs and what its detailed environment is.

You need to do this in an environment that is flexible enough to handle the kind of additional information you will be annotating (or coding) a variant with – something like a spreadsheet that can function like a simple database programme. Most of us use Excel because of the ubiquity of MS Office but obviously open source programmes like OpenOffice Calc will do the job as well. (Even if you are doing your coding in something like ELAN, you may find yourself taking advantage of the data manipulation options in a spreadsheet at some stage.)

Setting up a spreadsheet is simple and you can continue to mine it happily for some time *if* you follow some basic principles.

First, you need to have every example/token of the variable you're interested in in a different row of your spreadsheet. That means that you might have several rows in your spreadsheet for one sentence or utterance, because sometimes they have more than one token of the form you're studying. Figure 11.1 shows this for a study that's going to be looking at existential constructions in Bequia. We can immediately create a column with the context (sentence, clause, phrase) that has an existential in it; rows 10 and 11 have the same utterance but each row codes a different example of an existential. Next we add columns for the variable we'll be looking at. We had already noticed that existentials in Bequia English alternate between the *there is/are*-type forms used in Standard English and *it have/get*-type forms used in the Caribbean, so in this case we have created two columns for the variable. The first one allows us to annotate each token for the form of the subject (*there* or *it*) and the second one focuses on the form of the verb (*be*, *get* or *have*).

Make sure that you're working within the full envelope of variation (Chapter 2). That is, you should have every single token of where the variant you're studying occurs and also all the places where it doesn't occur. So in this case, because we were interested in when the local, Caribbean form was used, the rows in our spreadsheet include not only the tokens that are realised as *it have/get* (as in rows 5–11), but also the ones that are not realised in the local fashion, the ones using a Standard English-like construction (rows 2–4). In variationist terminology, we'd say we have to record not only the cases where you have the application value of your variable, but also the non-applications. If you were measuring vowels, the coding for each token would usually include a column for the F1 value and a

	A	B	C	D	E
1	Subject	Verb	Speaker	Line	Token
2	t	b	8	57	"there's a brown girl in the ring tra-la-la-la-la"
3	t	b	8	1364	There's a God, yeah.
4	t	b	8	225	There was more noise
5	i	h	8	622	But now it have all kind of thing they grinding and make seasoning now
6	i	h	8	112	where that house up there now it had a lot of mango tree up there
7	i	g	8	878	It get some beat bad.
8	i	h	11	1623	That too, and it had one in the upper corner of Friendship-Bay, so was Petit-Nevis island
9	i	h	11	1704	Oh, it had sailing boat here.
10	i	g	11	1764	It got six, [and it got seven coming down]
11	i	g	11	1764	[It got six,] and it got seven coming down

Figure 11.1 Screenshot showing tokens of existential constructions identified in interviews with two speakers of Bequia English – coded for the subject type (*it*, *there*) and the verb type (*be*, *have*, *get*)

Note: The same sentence appears in rows 10–11 because it has two tokens of an existential

separate column for the F2 value of each token (you'd have calculated this using something like the software programme Praat or vowel extraction software, see Chapter 7).

Even if you are just starting out with this kind of work, and even if you have very little time to complete a class project, this level of coding will allow you to do the bare minimum. You can, for instance, now much more easily report your findings as percentages and not simply as raw totals. Sometimes students doing a very simple quantitative study submit reports that have frequency counts as their final results. A frequency count (e.g. "The Caribbean forms of the existential construction occurred 123 times in my data") are useful ways of getting an overview of what your data looks like, but they aren't very informative. That's because one person, for example, might have spoken a lot longer than all the other people and their data is going to skew the frequency counts. So you should always *at least* report your results as percentages since this adjusts for differences in frequency in different contexts or by different speakers. See Chapter 12 for more on calculating and presenting percentages.

At this stage, if you have been transcribing zero tokens of arguments or verbs (as discussed in Chapter 10, example 2), you can also relatively easily extract cases where your variant doesn't appear and no other overt alternative fills the position it would appear in. If you haven't marked phonetically null or zero tokens

	A	B	C	D	E	F	G	H	I
1	Copula Expression	Grammatical Person	Subject Type	Following Grammatical Category	Preceding Phonological Context	Following Phonological Context	Speaker Number	Line Number	Context
2	f	6	n	n	s	c	306	75	Our games is marble
3	f	6	n	n	s	c	306	75	The boys games is cricket
4	0	6	p	n	v	c	306	78	they Ø teachers
5	f	3	n	p	c	c	306	96	the world is more enlightened
6	c	3	p	n	c	c	306	111	It's today with mine- mine associates, but outside
7	f	3	n	a	v	c	306	129	Bequia is just beautiful for a holiday
8	c	3	N	a	v	c	306	137	the heat of the sun today's much hotter than fourteen and fifteen years ago.
9	c	3	p	a	c	c	306	139	it's much hotter
10	c	3	p	n	c	v	306	142	it's a beautiful spot,
11	c	3	p	n	c	c	306	142	I think it's one the most beautiful spots in the island of Bequia, Mt–Pleasant
12	c	3	p	n	v	v	306	172	the people get more knowledge and is a wider experience of sewing
13	f	3	p	a	c	c	306	179	well I find tis more beautiful than now
14	f	3	w	?	c	/	306	184	They deal with they own problem according to what it is
15	0	3	p	n	c	c	306	184	But if it Ø difficulties they go to St-Vincent then.
16	c	3	p	n	v	c	306	204	um what you call whooping cough and what not, is bush, is these um herbal bush
17	c	3	d	a	c	c	306	206	that's right
18	c	3	d	n	c	v	306	236	That's all.
19	0	3	n	a	c	c	306	257	The lightning Ø first
20	c	3	p	a	c	c	306	257	and it's very hot,
21	f	3	w	a	s	c	306	259	which is very dangerous

Figure 11.2 Screenshot showing tokens and coding for copula presence and absence in a Mount Pleasant speaker of Bequia English (Walker and Meyerhoff 2006)

of your variable when you were transcribing, you may have to insert them as a separate code after rereading or relistening to your source files. In Figure 11.2, you can see an example of the coding underlying Walker and Meyerhoff's (2006) study of where the copula was and wasn't present in a variety of Caribbean English. Note the use of Ø in the 'Context' column to indicate where a form of the copula appears to be absent and the coding of this as 0 in the column 'Copula Expression'.

Once you have coded your variable for the different forms it is realised as, you can start coding for the factors that you think may be influencing the distribution of the different forms. For phonological variables, these are typically also related to other phonological or prosodic structures (preceding or following segment, stressed or unstressed syllable, position in the syllable, etc.). Many researchers also code for the individual word/lexeme, so they can see whether there are specific lexical effects on how variation is patterned.

For syntactic or discourse variables, the factors that might possibly be influencing the distribution of forms are likely to be more extensive. The immediate phonological environment may still be relevant, but so will the structure of the clause, and very often also relationships across clauses, e.g. whether the subject in the current clause was also some kind of argument in the preceding clause. Figure 11.2 shows that for the grammatical variable of copula presence/absence we coded for some phonological and some syntactic features (this is actually a subset of the things we coded for).

Deciding what to code for in your study is best guided by doing a thorough literature search on other analyses of that variable or related variables. You will find that experienced researchers use the previous literature to scaffold or motivate their own hypotheses in a literature review or in a section called something like 'Circumscribing the variable context', or 'Defining the envelope of variation'.

When you are setting up your spreadsheet, here are some useful principles that will make your life easier when you start to do your analysis.

1 Have a separate line for every token of the variable (see Figure 11.1).
2 Have a separate column for each of the linguistic factors that you think might be constraining the distribution of the form (e.g. thematic role of the referent in that clause, preceding/following phonological segment, word class).
3 Have a column for each of the non-linguistic (social) factors that you think might be relevant in predicting the distribution of the variable's forms (e.g. speaker's gender, individual speaker identification, speaker's age).
4 Keep clear records of what each column is documenting. The column labels in Figure 11.2 are reasonably transparent, but try working out what we were doing with 'Subject Type'; it may be a bit opaque to you without access to our coding guide.
5 Keep clear records of how you have coded each variable. This is essential for any study, but even if you are the only person doing the coding, you need to

document the decisions you've made at each step so you can be consistent in how you do your coding. In Figures 11.1 and 11.2 you can see how single character codes might become hard to reinterpret after only a short time, but what your coding notes will also do is record how you decided to code or exclude any complicated or unclear examples, and why.

A NOTE ON EXCLUSION

We have emphasised the importance of counting all places where your variable could possibly occur, and this is the general rule for analyses of variation. However, we should also note that in some analyses, researchers will make some principled exclusions. For instance, if you are analysing the deletion of final coronal stops in words like *praised* [pɹezd] and *bent* [bɛnt], then typically people ignore cases where the following word starts with a coronal stop (*bent top*) because we are not confident that we can reliably identify a deleted [d] or [t] in that context. Such environments are called *neutralisation contexts*. Some researchers also exclude very common words (with this variable, things like *and* and *just*) or alternatively they may cap the number of tokens they code from any one lexical type (e.g. take only a maximum of 20 tokens of any one word).

Your coding of each variable will identify the different values that each variable can have, e.g. the thematic role of the referent might be coded as 'agent', 'patient' etc., and the following phonological segment might be coded in a lot of detail. For social factors, this is probably fairly easy and may seem a bit boring but you still need to code each token for it. For example, the speaker's age won't change across different tokens of the dependent variable – though the time in the interview will and you might want to have a separate column showing this – so you can just enter age once (on the first token) and in Excel you can pull down and fill all the cells below with the same value (or in ELAN you can automatically label all the annotations in one tier with the same value).

Some people like to code for the specific realisations of the following segment, e.g. [t], [ð], [ʔ]. Later, you might find it is more informative to classify these on the basis of manner or place of articulation, e.g. grouping [t] and [ʔ] with other stops, or [t] and [ð] with other alveolar and post-alevolar segments, but if you code in detail at the start, you will have more flexibility in your analysis later on. If you are working on a project with other people and you are coding different speakers to the same system, you can imagine how useful it is to have a clear set of coding guidelines – what each coding abbreviation means and when it should be used. You'll need this when you come to write up your study, so it's worth spending time on it at the start for all sorts of reasons.

REPORTING YOUR CODING

Some researchers report their coding in more of a narrative and interweave the coding system with aspects of their literature review. Cheshire (2005: 481–485) takes this approach for the linguistic variables; the social variables are introduced with the analysis (2005: 486). Hazen (2000) introduces each independent variable and the results associated with it in the body of the report. Other people provide you with something more like their lab notes. Erker and Guy (2012: 533–535) introduce and exemplify in turn each of the linguistic factors that they coded null subjects in Spanish for. When you are starting out and learning how to report your work, the style used by Erker and Guy may provide the most helpful model for your own report.

The coding system should be as transparent as you can possibly make it. Some of the programmes that you may be doing your analysis in will have restrictions on the kind of labels you can use in your coding – Goldvarb, for instance, can only work with single character codes for the different values of each variable (this is what's shown in the figures earlier in this chapter). But other programmes will allow you to use whole words as your code, e.g. 'patient' might be coded as 'p' in Goldvarb but you can use the whole word 'patient' in R. We recommend you avoid using complex, multi-word labels though in any format because that can start to cause confusion because of the way different programmes handle them.

ZEN AND THE ART OF CODING VARIABLES

> You look at where you're going and where you are and it never makes sense, but then you look back at where you've been and a pattern seems to emerge.
>
> (Pirsig 1974: 170)

> Just keep swimming, swimming, swimming. What do we do? We swim, swim.
>
> (Stanton and Unkrich 2003)

Getting to the Zen stage of handling your variables – complete absorption in and satisfaction through the task – can require a bit of experimentation. For a lot of people, detailed coding of the dependent and independent variables can be a huge chore. For one of us, the breakthrough was being taught to do your coding with pleasing music as a backdrop. If you try this, start with something that doesn't have lyrics – plinky-plunky Baroque music seems to be especially well-suited to repetitive coding but we have known students to find Japanese pop equally effective as a sonic backdrop. It seems that lyrics (in a language you can understand) can distract you from the linguistic tasks associated with coding but this is clearly an area that needs further research. Other people prefer to keep their data coding experience pure and ascetic. Yet others handle it by working in short and intense bursts of activity.

There is no way around it: coding your variables can be slow and tiresome and the only way to get it done is by plugging away at it (as Dory says in *Finding Nemo*, "Just keep swimming"). Something to remember about this stage of your analysis is that you are in fact internalising a lot of distributional information and are starting to formulate hypotheses about how to further explore the patterns associated with particular variants in your data.

Code once and code a lot

It's a bit like the old adage about voting in Chicago – code once and code a lot. What do we mean by that? It's quite simple really. It means you should spend some time at the outset of your coding and think strategically about what you need to code for: it's always better to code for lots and lots of possible factors that could be influencing your variable from the outset and to code in a lot of detail within each of them. It's miserable getting to the end of your coding and realising that you have to go back and code for something useful that you missed. Minimally, your coding should have a timestamp for every token (our figures show line numbers from Word transcripts), which means that if you suddenly find yourself with more time than expected to do your coding, you can at least go back later and find all the tokens again without too much pain and agony.

In some cases, more detailed coding can save you time. For example, if you code for preceding phonological segment in detail, you can go back to your data later and code for whether those preceding segments were voiced or voiceless (say) by coding all the [t]s at once, all the [d]s at once, etc. This saves you from having to make the 'voiced/voiceless?' decision with every single token.

EMIC AND ETIC CODING

In other textbooks on (socio)linguistics, you may see reference to a distinction between 'emic' and 'etic' categories. We won't delve deeply into the theory behind this, given the practical nature of this guide, but we want to acknowledge the tradition. Essentially, emic categories are ones that make sense within the boundaries of the group or language that you are studying and etic ones make sense to a linguist or outsider and generally allow for easier cross-study comparisons. So, for example, if you code for the communities of practice that speakers participate in and that have meaning to them, that would be an emic coding system. If you code following segments as stops, fricatives, etc., that's an etic coding system. Some social factors are coded etically, e.g. if gender is coded as a binary based on the speaker's sex. Some linguistic features are coded emically, e.g. it's an empirical question whether languages treat nasals as + or – [continuant].

The distinction between emic and etic categories derives from the work of Kenneth Pike (1954). Pike believed that a combination of emic and etic approaches were essential for sound analysis of language. That advice is still good today.

Getting summary statistics

Once you have coded all your data in a spreadsheet, you can start to look over the distribution of the variants you're interested in. You can do this by sorting and summing across rows in Excel or by searching across tiers in ELAN or by importing the Excel data into a data analysis programme like Goldvarb or Rbrul and doing some basic cross-tabulations.

At this point, you will be able to see if there are any big gaps in your dataset that might require recoding or rethinking how you might undertake your analysis, e.g. you may find that when you sum up the thematic roles that your variable fills there's no examples of first person pronouns as patients of a clause. Or you might find that there are hardly any examples of a (th) variable occurring as [f] word-medially. If your data is skewed in this way, it's not the end of the world – on the contrary, congratulations, these are your first findings!

But what it does mean is that you'll want to amend your hypotheses and plans for further analysis to reflect what this information about the distribution of forms tells you.

EXERCISES

Exercise 1

Buchstaller (2008) studied the use of verbs of quotation in US and UK English, so the verbs *(be) like*, *go*, *say* and zero (as shown in example 11, below) constitute her dependent variable.

Below are the examples she gave showing how she coded her data for the independent variables of quote type (mimetic content, i.e. when the speaker imitates a specific sound vs linguistic content), and quote content (reported speech vs reported thought) (2008: 23–24).

1 Set up a table or spreadsheet and code all the examples in (3)–(18) for (i) the dependent variable and (ii) all the independent variables.
2 Now create a table or tables that summarise the distribution of the three forms of the dependent variable.
3 Based on your summary table, what are the next steps that you might undertake for the analysis of these verbs of quotation?

Reported Mimetic Quote

(3) USA I was just a youngster and I was **like** "oh my gosh".
(4) UK I'm **like** "uuups".
(5) USA He picks up a stick and **goes** "bang".
(6) UK Then so then he **went** he **went** "pfff".

Reported Linguistic Quote

(7) USA And we're **like** "who are you to judge?" you know "just report the facts".
(8) UK I'm **like** "yes I'll eat it but I'm not enraptured".
(9) USA She **goes** "well Frank opened his big mouth".
(10) UK I **went** "alright I'll give me a call back in a minute".

Reported Speech

(11) USA My daughter's like "Mommy can I help you with the laundry?"
Ø "Of course you can".
(12) UK And my mom was going "come on, try it on".
I was **like** "no I'm not trying it on".
(13) USA And he **goes** "do you want to dance?"
I **go** "no no".
(14) UK And he just kind of looked at me and he **goes** "you all right?"
and I said "yeah".

REPORTED THOUGHT

(15) USA Well I used to make the regular pudding and put it in the pie shell,
and it would sit in the refrigerator for a day,
where you cut the pie it would soak into the pie shell and it was
like red and I'm **like** "uuahh:: this is kind of groedy [sic.]".

(16) UK I mean I was like trapped,
rather like being a rabbit in the headlight you know,
it was **like** "ahhhh".

(17) USA The first year the deer ate my garden,
and I was just so astounded I'm **going** "deer right here in the city?"

(18) UK And the third time my hand went like straight through the window,
and there was like gropping plastic smashing down,
and I **went** "oh shit".

Source: Buchstaller (2008: 23–24)

References

Buchstaller, Isabelle. 2008. The localization of global linguistic variants. *English World-Wide* 29: 15–44.

Carroll, Lewis. 1876. *The Hunting of the Snark: An Agony in Eight Fits*. London: Macmillan & Co.

Cheshire, Jenny. 2005. Syntactic variation and beyond: Gender and social class variation in the use of discourse-new markers. *Journal of Sociolinguistics* 9: 479–508.

Erker, Daniel and Gregory R. Guy. 2012. The role of lexical frequency in syntactic variability: Variable subject personal pronoun expression in Spanish. *Language* 88: 526–557.

Hazen, Kirk. 2000. Subject-verb concord in a postinsular dialect: The gradual persistence of dialect patterning. *Journal of English Linguistics* 28: 127–144.

Nagy, Naomi and Miriam Meyerhoff. 2015. Extending ELAN into variationist sociolinguistics. MS, The University of Toronto/Victoria University of Wellington. www.individual.utoronto.ca/ngn/Resources/resources.htm.

Pike, Kenneth L. 1954. *Language in Relation to a Unified Theory of Human Behavior*. Vol. 1. Dallas, TX: Summer Institute of Linguistics.

Pirsig, Robert M. 1974. *Zen and the Art of Motorcycle Maintenance: An Inquiry into Values*. New York: William Morrow.

Stanton, Andrew and Lee Unkrich (dirs.) 2003. *Finding Nemo*. Pixar Animation & Disney Enterprises.

Walker, James A. and Miriam Meyerhoff. 2006. Zero copula in the Caribbean: Evidence from Bequia. *American Speech* 81: 146–163.

Further reading

Schilling, Natalie. 2013. *Sociolinguistic Fieldwork*. Cambridge: Cambridge University Press.

Tagliamonte, Sali A. 2006. *Analysing Sociolinguistic Variation*. Cambridge: Cambridge University Press.

12 Analysing your data

Preliminaries

Let's pause for a moment and take stock of where you are at this point in your project. You've identified a research question, selected the source of your data and coded a variable of interest. Now it's time to dig into your data to see what it reveals the answer to your research question to be.

In the following three chapters, we're going to discuss how this digging is done in the tradition of quantitative variationist sociolinguistics (Chapter 15 will incorporate qualitative data analysis). This research paradigm is based on Weinreich, Labov and Herzog's (1968) foundational theory of "orderly heterogeneity" in language variation. This is the proposal that, when speakers have a choice between two or more ways of saying the same thing (heterogeneity), their use of one or the other option is structured and systematic (orderly), rather than random. This was a ground-breaking proposal at the time, because previous linguistic work up to then had viewed variation in language as completely haphazard, with no pattern concerning when a speaker would use one or another variant.

What led Weinreich, Labov and Herzog to this conclusion was the quantitative analysis of linguistic variation. Specifically, following on from Labov's ground-breaking work in New York City, they pointed out that linguistic variants tend to correlate, or covary, with factors like style, age and social class. When these researchers probed the language variation within a speech community, they found that certain variants were used more or less by some groups of speakers or in some contexts than others.

How could they definitively say that a variant was used more or less? They looked at numbers: comparing, say, the rate of use of a variant by one group of speakers to the rate that variant was used by a different group. This quantitative approach blazed the trail for a new sociolinguistic tradition.

In the following chapters, we'll introduce you to the types of quantitative analysis variationist sociolinguists perform on their data. Before we get there, though, we'd like to take a moment to reassure some of you who may be thinking

"I thought I was going to be doing sociolinguistics – no one ever told me I'd have to use numbers!".

Many of our students balk when confronted with the idea of doing quantitative analysis, protesting that they are "not good at maths" or "terrible with numbers". In these students' minds, the population breaks down into 'maths people' and 'non-maths people', and they feel that they're in the latter group. However, psychologists have found that intelligence, including maths skills, is malleable (Jaeggi et al. 2008): with dedicated work, it can be improved, meaning that it's very unlikely that someone is doomed to be a 'non-maths person' forever. In fact, once students are told this, they start performing better in school (Blackwell, Trzesniewski and Sorich Dweck 2007)!

If you're one of those students who thinks they're bad at maths, we encourage you not to sell yourself short. Telling yourself you're bad at maths won't help you improve. But if you keep an open mind and a positive attitude, work hard and ask questions when something is unclear, you just might find you're capable of more than you realised.

Terminology

In the next few chapters, we'll be using a number of terms that are common parlance in quantitative data analysis. The first two are *dependent variable* and *independent variable* (also known in the hard sciences as *response* and *predictor*, respectively). The dependent variable is the linguistic feature or behaviour/attitude that you're studying (see Chapter 2). So, the dependent variable in your study could be the F2 of the GOOSE vowel, or the presence vs. absence of *-s*, or the alternation between *go*, *say* and *be like* to introduce a quotation, or people's attitudes towards a particular variety. An independent variable is any factor you've identified that could condition, or affect, the variation, be it social, stylistic or linguistic. Sociolinguists typically break these independent variables down into internal (linguistic) factors and external (social) factors. Some researchers are also beginning to note the place of cognitive factors (see, for instance, Labov 1994, 2001, 2010).

Two other terms refer to the nature of these variables: a variable can be categorical or it can be continuous (also called numeric). A categorical variable is one where each observation falls into a finite amount of categories. This is a variable that you code, assigning each instance to the relevant category. Your categories are typically referred to as levels or groups. Speaker sex is normally a categorical independent variable, and presence vs. absence of *-s* is a categorical dependent variable. A continuous variable is one where observations can take on a conceivably infinite number of different values. This is a variable that you measure, such as the age of a speaker, or their evaluation of an accent on a scale of 1–6 (see examples in Chapter 8). Continuous variables can be made into categorical variables when their values are grouped. For instance, if you measure the F2 of GOOSE, you've got a continuous variable, because formant frequency could conceivably take any point on a number line (though in practice, of course, F2 will manifest within a particular range). But if you decided to set a cut-off point above which you want to call an F2 value 'fronted' and below which you want to call a value 'not fronted', and subsequently coded each F2 value in your data using this coding scheme, you've converted a continuous variable into a categorical one.

NORMALISING CONTINUOUS DATA

Normalising data puts values from different speakers on the same scale. Data normalisation is commonly used in sociolinguistics for vowel formant data. Different speakers have different vocal tract sizes, which causes their formant values to differ in predictable ways. For instance, women tend to have higher formant values than men due to the fact that women tend to have smaller vocal tracts than men. Children tend to have higher formant values than adults for the same reason. As sociolinguists, we are interested in vowel formant differences that cannot be explained simply by physiological differences like this. Normalisation transforms raw formant measurements in such a way that physiological differences are filtered out but sociolinguistic differences remain. The NORM suite online (search: *NORM Vowel Normalization*) provides a detailed overview of normalisation techniques and a useful web tool that normalises your data for you.

The techniques for analysing a categorical dependent variable are different from those for analysing a continuous dependent variable. Because most of the dependent variables that introductory sociolinguistics students will be working with are categorical, we'll focus more of our attention on those in the following discussion. Hay (2011) provides an excellent introduction to the analysis of continuous dependent variables.

In the rest of this chapter, we'll guide you through the best practices for summarising and analysing your data, which will set us up for Chapter 13, where we'll discuss best practices for graphing your findings. For the moment, we'll assume that you are examining the effects of only one independent variable at a time. (Consult Chapter 14 for the analysis of two or more independent variables.)

Summarising a categorical dependent variable

As discussed in Chapter 11, coding a categorical dependent variable entails assigning each observation, or token, of that variable to a particular category.

verb.of.quotation	sex	age	subject	tense	token
be like	f	25	1.sg	past	And I was like *raises eyebrows*
be like	f	25	1.pl	past	And we were like, "[Gesture]."
be like	m	15	1.sg	past	I was like "meh"
be like	f	25	3.pl	present	They're like you wanna come
go	f	25	3.sg	present	And he goes "unintelligible imitation"
go	f	35	3.sg	present	She goes "what are you doing"
say	f	19	3.sg	past	She said, "Nope you're not leaving this house, don't even try."
go	f	56	NP	past	What was the name of that video with the girl who went, "I like my house!"
go	f	78	3.sg	past	So she picked up my hand and went, "AhEww!" *Comical expression of disgust*
say	f	35	3.sg	past	She said, "Look for it in the back."
be like	m	35	1.sg	present	I'm like (motions with hands) and she like got in the truck
be like	m	35	1.sg	past	I was like, "awwwww"
say	f	35	2.sg	past	You said, "Five minutes!"

Figure 12.1 Sample data from a study of verbs of quotation

When you've finished with that task, you'll be left with a spreadsheet full of observations, looking something like Figure 12.1.

Figure 12.1 is an excerpt of data from a study of verbs of quotation carried out by students at the University of Pennsylvania in 2010. The dependent variable is the verb speakers used to introduce a quotation, and a number of independent variables, both internal and external, have been coded for.

In a quantitative sociolinguistic analysis, the operative question is whether and how the dependent variable is conditioned by the independent variable(s) of interest. For this example, let's say we're interested in how speakers of different ages use the various verbs of quotation. We'll break the ages up into three groups to make them easier to work with (that is, we'll make this continuous variable categorical).

Obviously we can't answer our question simply by looking at the spreadsheet alone: there's too much data to make sense of. The first step is to summarise the data so that we can look for patterns.

Many students initially think that simply counting up the number of times each variant is used by the different age groups is an acceptable way of summarising the data. But take a look at Table 12.1 to get an idea of why this is the wrong way of dealing with a categorical dependent variable.

As Table 12.1 reveals, our data contains many more tokens from speakers under 30 than from speakers of the other age groups (a fact which is unsurprising given that the data was collected by undergraduate students). It's thus very difficult to compare verb of quotation use across the different age groups because *every* verb of quotation is used more often among the under 30s than it is among the other age groups. This isn't a fact about how speakers under 30 use language; it's simply due to the fact that we collected more data from those speakers.

To prevent the confusion that raw counts like this engender, we calculate percentages to indicate how often each variant of the dependent variable is used by each group. Percentages control for differing sample sizes: they put each group on the same scale, regardless of how much data we collected from them.

The appropriate way to calculate percentages for sociolinguistic data is to take the number of times a variant is used by some group and divide it by the total number of tokens from that group. For instance, if we want to know the percentage use of *be like* by speakers under 30, we take the number of times

Table 12.1 Counts for a study of verb of quotation use by age group

	under 30	*30–50*	*over 50*
say	98	36	52
go	49	11	11
be like	326	27	10

Table 12.2 Percentages for a study of verb of quotation use by age group

	under 30	*30–50*	*over 50*
say	21%	49%	71%
go	10%	15%	15%
be like	69%	36%	14%
N	473	74	73

speakers under 30 used *be like* (here, 326) and divide it by the total number of tokens from speakers under 30 (here, 98 + 49 + 326 = 473). In this case, we get a percentage of 69 per cent.

A common mistake we see students make is to calculate their percentages by taking the number of times a variant is used by some group and dividing it by the total number of tokens of that variant: in this case, say, dividing the 326 tokens of *be like* from speakers under 30 by all 363 tokens of *be like* in our study (326 + 27 + 10 = 363). This is incorrect, however, and if you think about it as follows, the reasoning should be clear.

Every speaker has a choice whenever they utter a quotation of which verb of quotation to use, and the object of this study is to determine how often young people, middle-aged people and older people chose *be like*, *go* or *say* as that verb of quotation. Accordingly, we ask: out of all young people, how many of them chose *be like*, *go* or *say*? Out of all middle-aged people, how many of them chose *be like*, *go* or *say*? And so forth. Dividing by the total number of young people in the study is the mathematical equivalent of saying 'out of all young people'. By contrast, it is *not* the case that every time *be like* is uttered, a speaker has a choice of whether to be young, middle-aged or old! So the total number of *be likes*, or of any linguistic variant, should not be in the denominator of your fraction. Similarly, it is not correct to calculate your percentages by dividing by the total number of data points in your study.

Correct calculation of percentages for the data in Table 12.1 looks like what you see in Table 12.2. Note the last row, labelled 'N'. This represents the total number of tokens in each age group, and tells your reader how many tokens each percentage was calculated out of. When presenting any data that represents the summary of a larger set of tokens, it's important to accompany it by this measure. Ns are crucial for the interpretability of summary statistics like percentages. They can give the reader a warning that a percentage calculated from very few tokens should not be heavily relied on (and we'll talk more about why small datasets are unreliable later), or reassure the reader that enough data was collected for the summary to be reliable.

Summarising a continuous dependent variable

A few ways of condensing a set of continuous data into a single metric exist. The best-known is probably the (arithmetic) mean, also known as the average; you are probably also familiar with the median, the mid-point of your data when it is arranged from smallest to largest. Though the mean tends to be what is reported in sociolinguistic studies where the dependent variable is continuous (most typically vowel formant values), it is not always preferable. This is because the mean can be strongly skewed by outlier points, i.e. points that are extremely different from the majority of your data. Hay (2011) discusses best practices for summarising a continuous dependent variable. As she points out, it is important to visualise your data first, by plotting it with a histogram or a boxplot (see Chapter 13). This will allow you to determine to what extent the data contains outliers.

Once you have established general tendencies, you may want to find out whether two variables are correlated, or working together in some way. A correlation is a measure of dependence between two variables. A correlation could be used to determine, say, whether the F2 of GOOSE is tied to speaker age in a community, or whether the duration of vowels is tied to speaking rate. Correlation is most commonly assessed using Pearson's correlation, abbreviated as *r*, which takes the form of a value that ranges between −1 and +1. When *r* is positive, the two variables are positively correlated: as one measure increases or decreases, the other does the same. When *r* is negative, the two variables are negatively correlated: as one measure increases or decreases, the other does the opposite. A value of *r* that is close to zero means that there is basically no correlation: the two measures have no relationship. Pearson's correlation can be heavily affected by outliers; other measures of correlation, like Spearman's correlation, are not (Hay 2011; Johnson 2013).

Statistical significance

Above, we mentioned that quantitative variationist sociolinguistics is interested in when and where a particular variant is used more or less than another. It may initially seem obvious how to determine whether Variant A is used more often than Variant B: you count how often the two are used, and if the number of uses of Variant A is greater than the number of uses of Variant B, your question is answered in the affirmative. However, linguists, like all researchers in the social and hard sciences, actually use a much more stringent means of comparison than this.

A stringent means of comparison is necessary because findings based on small datasets are subject to errors introduced by chance. This is easiest to make sense of if we take an extreme example (and step out of the domain of linguistics for a moment). We've all experienced weather that was somehow unseasonable:

for instance, Laurel remembers a particular January day in Philadelphia when the temperature reached 72° F (22° C). Should an outside observer conclude from this observation that January is the warm season in that city? Not at all – looking at more data points reveals that this day was a fluke (and that the average high temperature in Philadelphia on that day in January, based on the 39 data points available from WeatherSpark.com, is 40° F (4° C)). Our original dataset of one observation was subject to an error introduced by chance.

The best way to reduce the effect of errors introduced by chance is to gather a large body of data. The bigger our dataset, the more likely it is that any differences between groups we find are meaningful, and not flukes. But unless we can record and study every single linguistic utterance that our subjects produce – something that would be impossible for even the most dedicated researcher – we are working only with a sample of data. And a sample of data can always only approximate the actual data that's out there in the world.

Luckily, there are mathematical procedures – called (statistical) significance tests – that can tell us how likely it is that the findings we observe in our sample are representative of what we would have found had we examined all possible data (what statisticians call the population). These tests tell us how likely it is that our findings are due to chance, i.e. are a fluke, like the one warm day in January. If the test concludes that our findings are not likely to be due to chance, it means that our results would most likely continue to hold even if we gathered more data: they are representative of real trends in the population.

Statistical tests are predicated on what's called a null hypothesis (commonly abbreviated as H_0). This is the hypothesis that our dependent variable is not affected by the independent variable we're examining. For instance, if our dependent variable is the variation between the realisations [ɪn] and [ɪŋ] for the suffix *-ing*, and our independent variable is a speaker's sex, then our null hypothesis is that the sexes use [ɪn] and [ɪŋ] at the same rate as each other. At the same time, we also have an alternative hypothesis (H_A): that the independent variable *does* have an effect, or, in this case, that there is some difference in the use of [ɪn] and [ɪŋ] between males and females. The significance test adjudicates between these two hypotheses. Gries (2013, chapter 1) has more on hypothesis generation in linguistics.

If the test finds that the dependent variable differs substantially between the levels (groups) of the independent variable that we're studying, the null hypothesis is rejected: it could not be a possible explanation of the patterns in our data. In our example, this would mean that men and women differ in their use of [ɪn] and [ɪŋ]: an interesting sociolinguistic finding! If the test does not find a substantially large difference between groups, we can't reject the null hypothesis.

What counts as 'substantially large' for our purposes? We need to look at the output of the significance test, which is called a *p*-value. The *p*-value effectively represents the probability that our findings are due to chance. A probability, as you may have learned in maths, is a number that ranges between 0 and 1, and a *p*-value is no different. The smaller the *p*-value, the less likely it is that our findings are due to chance. How small is small enough? The convention in sociolinguistics (and in many scientific fields) is to reject the null hypothesis only if our *p*-value is less than 0.05. A *p*-value of less than 0.05 means that the probability of our findings being a fluke is no more than five out of 100. That is, if there was truly *no* difference between men and women's variation in *-ing*, and we studied our interviewees' language 100 times, we would get a range of results, but those results would *only* produce the kinds of differences that *we* found fewer than five times out of those 100. That's an unlikely enough scenario that it allows us to conclude that the difference we see is not due to chance: it's very likely to be real.

When our *p*-value is below 0.05, we say that the difference we see between groups is statistically significant: that is, statistically reliable – not likely to be a fluke. It's not appropriate to describe a finding as 'significant' unless your data has passed this test.

There's a wealth of different significance tests in existence, because categorical and continuous dependent variables require different tests, as do studies where only one independent variable is examined as opposed to those that test the competing effects of multiple independent variables. The tests described in the remainder of this chapter can only test for the significance of one independent variable at a time. To test for significance when multiple independent variables are in consideration, consult Chapter 14.

The simplest significance tests can be performed in basic spreadsheet programmes like Excel, or even largely by hand. For more complicated significance tests, you'll need to use dedicated statistical software. We recommend the free software R, but you may also have access to SPSS through your university. Textbooks covering the use of R in linguistics are in the Further Reading section for this chapter.

Testing a categorical dependent variable for statistical significance

The simplest test of a statistically significant difference between groups when a dependent variable is categorical is called the chi-square test (properly, the *chi-square test for independence*). The chi-square test is performed on what's called a contingency table: a table of raw numbers with marginals (totals of the rows and columns). What we said earlier about percentages still holds, of course: they are still the best way to look for trends in a categorical dependent variable. You just can't perform the chi-square test on them. Table 12.3 contains a contingency table appropriate for performing the chi-square test on. Note that you don't need to have the same number of tokens (or even the same number of speakers) in each speaker group to perform this test.

Table 12.3 A contingency table for a study of verb of quotation use by age group

	under 30	*30–50*	*over 50*	*N*
say	98	36	52	186
go	49	11	11	71
be like	326	27	10	363
N	473	74	73	620

The chi-square test, like any statistical test, is predicated on the null hypothesis that there is no difference between the groups under study (in this case, the hypothesis that each age group uses the three verbs of quotation at the same rate as the other age groups do). Accordingly, performing the test requires determining how the collected data would be distributed across the three age groups if this were the case, and then determining how different that scenario is from the patterns displayed by the *actual* data that was collected. Any elementary statistics textbook should walk you through how to perform the chi-square test by hand, and there are a number of online calculators (search: *interactive chi-square calculator*) that will calculate marginals and perform the test on data you enter yourself. Note that when the number in any cell of a contingency table is less than ten, Fisher's Exact test should be performed instead.

Technically, when a chi-square test is performed on more than two groups, a significant result from such a test just means that there's a significant difference in your table *somewhere*: in this case, that age is having a significant effect on verb of quotation use. It doesn't mean that every group significantly differs from every other. (You can see this for yourself by performing the chi-square test on a table containing three groups, two of which show identical behaviour with regard to the dependent variable and one of which is extremely different from the other two.) To tease apart exactly where the differences lie, you need to compare the groups by pairs, so in our example you'd run three tests rather than one. Gries (2013: 366) discusses things you should be aware of when performing multiple comparisons like this.

When reporting the results of a chi-square test (or any significance test, for that matter), good practice is to mention at least the name of the test and the *p*-value. For the chi-square test, most researchers also report three numbers involved in its calculation, the degrees of freedom, the total number of tokens and the chi-square statistic. We suggest rounding your *p*-values to two or three decimal places to keep them from being unwieldy. If your *p*-value is so small that rounding it would give 0.00 (or 0.000), report it as < 0.01 (or < 0.001), or use scientific notation. For example, in Table 12.3, age has a significant effect on verb of quotation use, $\chi^2(4, N = 620) = 105.535, p < 0.001$.

Testing a continuous dependent variable for statistical significance

You can't use a chi-square test on a continuous dependent variable. Instead, the most common test of a significant difference between groups is the t-test. This test (which you can run in Excel) compares the means of two samples to determine whether they could have come from the same larger population (recall the technical definition of *population* given earlier). Just like the chi-square test, the t-test is predicated on a null hypothesis: that the two groups were drawn from the same population, and there is no real difference between them. When your t-test returns a *p*-value below 0.05, this means that, fewer than five times out of 100, two samples drawn from the same population would look as different as your two samples did.

Note that t-tests can compare only two groups. If your independent variable is divided into more than two groups – for instance, the three age levels we differentiated above – you need to use a different test, an analysis of variance (ANOVA), which you can learn about in Johnson (2008).

Note also that the t-test and ANOVA make a particular assumption of your data – that it is normally distributed (basically, that it fits a canonical bell-shaped curve) – which may not hold. Sometimes sociolinguistic data has a more bimodal distribution, which means there are a bunch of people or responses at one end of the scale and a bunch at the other. Gries (2013) discusses how to test whether your data is normally distributed, and introduces an alternative to the t-test, the U-test, to use when it is not.

EXERCISES

Exercise 1

Consult the following classic sociolinguistic studies and determine what the dependent and independent variables are. Are they categorical or continuous?

- Labov (1972) on language variation in New York City department stores
- Eckert (1988) on Jocks, Burnouts and In-betweens at Belten High
- Labov (1990) beginning on p. 227, on vowel change in Philadelphia

Exercise 2

Consult our companion website for a sample dataset and an analysis exercise.

References

Blackwell, Lisa S., Kali H. Trzesniewski and Carol Sorich Dweck. 2007. Implicit theories of intelligence predict achievement across an adolescent transition: A longitudinal study and an intervention. *Child Development* 78: 246–263.

Eckert, Penelope. 1988. Adolescent social structure and the spread of linguistic change. *Language in Society* 17: 183–208.

Gries, Stefan Th. 2013. Basic significance testing. In Robert J. Podesva and Devyani Sharma (eds) *Research Methods in Linguistics*. Cambridge: Cambridge University Press, 316–336.

Hay, Jennifer. 2011. Statistical analysis. In Marianna Di Paolo and Malcah Yaeger-Dror (eds) *Sociophonetics: A Student's Guide*. London: Routledge, 198–214.

Jaeggi, Susanne M., Martin Buschkuehl, John Jonides and Walter J. Perrig. 2008. Improving fluid intelligence with training on working memory. *Proceedings of the National Academy of Sciences* 105: 6829–6833.

Johnson, Keith. 2008. *Quantitative Methods in Linguistics*. Malden, MA: Wiley-Blackwell.

Johnson, Daniel Ezra. 2013. Descriptive statistics. In Robert J. Podesva and Devyani Sharma (eds) *Research Methods in Linguistics*. Cambridge: Cambridge University Press, 288–315.

Labov, William. 1972. The social stratification of (r) in New York City department stores. Reprinted in N. Coupland and A. Jaworski (eds) 1997. *Sociolinguistics: A Reader and Coursebook*. London: Macmillan Press Ltd, 168–178.

Labov, William. 1990. The intersection of sex and social class in the course of linguistic change. *Language Variation and Change* 2: 205–254.

Labov, William. 1994. *Principles of Linguistic Change: Internal Factors*. Malden, MA: Blackwell.

Labov, William. 2001. *Principles of Linguistic Change: Social Factors*. Malden, MA: Blackwell.

Labov, William. 2010. *Principles of Linguistic Change: Cognitive and Cultural Factors*. Malden, MA: Blackwell.

Weinreich, Uriel, William Labov and Marvin Herzog. 1968. *Empirical Foundations for a Theory of Language Change*. Austin, TX: University of Texas Press.

Further reading

Baayen, R.H. 2008. *Analyzing Linguistic Data: A Practical Introduction to Statistics Using R*. New York: Cambridge University Press.

Gorman, Kyle and Daniel Ezra Johnson. 2013. Quantitative analysis. In Robert Bayley, Richard Cameron and Ceil Lucas (eds) *The Oxford Handbook of Sociolinguistics*. Oxford: Oxford University Press, chapter 11, 214–240.

Gries, Stefan Th. 2013. *Statistics for Linguistics with R: A Practical Introduction*. New York: Taylor & Francis.

13 Presenting your data

In the previous chapter, we introduced you to the ways researchers turn a spreadsheet of data tokens into meaningful summaries. In this chapter, we'll walk you through the best practices for presenting that summarised data.

We're assuming here that the end goal of your data analysis is going to be the presentation of your findings in a paper for a reader who is unfamiliar with your work. Accordingly, you should keep in mind that your reader's understanding is your main objective. Quantitative findings should always be presented in a way that is maximally informative and requires a minimum of effort on the part of your reader to understand them. In what follows, we'll walk you through what this looks like, and exemplify some common errors that we've run across.

What should a graph do?

Think back to the previous chapter, where we established that the goal of much variationist sociolinguistic work is to determine whether particular linguistic variants are used more or less by some group or in some context as compared to some other group(s) or context(s). Presenting your data in a table, and calculating its statistical significance, goes a long way towards achieving this objective, but it can be very difficult for a reader to see the bigger picture of 'more' and 'less' when confronted with a table full of numbers. Much easier on your reader is to present your findings in a graph, where the relationships of more and less are made transparent and instantly easy to grasp. As Cleveland and McGill (1984: 535) put it, "The power of a graph is its ability to enable one to take in the quantitative information, organize it, and see patterns and structure not readily revealed by other means of studying the data".

Figure 13.1, reproduced from Labov's (1990) Figure 6, manages to show a tremendous amount of data, but in a clear and space-conserving way. Labov plots the overall mean first and second formant values for 22 vowels in a corpus of sociolinguistic interviews among Philadelphians. The direction of each vowel's movement in apparent time is indicated by the direction of the arrow passing

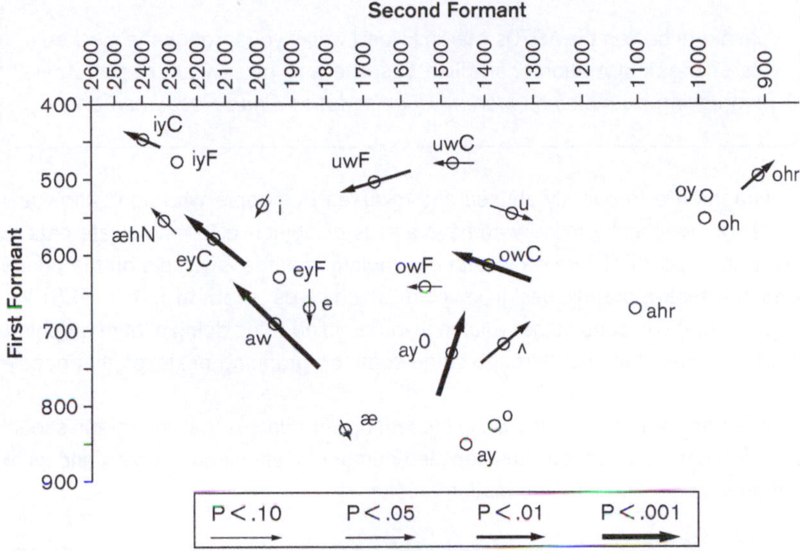

Figure 13.1 Philadelphia vowel movements in apparent time

Source: Labov (1990)

through the circle representing the mean, with the mean F1 and F2 values for speakers 25 years younger than the average represented by the tip of the arrow, and the mean F1 and F2 values for speakers 25 years older than the average represented by the tail of the arrow. The weight of the arrow additionally corresponds to *p*-values representing the significance of this apparent-time movement. Imagine how unwieldy a table representing all of this information would be, and compare that to how easily presented it is by the graph!

ANIMATION

Though it's not helpful for those who are presenting their data on the printed page, animation has been used as a wildly successful tool for displaying change over time in data that is presented digitally. Search the web for *Josef Fruehwald Philadelphia Language in Motion* to see an animated plot that makes use of real-time data to bring Labov's diagram in Figure 13.1 to life. This allows the presentation of non-linear vowel trajectories, like the reversal of previous movements. For instance, select the vowel 'aw' (as in *house*) in Fruehwald's diagram, press play and watch the fronting and raising of /aw/ in Philadelphia reverse beginning with speakers born in the 1970s. Martin Hilpert walks you through the mechanics of creating motion charts like this one and gives you several other engrossing examples on *Martin Hilpert's Motion Chart Resource Page.*

Graphs are frequently abused and misused by people who don't know any better (as well as by those who have a sinister objective to manipulate data to prove their point!). There's a wealth of scholarly material available on the principles of effective graphic design, much of which owes a debt to Tufte (1983). We suggest that you consult that volume if you're going to be doing a lot of graphing, but below we'll take you through some common graphing mistakes that people make.

The general rule of thumb when presenting your data is that your graph should communicate the relationships between numbers clearly and honestly and without providing redundant information.

Clarity

To see what we mean by presenting results clearly, consider the two sample graphs in Figure 13.2. The graph on the top uses three-dimensional bars, which

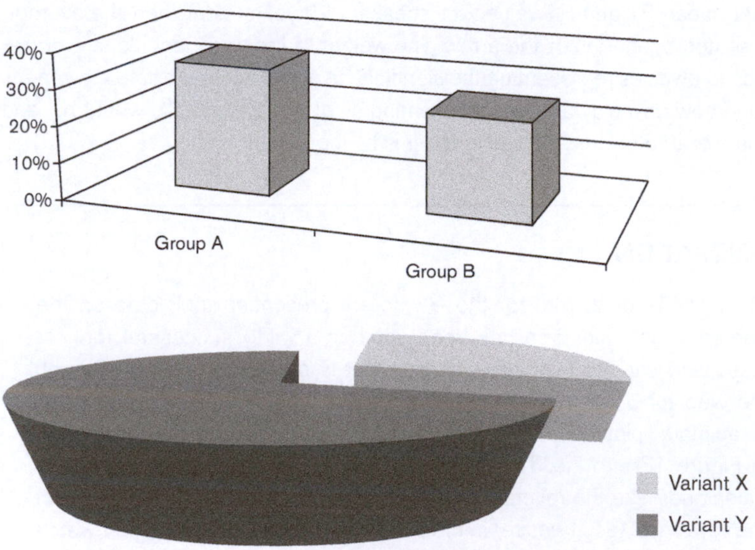

Figure 13.2 Two sample graphs exemplifying a lack of clarity

means that the front of each bar hits the y-axis (vertical axis) in a different place than its back. This makes it impossible for a reader to determine what the height of each bar – and, hence, the number that is plotted – actually is. For instance, Group A looks like it could be either 25 per cent (based on where the front of the bar hits) or 30 per cent (based on the back). (In fact, the value plotted for Group A is neither: it's 35 per cent, but you certainly can't tell that from the chart!) Note, additionally, that with no label on the y-axis, a reader has absolutely no idea what the graph is meant to be showing.

The graph on the bottom is tilted in such a way that the smaller piece of the pie is hidden behind the larger one, making their sizes very difficult to gauge. Moreover, rounded charts, like pie and donut charts, are to be avoided when you are asking your reader to compare proportions across groups, as people tend to be less accurate at comparing the angles that distinguish the slices of a pie than they are at comparing the heights that distinguish the columns in a bar chart (Simkin and Hastie 1987). Though it can be tempting to want to use a pie chart when your dependent variable has several levels which all add up to 100 per cent, we recommend a bar chart in such cases instead. These bar charts can be 'stacked', like the upper graph in Figure 13.3 (from Foulkes, Docherty and Watt 2005, Figure 1), or not, like the lower graph in Figure 13.3, which we generated based on Foulkes et al.'s data. We find the upper figure easier to read, as each variant can be directly compared across the three groups without the other variants intervening and cluttering things up.

Your results can also be rendered unclear when you choose the wrong type of graph for your data. A line graph is conventionally used when the variable on the x-axis (horizontal axis) is ordered in a meaningful way. Line graphs connect each point to the next and allow the reader to track the trend in the dependent variable as the elements on the x-axis move along their scale. They also allow the reader to interpolate – to estimate – the value of the dependent variable that would be present in between each tick on the x-axis, by tracing along the line. For instance, if the creator of the graph has calculated a value of the dependent variable for subjects at ages 14 and 15, and connected them with a line, the reader can estimate what the value for subjects of age 14.5 must have been, even though they weren't studied: it's presumably a value in between the value for age 14 and the value for age 15.

The upper graph in Figure 13.4, reproduced from Milroy and Milroy's (1985) Figure 3, is a line graph that creates a misleading impression. There is no meaningful way to order men and women of different age groups, and no speakers are 'in between' men age 40–55 and women age 40–55. So there is no reason for the points to be connected with a line. Compare this to the lower graph in Figure 13.4, reproduced from Gorman's (2010) Figure 3, which plots use of negative concord by occupation level. The values on the x-axis are ordered in a meaningful way (from lowest to highest occupation level), and it's clear that the

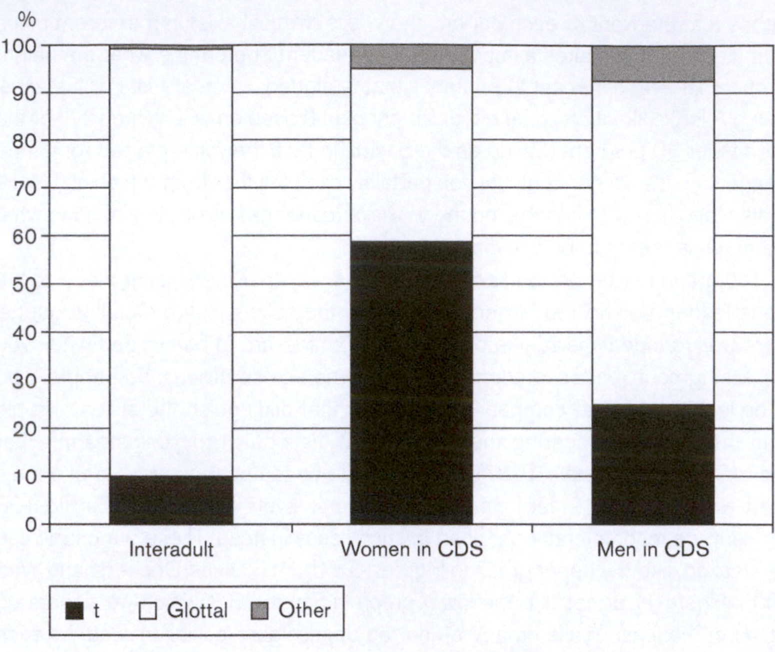

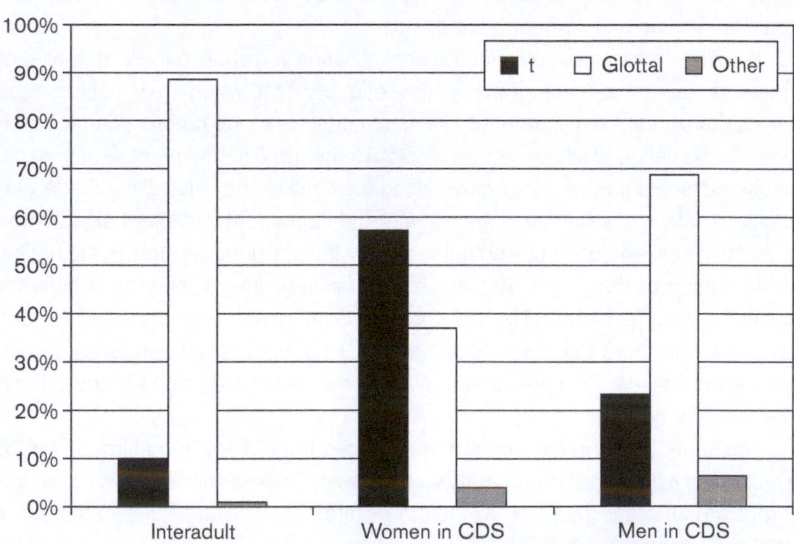

Figure 13.3 Two graphs showing interadult and child-directed speech (CDS) in which the dependent variable has several levels, or realisations

Source: Foulkes, Docherty and Watt (2005), Figure 1

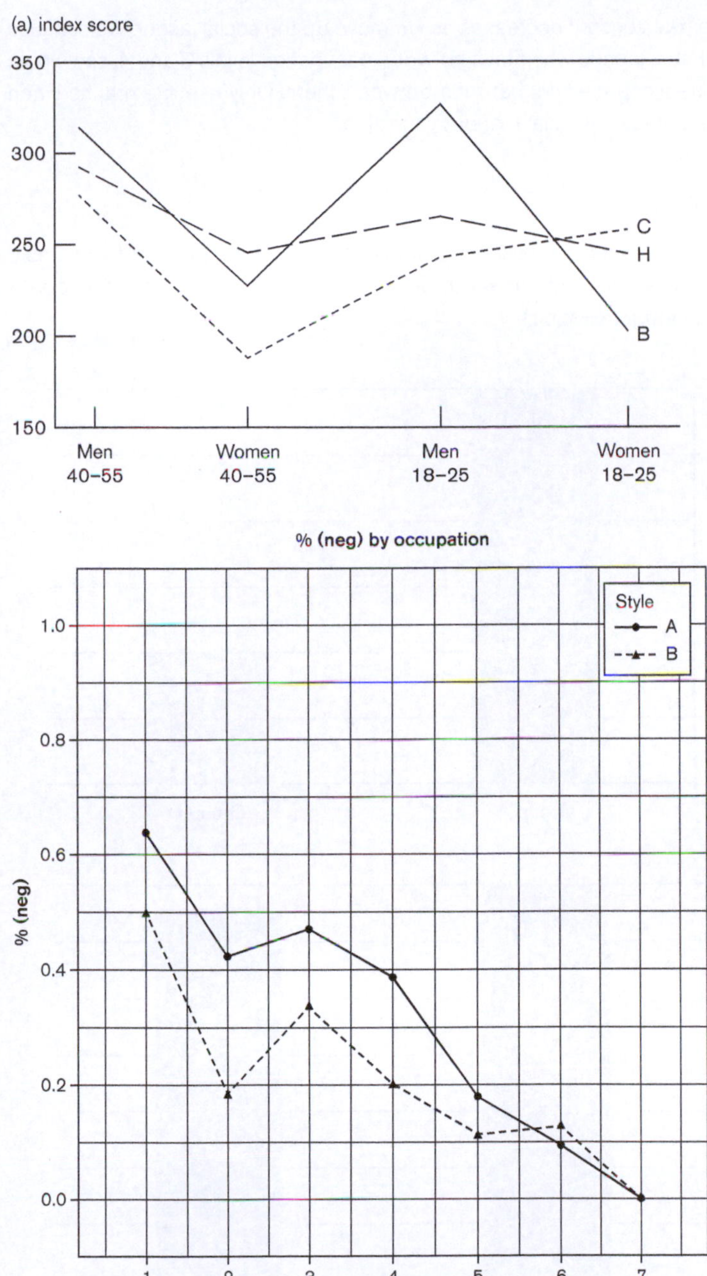

Figure 13.4 Two line graphs, only one of which is appropriate to the data

Source: Milroy and Milroy (1985), Figure 3; Gorman (2010), Figure 3 use of negative concord decreases as we move up the social ladder. We can also estimate that someone who fits in between occupation levels 3 and 4, say, would have a value along the line that runs between them. Only use line graphs when they make a meaningful claim about your data.

Honesty

To see what we mean by presenting results honestly, compare the two sample graphs in Figure 13.5, both of which plot the values of 35 per cent for Group A and 33 per cent for Group B.

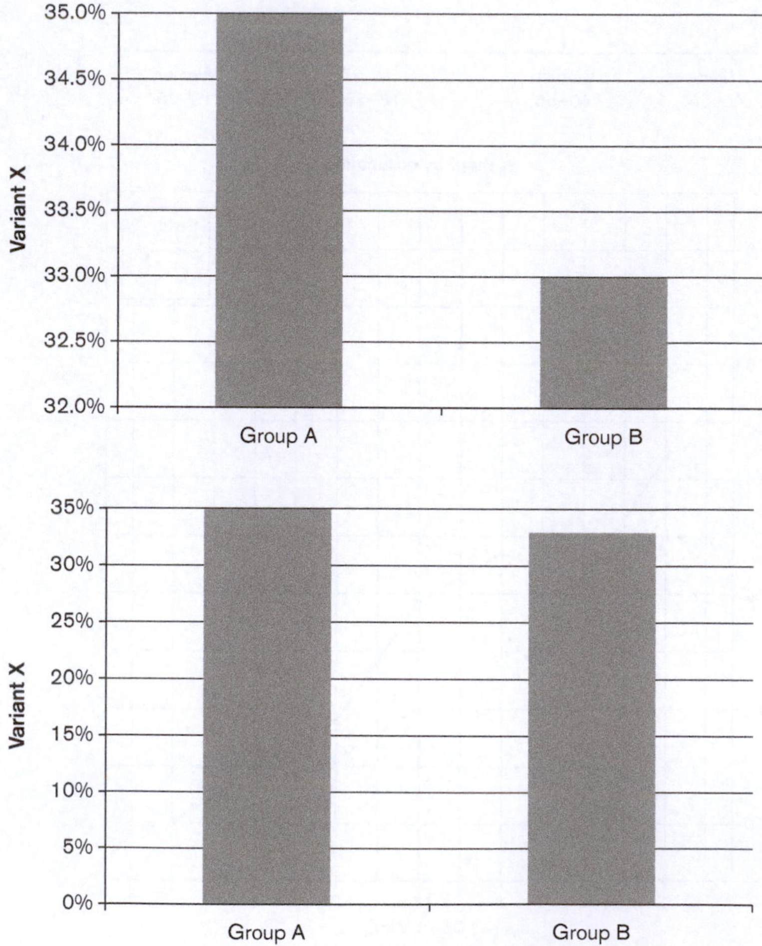

Figure 13.5 Two bar graphs, one of which is misleading

The only thing that differentiates the two graphs is the value at which the y-axis starts (32 per cent for the upper graph, 0 per cent for the lower graph), but look what an effect it has! The tiny difference of 2 per cent between the two groups is massively exaggerated in the upper graph in a way that it isn't on the lower graph. The upper graph thus provides a misleading picture of the data. When graphing percentages, always start your y-axis at 0 per cent.

Eliminating redundancy

To see what we mean by eliminating redundant information, consider the two sample graphs in Figure 13.6. Both graphs contain redundancies. In the lower graph, group identity is indicated twice: by the labels of the bars and by the colours of the bars. The value of each bar is also indicated twice: by the height of the bar and by the number at the top of it. For both of these variables, only one means of representation is necessary.

This is not to say that *any* numbers represented directly on a graph are inherently bad. Some researchers use the space at the top of a bar to provide the N (total number of tokens that a percentage is based on; see Chapter 12). This is an efficient use of space and a clear way of providing multiple pieces of information at once.

The upper graph contains a legend identifying both bars as plotting Variant X, but this is made perfectly clear by the title and the y-axis label – what else could the bars have been plotting? (Be aware that the inclusion of a redundant legend like this is default behaviour in Excel.)

Another type of redundancy can come about through how the researcher decides to plot the variants of the linguistic variable under study. Many linguistic variables are inherently binary: they have only two variants, meaning that speakers have an 'either/or' choice. For instance, for the variable (ing), a speaker can pronounce the *-ing* suffix either as [ɪn] or as [ɪŋ]; in a situation of /s/-deletion, a plural marker *-s* can either be deleted or it can be present. Other variables are construed by the researcher to be binary: a speaker either uses *be like* as their verb of quotation, or they use some other, more traditional verb of quotation which the researcher is not interested in the specifics of. In the case of binary variables like these, there is no need to graph the rate of both variants. Because they will necessarily sum to 100 per cent, the rate of one of them is completely predictable from the other. Thus, we suggest removing either both grey bars or both black bars from the graph in Figure 13.7: if Group A deleted [s] 65 per cent of the time, then it goes without saying that they retained it 35 per cent of the time.

The nature of your study may dictate which variant you choose to graph and which you choose to remove: for instance, if you are showing the progression of a change in progress, you'll want to graph the novel variant. Regardless of which

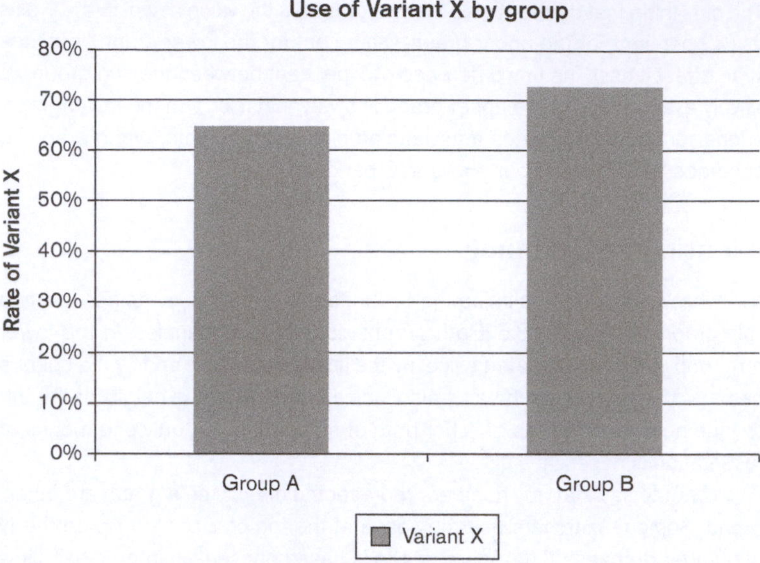

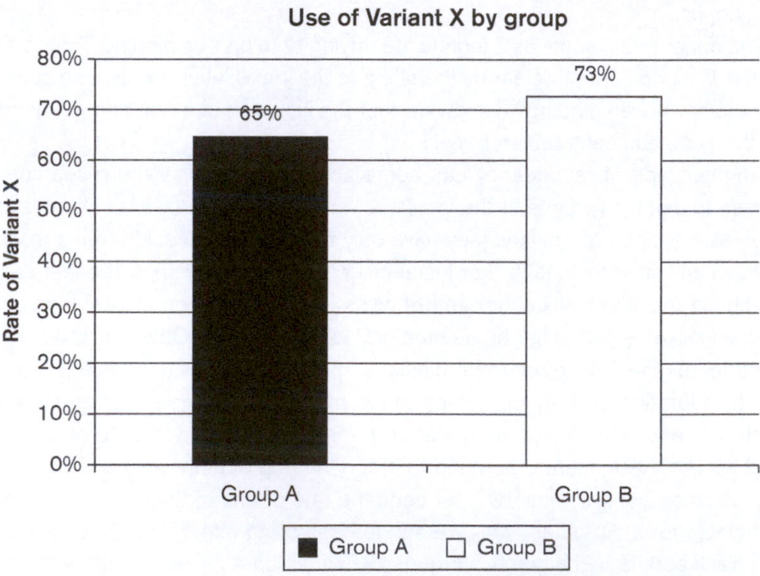

Figure 13.6 Two bar graphs displaying redundancies

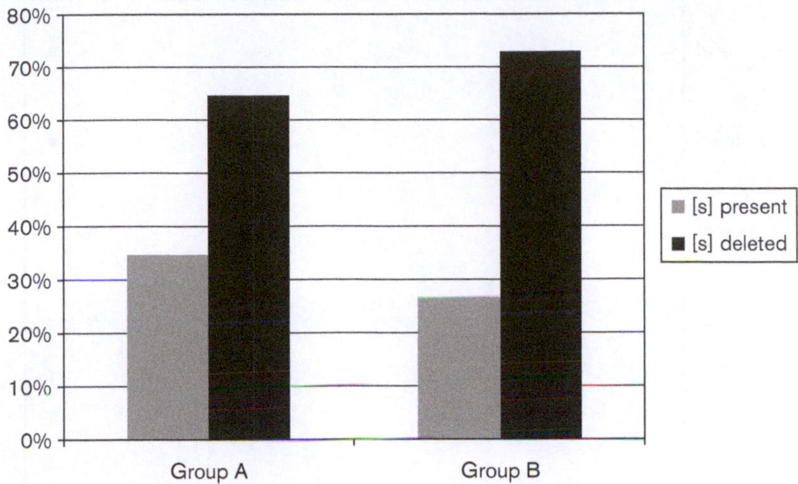

Figure 13.7 A bar graph that redundantly plots both variants of a binary dependent variable

variant you select, your graph must make it abundantly clear to your reader which one is being plotted.

Though these redundancies may seem like minor issues when compared with the misrepresentation of data shown in Figures 13.2 and 13.5, they can still result in confusion and frustration on the part of your reader, who has wasted their time figuring out what the various components of the redundant graphs are supposed to indicate, only to discover that they provide absolutely no new information. For a similar reason, you should think critically before including both a graph and a table in your paper if they contain exactly the same information.

Now that you know what *not* to do . . .

We'll close this chapter with some general recommendations for visually presenting your data.

If you're analysing a categorical dependent variable – the kind of data you would summarise with percentages and test for significance with a chi-square test (see Chapter 12) – there are a few options for representing the differences between groups. Both bar graphs and line graphs are acceptable, depending on the nature of the variable on your x-axis (see earlier in this chapter). Another possibility is a dot plot (Cleveland 1993), which serves the same function as a bar graph but is less cluttered. Figure 13.8 presents a dot plot of the variable voicing of stem-final voiceless fricatives in plural nouns (as in [bæθs] ~ [bæðz]), in an unpublished analysis of the Switchboard corpus (Godfrey, Holliman and McDaniel 1992) carried out by Laurel. Each plural form of the 11 words under study was

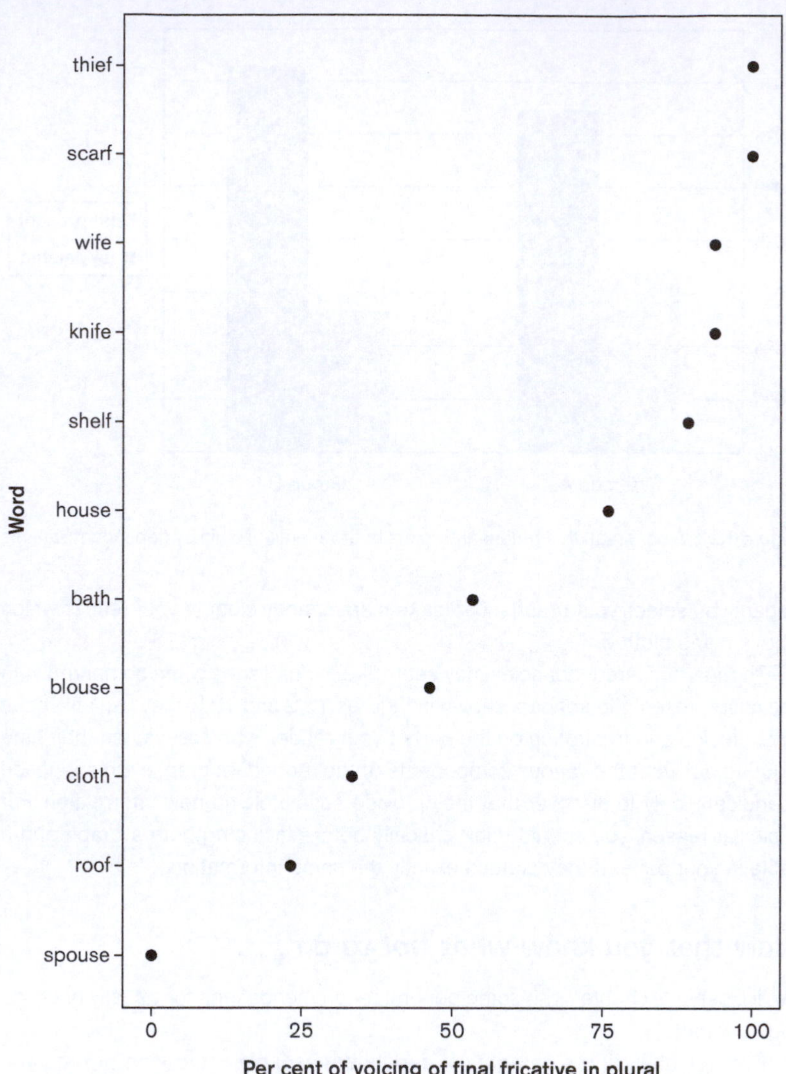

Figure 13.8 A dot plot of the rate of voicing of stem-final voiceless fricatives in plurals, with data from the Switchboard corpus (Godfrey et al. 1992)

Note: The categorical dependent variable here is whether a final voiceless fricative remained voiceless or was voiced in the plural coded for whether its stem-final fricative was voiced or voiceless, and the graph plots the per cent of voicing for each word. It's easy to see from the plot that nouns ending in /f/ are voiced in the plural more often than nouns ending in /θ/ or /s/.

A continuous dependent variable is the type of variable you would summarise with a mean or median, and test for significance with a t-test if it's normally distributed, or a U-test if it isn't (see Chapter 12). One common way of visualising a continuous variable is a histogram, which plots the number of times each unique value appears in your data. On the x-axis of a histogram are the unique values themselves, and on the y-axis is the count of how many times each of those values occurs. If there are a whole lot of unique values, the histogram puts them in 'bins', or ranges. So rather than plotting how many times each unique value occurred, it plots how many times values within particular ranges occurred. Histograms allow you to eyeball your data and get an idea of whether or not it's normally distributed (see Chapter 12).

The histogram in Figure 13.9 plots the occurrence of different fundamental frequencies (F0, perceived as pitch) of American English vowels as uttered by 76

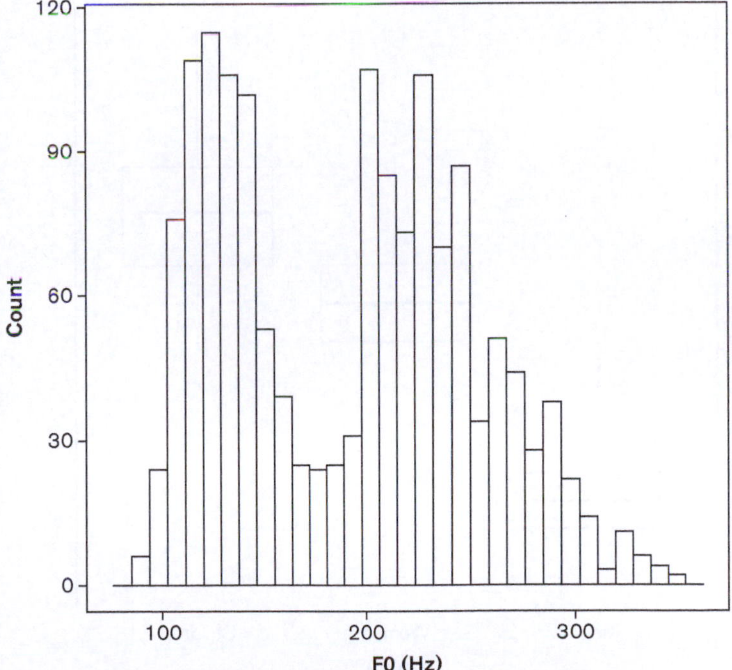

Figure 13.9 A histogram of F0 measurements for vowels spoken by men, women and children, using data from Peterson and Barney (1952)

Note: F0, or pitch, is a continuous dependent variable

speakers comprising men, women and children (data from Peterson and Barney 1952, available through the CMU Artificial Intelligence Repository). Each bar represents the number of observations that fell within a particular range: here, the ranges span about 8.5 Hz. We can see, for instance, that very few vowels were uttered with an F0 below 100 Hz (it looks like only about five observations, based on the y-axis), and that many vowels were uttered with an F0 between approximately 115 Hz and 123 Hz (close to 120 observations). The distribution has two clear peaks, and possibly a third one on the right edge: these correspond to the lower-pitched voices of men as opposed to the higher-pitched voices of women and children.

Another common choice for this kind of variable is a boxplot (Figure 13.10), which marks quartiles of a set of data using boxes. Quartiles divide a dataset into four groups of equal size. The bottom of a box represents the first quartile of the data (the value below which 25 per cent of the data fall), the thick line through the middle represents the second quartile, or median, of the data (the value below which half of the data fall) and the top of the box represents the third quartile

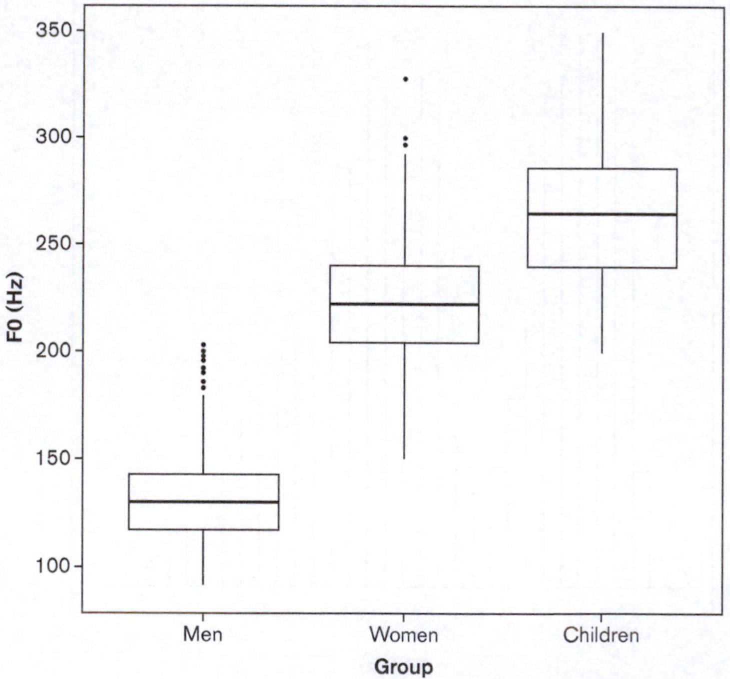

Figure 13.10 Boxplots of men's, women's and children's F0, using data from Peterson and Barney (1952)

Note: A boxplot summarises a continuous dependent variable and makes it easy to compare groups

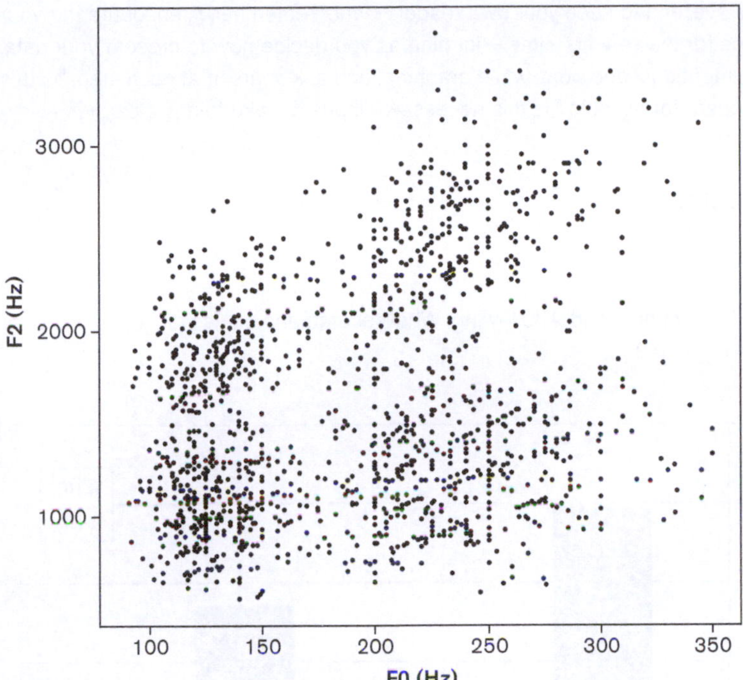

Figure 13.11 Scatter plot showing F2 by F0, using data from Peterson and Barney (1952)

(the value below which 75 per cent of the data fall). Boxplots frequently also have 'whiskers', lines extending out on either end. In Figure 13.10, the upper and lower whiskers mark the highest and lowest values (respectively) falling within a particular range. Here, the upper bound of that range is calculated as the third quartile plus 1.5 times the interquartile range of the data (which itself is calculated as the third quartile minus the first quartile), and the lower bound is calculated as the first quartile minus 1.5 times the interquartile range. Any observations outside this range are plotted as points. This follows Tukey (1977).

To represent correlation between two continuous variables, choose a scatter plot (Figure 13.11). Correlation is assessed using Pearson's correlation when the data is normally distributed, and Spearman's correlation when it's not (Chapter 12). Figure 13.11 plots the second formant (F2) by F0; it does indeed look like speakers with higher-pitched voices have higher second formants, which makes sense articulatorily.

We haven't covered the full range of 'what to do and what not to do when graphing' here, but we hope that the examples in this chapter have given you some food for thought. Remember to look at other researchers' graphs with a critical eye, and to keep your own reader – who, remember, is encountering your findings for the very first time – in mind as you decide how to present your data. Make intentional decisions while graphing, and ask yourself at each step, "Is this appropriate for my data? Is this necessary? Does it make things clearer?"

EXERCISES

Exercise 1

Consider Graphs 1 and 2, following. What recommendations would you make for improving them?

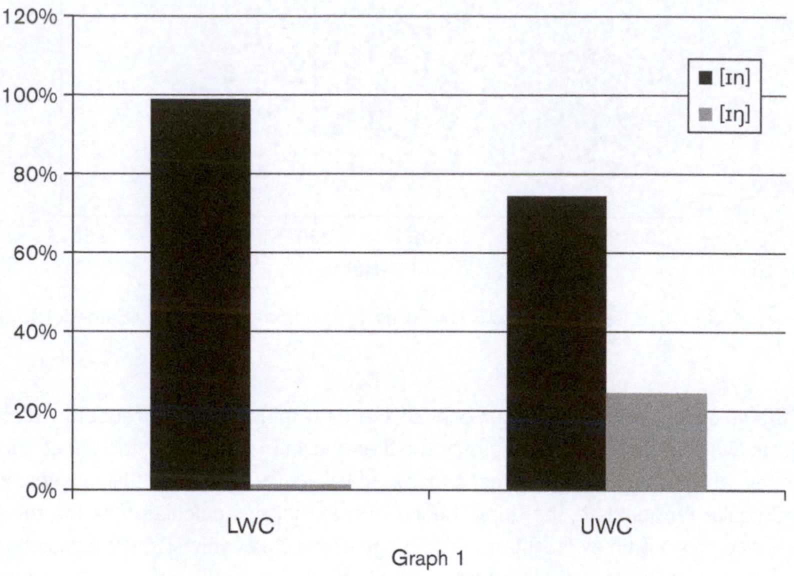

Graph 1

Exercise 2

Consult our companion website for a sample dataset and an analysis exercise.

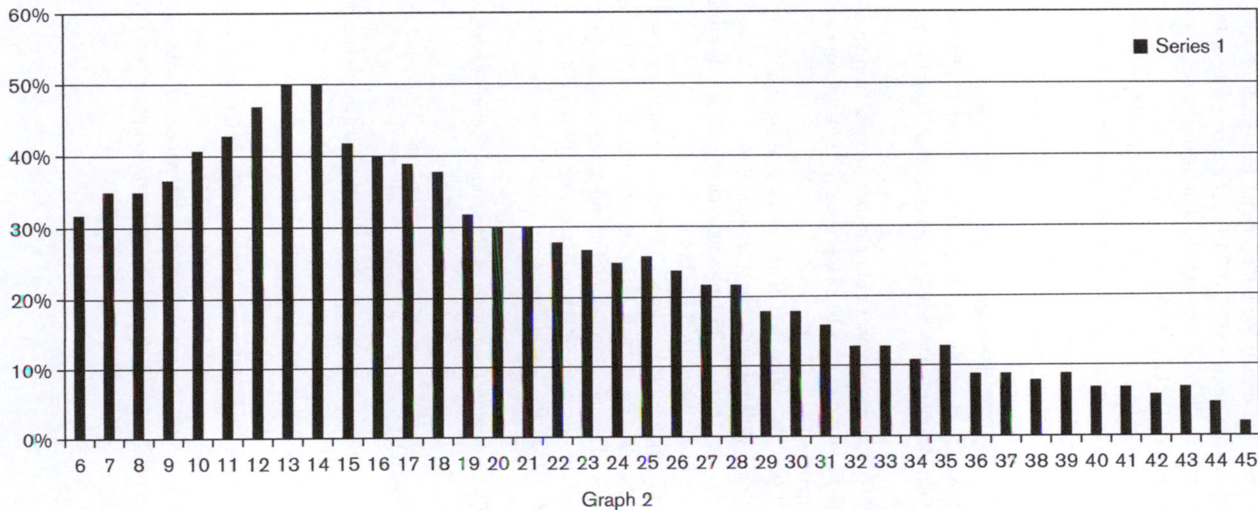
60%
50%
40%
30%
20%
10%
0%
Series 1
6 7 8 9 10 11 12 13 14 15 16 17 18 19 20 21 22 23 24 25 26 27 28 29 30 31 32 33 34 35 36 37 38 39 40 41 42 43 44 45
Graph 2

References

Cleveland, William S. 1993. *Visualizing Data.* Summit, NJ: Hobart Press.

Cleveland, William S. and Robert McGill. 1984. Graphical perception: Theory, experimentation, and application to the development of graphical methods. *Journal of the American Statistical Association* 79: 531–554.

CMU Artificial Intelligence Repository. Peterson Barney: Vowel formant frequency database. Available at www.cs.cmu.edu/afs/cs/project/ai-repository/ai/areas/speech/database/pb/0.html (last accessed 7 November 2014).

Foulkes, Paul, Gerard Docherty and Dominic Watt. 2005. Phonological variation in child-directed speech. *Language* 81: 177–206.

Godfrey, John J., Edward C. Holliman, and Jane McDaniel. 1992. SWITCHBOARD: Telephone speech corpus for research and development. In *Proceedings of the IEEE International Conference on Acoustics, Speech, and Signal Processing, Volume 1,* 517–520.

Gorman, Kyle. 2010. The consequences of multicollinearity among socioeconomic predictors of negative concord in Philadelphia. *University of Pennsylvania Working Papers in Linguistics* 16: 66–75.

Labov, William. 1990. The intersection of sex and social class in the course of linguistic change. *Language Variation and Change* 2: 205–254.

Milroy, James and Lesley Milroy. 1985. Linguistic change, social network and speaker innovation. *Journal of Linguistics* 21: 339–384.

Peterson, Gordon E. and Harold L. Barney. 1952. Control methods used in a study of the vowels. *The Journal of the Acoustical Society of America* 24: 175–184.

Simkin, David and Reid Hastie. 1987. An information-processing analysis of graph perception. *Journal of the American Statistical Association* 82: 454–465.

Tufte, Edward R. 1983. *The Visual Display of Quantitative Information.* Cheshire, CT: Graphics Press.

Tukey, John. 1977. *Exploratory Data Analysis.* Reading: Addison-Wesley.

Further reading

Fung, Kaiser. Junk Charts. Available at http://junkcharts.typepad.com/ (last accessed 7 November 2014).

Gries, Stefan Th. 2013. *Statistics for Linguistics with R: A Practical Introduction.* New York: Taylor & Francis.

Kosara, Robert. eagereyes: Visualization and Visual Communication. Available at https://eagereyes.org/ (last accessed 7 November 2014).

Seltman, Howard J. 2014. *Experimental Design and Analysis*, chapter 4. Available at www.stat.cmu.edu/~hseltman/309/Book/chapter4.pdf (last accessed 7 November 2014).

14 Analysing multiple independent variables

In Chapters 12 and 13 we discussed how to summarise, graph and test data for significance when focusing on one independent variable at a time. This is the simplest way to begin your data analysis, but most sociolinguistic studies are of course going to be examining the effects of more than one factor on the dependent variable.

A number of new questions arise when you've got more than one independent variable in the mix. For instance, you can ask whether two of your independent variables interact: that is, whether your dependent variable behaves differently when their effects combine. You can also determine the relative strength of your various predictors: do they all have an equally strong influence on your dependent variable, or are some doing more work than others in conditioning the variation? This chapter will introduce you to quantitative methods that can address these questions.

Cross-tabulating two independent variables to check for interactions

In Chapter 12, we saw that the behaviour of a categorical dependent variable with regard to an independent variable is summarised with percentages. It's also possible to summarise the behaviour of a categorical dependent variable with regard to *two* independent variables at once, and this is something that we do often to look for what are called interactions.

A statistical interaction is in evidence when the effect of an independent variable on a dependent variable differs based on some additional independent variable. Interactions pop up frequently in sociolinguistic data, and one is exemplified in Figure 14.1. This figure comes from a study by D'Arcy et al. (2013, Figure 8) examining the alternation between *-body* and *-one* in pronominal quantifiers like *somebody/someone*. In this figure, D'Arcy et al. compare how often the *-body* quantifiers are used among different age groups (old vs. young) and with or without postnominal modifiers (like *somebody/someone different*). You can think

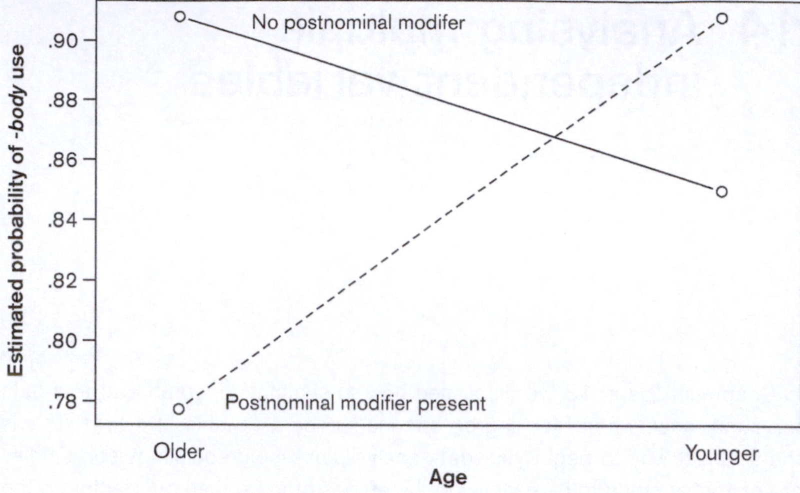

Figure 14.1 An interaction between age and postnominal modifier presence in the use of *-body* pronouns

Source: D'Arcy et al. (2013), Figure 8

of the 'estimated probability' values on the y-axis as if they were percentages of the use of the *-body* pronouns (and we'll talk about how they're different from percentages later on).

Figure 14.1 shows an interaction between the two independent variables on the use of *-body* pronouns. For older speakers, *-body* pronouns are more likely to be used than *-one* pronouns when there is no postnominal modifier. For younger speakers, by contrast, *-body* pronouns are more likely to be used when there is a postnominal modifier. The effect of a postnominal modifier on *-body* pronoun use thus depends on a speaker's age, meaning that the two conditioning factors interact.

You can look for interactions in your data by cross-tabulating two independent variables. Cross-tabulating is simply calculating the frequency of one variant of your dependent variable in each combination of two independent variables. Table 14.1 gives an example of a cross-tabulation, carried out by students at the University of Manchester who examined Victoria Beckham's /l/-vocalisation

Table 14.1 Cross-tabulation of Victoria Beckham's vocalised /l/ by age and phonological context

	_#V (e.g. all of it)	_#C (e.g. all the things)	_C (e.g. alternate)
age 23	32% (N=19)	90% (N=49)	82% (N=22)
age 38	31% (N=13)	61% (N=79)	52% (N=73)

across her lifespan. Vocalisation of /l/ is the chosen variant, and the two independent variables are Beckham's age and the phonological context in which a particular token of /l/ arose: word-finally before a vowel, word-finally before a consonant and word-internally before a consonant.

We can interpret this table as follows: at age 23, Beckham vocalised word-final pre-vocalic /l/ 32 per cent of the time (out of 19 total tokens of word-final pre-vocalic /l/); at age 38, 31 per cent of the time (out of 13 total tokens of word-final pre-vocalic /l/), and so forth. The cross-tabulation reveals an apparent interaction: Victoria Beckham decreased her rate of /l/-vocalisation in both pre-consonantal contexts over time, but showed no lifespan change pre-vocalically. (Of course, we can't say whether this effect is statistically significant based on a cross-tabulation alone; see below for how to test for significance on data like this.)

Note that the columns of percentages in Table 14.1 do not sum to 100 per cent, as they did in the simple table of percentages in Table 12.2. This is because the denominator in each cell of a cross-tabulation comes from a different count. This is clearly indicated in Table 14.1 by the Ns in each cell. Note also that cross-tabulation entails focusing on one variant of your dependent variable. This requires you to make a choice of which variant you want to analyse, and it's your responsibility to clearly communicate that choice to your reader (say, by indicating it in the caption or title of your table or graph, as we've done here). A cross-tabulation is really uninterpretable without that information.

Graphing your cross-tabulation

When graphing more than one independent variable, you get to introduce additional parameters into your plot, like colours and line types. Because a cross-tabulation implicates two independent variables, there are two different ways of graphing it, as depicted in Figure 14.2 (based on the data from Table 14.1).

The upper graph in Figure 14.2 puts phonological context on the x-axis and represents age with colour, while the lower graph does the reverse using line type. Neither way is inherently better; the choice between the two simply depends on what story you want to convey with your graph. To our eyes, the lower graph brings the trends in real time to the fore, and communicates the differences between the contexts secondarily.

Checking your cross-tabulation for significance

You can't perform a chi-square test (see Chapter 12) on a cross-tabulation as it is. Recall how a chi-square test is set up (Table 12.3): each row of the contingency table contains counts from a different variant of the dependent variable. A cross-tabulation, which tabulates only one variant at a time, is incompatible with this. One way to test for significance of an interaction is by breaking up your

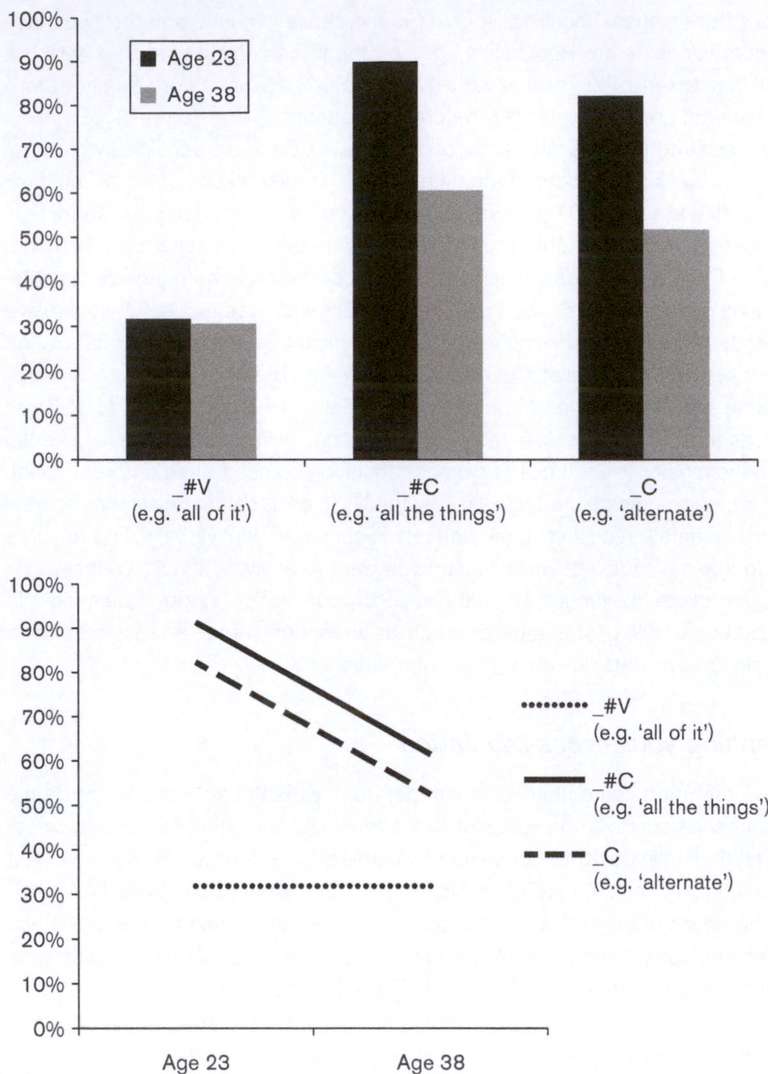

Figure 14.2 Two different ways of graphing the cross-tabulation in Table 14.1

cross-tabulation into multiple contingency tables containing the dependent variable and one independent variable each: for instance, in the case of the /l/-vocalisation data, one table testing the significance of phonological context at age 23, and another testing it at age 38. There are better ways of testing for significance when you have multiple independent variables, though. These fall under the heading of multivariate analysis.

Multivariate analysis

Why should we use multivariate analysis?

When you have multiple independent variables, performing multiple chi-square tests (or t-tests, in the case of a continuous dependent variable) is often not appropriate. To see one major reason for why this is, consider a study of (ing) in which speaker age and the grammatical class of the *-ing* word were examined. Let's say, in this study, younger speakers happened to produce mostly verbal *-ing* words, and older speakers mostly nominal *-ing* words, and a chi-square test finds a significant difference between the ages, with older people using more of the velar variant. Would we want to say that this is indicative of an age difference in (ing)? It could be – but it could also be attributable to the well-known grammatical class effect on (ing), whereby nominal words favour the velar variant (Houston 1985). Because age and grammatical class were confounded – tied up with each other – in our data collection, we can't tease their effects apart.

Multivariate analysis is a statistical test that can tease apart independent variables when they are tied up with one another like this. Multivariate analysis is also known as 'regression': specifically, 'logistic regression' in the case of a categorical dependent variable and 'linear regression' in the case of a continuous one. Performing a multivariate analysis on data that has been coded for more than one independent variable will tell us 'all other things being equal, what effect does each independent variable have on the dependent variable?' In our (ing) example, multivariate analysis could tell us if it *weren't* the case that most of our (ing) words from older speakers were nouns – if tokens of nouns and tokens of verbs were more evenly distributed across the ages – whether (ing) variation would still show a significant age difference.

The 'estimated probabilities' plotted in Figure 14.1 are based on multivariate analysis: they represent the rate at which the different age groups under study would use *-body* pronouns with or without postnominal modifiers, all other linguistic and social factors being equal. Even if you have made every effort in your data collection to avoid confounds in your speakers' sociodemographic characteristics, it's important to perform multivariate analysis, because confounds involving linguistic conditioning factors can be very difficult to avoid (see Chapter 2).

Sociolinguists have traditionally performed multivariate analysis using software called Goldvarb and Varbrul. As our statistical knowledge and computational tools have evolved, new techniques have become available. One programme which is widely used among sociolinguists at the time of publication is Rbrul, which is freely available online and runs within the software R (also free). Rbrul has a number of improvements over its predecessor Varbrul (Johnson 2009), but it still outputs its results in the same way, which means that sociolinguists who have started using it haven't had to change the way they talk about or present their findings. You can also do regression analysis directly in R without Rbrul (or in another dedicated statistics programme such as SPSS); you'll get your results in a somewhat different format than you'd get from Rbrul, but you'll be using a method that is standard among researchers in other subfields of linguistics, and even in fields outside of linguistics.

In the rest of this chapter, we'll introduce you to the kind of results an Rbrul-type analysis provides, which will allow you not only to perform your own analyses down the road, but also to understand others' analyses when you encounter them in the literature. Hay (2011) provides a useful introduction to regression as it is performed directly in R, and the Further Reading section at the end of this chapter provides references to books containing even more in-depth guides to regression.

What does multivariate analysis tell us, and how does it do so?

Multivariate analysis considers all of our independent variables at once, and tells us which (if any) of them has a significant effect on our dependent variable. This is communicated through *p*-values (see Chapter 12); as we saw before, a *p*-value below 0.05 can be taken to mean that a particular independent variable has a significant effect on the variation.

Multivariate analysis also gives us details concerning the nature of the effect those significant independent variables are having on the dependent variable. We'll illustrate this with a categorical dependent variable, say, (ing). To perform multivariate analysis on such a dependent variable, you'll be required to choose one variant to focus on (say, use of the alveolar [ɪn] form), called the 'application value'. You'll then interpret your results with this one variant in mind, just as we did when cross-tabulating two independent variables above.

In the output of your regression, each categorical independent variable which the analysis has found to be significant will be associated with what are called factor weights, which are numbers ranging between 0 and 1. There will be one factor weight for each level of each of your categorical independent variables. A factor weight tells us what kind of effect its associated level has on the variant you selected to focus on. (The term 'factor weight' is used because independent variables are also sometimes known as 'factor groups', and their levels, 'factors'.) A factor weight of greater than 0.5 means that the application value is more likely to be used in the context associated with that factor weight: the context 'favours' the application value. A factor weight of less than 0.5 means that the application value is less likely to be used in the associated context: the context 'disfavours' it. A factor weight of 0.5 indicates no effect on the application value. You can thus interpret factor weights in a similar way to percentages, but with higher factor weights indicating a greater likelihood of use of the application value in the associated environment, and lower numbers, a lower likelihood.

Figure 14.3 shows you what the Rbrul output looks like when we perform logistic regression on the data from Labov's (1972) department store study (available from the Rbrul website). The application value in this case was set to rhoticity; factor weights are in the last column.

As expected, Rbrul reports that rhoticity was most favoured in Saks and least favoured at Klein's, with Macy's in between, and favoured in the word *floor* and disfavoured in the word *fourth*. Both store and word are found to have a significant effect on rhoticity. You can compare the factor weights to the percentages in the column to their left and observe that, though the factor weights go in the same direction as the percentages, they are not identical in value. For this reason, many students find it helpful to think of factor weights as 'adjusted percentages'.

Regression is very flexible to different types of data. The variables in Labov's study were all categorical, but regression can be performed with continuous independent variables too (like word frequency or vowel duration), and with a continuous dependent variable (like F1 or F2). A particular type of regression, called mixed-effects regression, allows for predictors of different types to be differentiated. Two types, known as random effects and fixed effects, are possible. Random effects are those independent variables whose levels have been drawn from a larger population that you couldn't possibly have sampled in its entirety: think the individual speakers in your sample (as presumably you haven't interviewed the entire speech community), or the individual words that your speakers uttered (as presumably you didn't record them uttering every word in the language!). Fixed effects, by contrast, are those independent variables that you can reasonably sample all levels of in your study, like speaker sex, social class or word class. As Johnson (2009) explains, regression analyses on typical sociolinguistic data that do not include a random effect for individual speakers run the risk of allowing one particularly deviant speaker to skew the results. This is because the analysis

BEST STEP-DOWN MODEL IS WITH store (1.17e-19) + word (8.18e-09)
[p-values dropping from full model]

$store

factor	logodds	tokens	rhotic/rhotic+non-rhotic	centered factor weight
Saks	0.900	177	0.475	0.711
Macy's	0.436	336	0.372	0.607
Klein's	−1.337	216	0.097	0.208

$word

factor	logodds	tokens	rhotic/rhotic+non-rhotic	centered factor weight
flooR	0.493	347	0.412	0.621
fouRth	−0.493	382	0.228	0.379

Figure 14.3 Rbrul output for an analysis of rhoticity in three New York City department stores

will erroneously treat that speaker's behaviour as characteristic of all speakers who share their demographics. Including a random effect of speaker, by contrast, lets the analysis allow for idiosyncratic behaviour. Regressions performed in R and Rbrul can handle mixed-effects models like this.

Though it may feel like your analysis tasks multiply in complexity the more independent variables you incorporate, don't despair. There are plenty of resources available to help, many written with students like you in mind, and the joy and satisfaction you'll derive from exploring and analysing your own data will be worth it.

EXERCISES

Exercise 1

Consider the following excerpt from the methods section of Haddican et al. (2013). Even if you don't understand every detail, you should be able to answer the following questions about their multivariate analysis:

1 Is their dependent variable categorical or continuous?
2 Which of their independent variables were random effects and which were fixed effects? What makes each independent variable appropriate for its particular type (random vs. fixed)?
3 What significant effects on the dependent variable did the researchers find?

GOAT diphthongization

We examined linguistic and social effects on diphthongization by fitting a series of linear mixed effects regression models, with normalized Euclidean distance measurements of FACE and GOAT tokens as the dependent variable and random intercepts for speaker and lexical root. The analysis was conducted using the lmer() function in the lme4 package in R (Bates, Maechler, & Bolker, 2011). The fixed social predictors tested were the speaker's attitudinal index score, style, speaker sex, and speaker age group. [. . .] We treated the attitudinal score as a continuous variable with possible values ranging from −4 to +4 (though in practice the scores ranged from 0 to +4). Style and sex were factors with two levels each: word list versus conversation and male versus female respectively. The age factor had three levels: 1998 older, 1998 younger, and 2008. The fixed linguistic predictors tested were the natural log of vowel duration (Klatt, 1973), and following and preceding voicing, manner, and place of articulation. [. . .]

Variables were selected using a step-up procedure similar to that employed in Goldvarb (Sankoff, Tagliamonte, & Smith, 2012) and Rbrul (Johnson, 2012). Fixed predictors improving the model significantly (α = .05) were added level by level. We then used this same step-up procedure to evaluate two-way combinations of variables where plotting suggested a possible interaction. The analysis revealed no significant interactions with >2 predictors.

We begin by describing a model of GOAT diphthongization, with all three age groups (n = 1,712, r-squared = .40). The step-up procedure selected interactions for preceding sound*age group, following sound*age group, and log-duration*age group. The analysis revealed no significant main effects or other interactions.

Source: Haddican et al. (2013)

Exercise 2

Consult our companion website for a sample dataset and an analysis exercise.

References

D'Arcy, Alexandra, Bill Haddican, Hazel Richards, Sali A. Tagliamonte and Ann Taylor. 2013. Asymmetrical trajectories: The past and present of *-body/-one*. *Language Variation and Change* 25: 287–310.

Haddican, Bill, Paul Foulkes, Vincent Hughes and Hazel Richards. 2013. Interaction of social and linguistic constraints on two vowel changes in northern England. *Language Variation and Change* 25: 371–403.

Hay, Jennifer. 2011. Statistical analysis. In Marianna Di Paolo and Malcah Yaeger-Dror (eds) *Sociophonetics: A Student's Guide*. London: Routledge, 198–214.

Houston, Ann. 1985. Continuity and Change in English Morphology: The Variable (ING). Doctoral Dissertation, University of Pennsylvania.

Johnson, Daniel Ezra. 2009. Getting off the GoldVarb standard: Introducing Rbrul for mixed-effects variable rule analysis. *Language and Linguistics Compass* 3: 359–383.

Labov, William. 1972. *Sociolinguistic Patterns*. Philadelphia, PA: University of Pennsylvania Press.

Further reading

Baayen, R.H. 2008. *Analyzing Linguistic Data: A Practical Introduction to Statistics Using R*. New York: Cambridge University Press.

Gries, Stefan Th. 2013. *Statistics for Linguistics with R: A Practical Introduction*. New York: Taylor & Francis.

Johnson, Keith. 2008. *Quantitative Methods in Linguistics*. Malden, MA: Wiley-Blackwell.

15 Mixing qualitative and quantitative analysis

Most of the chapters in this book have focused on quantitative approaches for exploring and analysing your data. This partly reflects our own research expertise and it's partly because our experience tells us that quantitative methods are what cause students the most headaches when they start studying sociolinguistics. But real language data is not only suited to number crunching. In fact, some approaches – like ethnography – reject quantification entirely and instead place value on exploring the quality of the data, delving into the specifics of how speakers use language and analysing forms in light of the larger social and conversational context that they occur in. We have touched on some of these more discourse-based approaches in some of the earlier chapters and the purpose of this chapter is to discuss ways in which the two modes of analysis – the quantitative and the qualitative – can be usefully combined. The reason some researchers like to combine quantitative and qualitative is that it enables them to understand better the full range of social and linguistic functions that language variation serves.

A word on terminology

The phrase 'mixed methods research' is increasingly common in the social sciences. Reviewers of some of our own work have referred to the combination of qualitative and quantitative analyses as 'mixed methods', but we ought to note that what we are talking about in this chapter is not exactly archetypal mixed methods research – very few sociolinguists do that. There is some disagreement in the literature about precisely what counts as mixed methods (Creswell and Plano Clark (2011) and Johnson, Onwuegbuzie and Turner (2007) are useful introductions and guides) – is it about an underlying philosophy or just the design for data collection? Is it about *why* you are doing the analysis or just about *how* you do the analysis? Beneath the disputes over the coverage of the term, there is some agreement that mixed methods research involves the preplanned blending of qualitative and quantitative data. In addition, these data are often designed to come from different sources rather than applying different analytic methods to the same data.

In practice, the mixing of qualitative and quantitative seems to often be more ad hoc in sociolinguistics (see the case studies later in this chapter). On the other hand, foundational studies in sociolinguistics (e.g. much of Labov's work) drew on qualitative data alongside quantitative data in the analysis of variation, so arguably sociolinguistics 'got' the point of mixing methods long before it became trendy in other social sciences.

Combining quantitative and qualitative: Learning by example

For some researchers, the difference between qualitative and quantitative analysis is simply one of scale – quantitative analysis is what you can do when you have enough qualitative observations. For other people, the decision to combine qualitative and quantitative methods may be based on more pragmatic considerations – if you have relatively few observations of a variable what is interesting about it may not be that it occurs in this person's speech three times and that person's speech not at all, but rather how the first person is using the feature when they do use it. We have no prescription for when you should try and mix qualitative and quantitative methods, issues of scale and availability of data may not exhaust all the reasons for mixing qualitative and quantitative methods.

However you have designed your project, it is worth remembering that you can always supplement your quantitative data with more evaluative and subjective information. This is true even if you collect data with closed answer questionnaires (Chapter 8), which you might think are entirely quantitative. When you are debriefing people, they may be eager to talk about what their impressions were of the questions you posed. You can learn a lot from their interpretation of what they were doing or from their reaction to your debriefing.

A sociolinguistic study can be designed so that it includes the collection of complementary quantitative and qualitative data. For example, during a single recording session with a speaker, you might ask them to read aloud a word list that you have carefully constructed so that it includes tokens of the variable you are studying in tightly controlled environments, such as you might *not* elicit in spontaneous speech. On another occasion, by simply chatting to the same person you might end up collecting a lot of information about their attitudes towards authority figures. These complementary forms of data can then enrich an analysis of why that person is or is not in the vanguard of language change. Labov (2001) did precisely this with his analysis of the Corcorans in Philadelphia: he considered each of the vowels under investigation in the speech of Barbara and Rick and compared their pronunciations against other members of the family, then against other members of their block on Wicket St, and finally against their social peers in wider Philadelphia. Labov notes that Barbara's position as a leader of change is consistent with her "determination to escape from unreasonable adult controls" (2001: 402).

Comparatively few studies these days undertake the repeated recordings that in the early days of the field were central to establishing rapport and encouraging speakers to relax into their vernacular. Where researchers do have multiple recordings to draw on, it is clear that this affords them qualitative data that can be very helpful in their analysis. A famous example of this is Rickford and McNair-Knox's (1992) series of interviews with Foxy Boston, a Palo Alto teenager who was bound for Stanford University. Their lengthy association with Foxy meant that they could interpret quantitative changes in her speech over time in terms of changes in how she positioned herself as an individual.

Similarly, Patricia Cukor-Avila and Guy Bailey have been engaged in research in a small town in Texas since 1986. They have seen people be born and grow up there, age and die, and by now some of the Springvillers who were children when they started working there have kids of their own. This all means that they have a huge amount of high quality data on how the community works and how different individuals interact with each other. Their work, based on their decades of recordings in Springville, tries to use the very rich qualitative data they have about speakers and the social structure of the community to inform their quantitative analyses of language variation and change. For example, in Cukor-Avila and Bailey (2011) they examine two linguistic features: the use of invariant habitual *be* and the use of quotative verbs, including the relative newcomer, *be like*. They draw on longitudinal data when discussing who uses which of the forms they are interested in and they also draw on observations about an individual speaker's movements in and out of the community. Based on this, they argue that the diffusion of some variables occurs in fits and starts, and relies on contact with urban social networks.

In another form of privileged and long-term contact with a speech community, Kirk Hazen (2002) was licensed to behave and be treated like a community insider in a small town in North Carolina because he married into it, but his dual role as a member of the extended family and as an outsider-researcher enabled him to make a qualitative distinction between residents who were more locally oriented and those who were more oriented to larger towns and cities. We realise that marrying into a speech community and acquiring the qualitative knowledge your extended family possesses is not necessarily an option for all studies (it's perhaps particularly unrealistic for a semester-long project), but it's worth mentioning as a model of mixing qualitative and quantitative forms of analysis.

More often, time constraints on data collection mean that a study will not have multiple independent sources of quantitative and qualitative data. Instead, a single recording session or interview will be mined for both kinds of information. In their study of the dialect of Pittsburgh, Barbara Johnstone and Scott Kiesling explain that:

> In the final module of the sociolinguistic interview, the fieldworker invited participants to talk about local speech via the question, 'Have you ever heard of "Pittsburghese"?' If they said they had, the fieldworker asked for a definition and some examples. So both here and, spontaneously, in other parts of the interview, participants provided metalinguistic talk that sheds direct light on how linguistic form and social meaning are linked for them, some of it about monophthongal /aw/ [i.e. the MOUTH vowel] in particular.
>
> (Johnstone and Kiesling 2008: 18)

As we noted already, there are different reasons why you might not have many observations – perhaps because you're investigating a rare sound or construction, or perhaps because you have caught something at an early stage in its development. Jenny Cheshire's (2013) work on the emergence of a new pronoun in London English appears to have caught the innovative use of *man* to refer to first, second and third singular referents at such an early stage in its development that it suffices to simply give all the examples in the corpus (a much richer source of the pronouns in London English recorded slightly after that linguistic survey can be found in *Attack the Block*, Cornish 2011).

EXERCISES

Exercise 1

Read the following extract from Penelope Eckert's (2011) paper on the pronunciation of the diphthong /ow/ (also known as the GOAT vowel). Eckert has just been talking about how Rachel, like most of the other kids in her class, tends to use fronted pronunciations of /ow/ when it follows an apical /t/ and more backed pronunciations when it precedes an /l/. While you are reading, pay attention to how Eckert introduces both qualitative and quantitative data.

1. Working with a partner, identify the key words and phrases that indicate to you that the analysis is qualitative or quantitative and circle them in different colours.
2. Was there any disagreement between you or features that one person identified but the other did not?

> In what follows, I will focus on the relation between Rachel's teenage persona and the fronting of /ow/.
>
> A clear example of the function of fronting is offered by Rachel's pronunciation of *go*, which serves as a common quotative in Rachel's speech.

Use of quotation in narrative is a well-known way of showing involvement—of making narratives come to life and creating voices rather than simply reciting actions (e.g., Schiffrin 1981; Tannen 1982). Quotation takes on increased importance in preadolescence as narrative becomes a central genre in social drama and an important means of enacting a teenage, crowd-member stance. There are 16 quotative occurrences of *go* in the speech sample under study here, and all of them introduce narratives about Rachel and her peers, more specifically about their relationships and events in the crowd. One can, therefore, take the use of quotative *go* as indexing aspects of her crowd status. For example, in the following, Rachel is telling me why she doesn't like Brenda, a girl in the crowd. Apparently Brenda has written something dirty in the slam book that is going around the crowd. A slam book is a notebook initiated by one or a few individuals. It contains one or more questions and circulates among peers for them to write their answers. This slam book had a bunch of questions about favorite things, one of which was "favorite body part." Harry, a popular boy, told Rachel that Brenda had tried to convince him to write dirty stuff:

> And she's all, "No, put grosser, like, really disgusting body parts." Um. And he's all, uh, "I don't know, I don't wanna say." And then, she's all, "How about dick." And then, he's all, "Whatever. I don't, you know, I don't wanna get into this." [. . .] But nobody knows that. You know, Harry told me. But I would believe Harry, but I would never believe Brenda. Brenda lies. Like Brenda, when I was playing, um, tag, she goes, um, cuz she got tagged, and then she–, um cuz she was in there for four times, and um, and then she goes, but Kristin tags her, and then she goes back to me and she goes, "Rachel, that wasn't a fair tag cuz you just went like this to me. And, you tagged me bare–, barely. And, I, you hardly even tagged me." I go, "Excuse me, Kristin tagged you." She's like, "Oh. Kristin, you, you tagged, you tagged me the wrong way." I go, "What is she doing? She's like totally lying."

Figure 1 [Figure 15.1] shows all 142 measurable occurrences of /ow/ in this interview. As the figure shows, Rachel's occurrences of /ow/ in quotative *go* are significantly more fronted than those in nonquotative occurrences of *go* (F2 $t[20] = -3.686$, $p < .001$; F1 $t[20] = -2.479$, $p < .01$). In fact, occurrences of quotative *go* are significantly more fronted than all other occurrences of /ow/, including those following apicals (F2 $t[141] = 2.114$, $p < .025$).

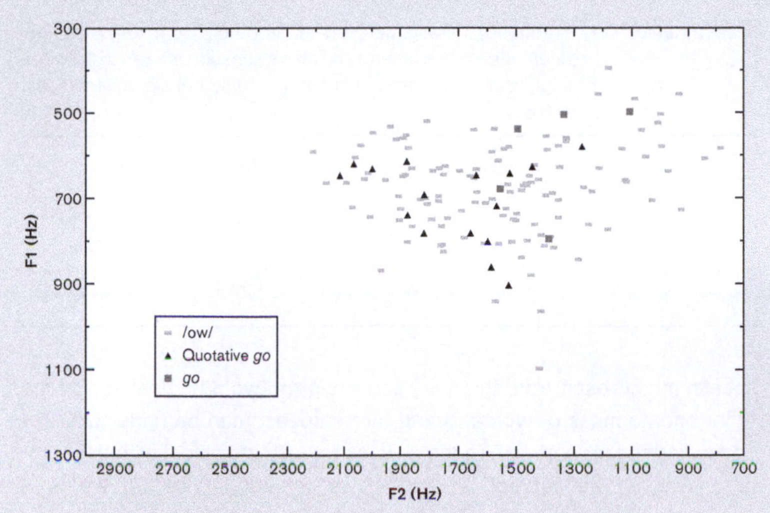

Figure 1 [Figure 15.1] Rachel's fronting of the nucleus of /ow/

Source: Eckert (2011: 93–95)

Exercise 2

In this exercise we have reprinted part of the discussion of results in a paper by Miriam that looked at the use of the word *sore* (meaning 'sorry') in Bislama (a Pacific creole). She has already established that in Bislama *sore* (like its English analogue) can be used to express regret and also to express empathy (i.e. *sorry for something* vs *sorry about something*). Read the extract and answer the questions that follow.

Interpreting the distribution

The question now becomes: Why do men and women prefer to express empathy with others through different behaviors? What, if anything, can we infer or learn about different members of the speech community from the distribution of *sore*? Why is the empathetic use of *sore* marked for men and unmarked for women? What social information is conveyed when speakers use *sore* with one meaning or another? First, we must determine whether the distributional differences noted above reflect a genuine difference in women's and men's use of *sore*, or whether they are a byproduct of other factors. That is, if women's speech is always more other-oriented than men's, then the different distribution of *sore* in men's and women's

Table 2 [Table 15.1] Frequency of 2sg. subjects vs all others as a test of other-orientedness in women's and men's speech. Difference between specifically addressee-oriented discourse not significant (t-test = 0.87)

	Women %	*N*	*Men* %	*N*
2sg. 'you'	8	249	7	190
Other subjects	92	2918	93	2349
Total Ns		3167		2539

speech might result from this. [. . .] one straightforward comparison of the other-orientedness of women's and men's speech can be undertaken by comparing the proportion of finite clauses with a 2sg subject with the number of clauses with subjects of all other persons and numbers, in women's and men's conversations. [. . .]

Table 2 [Table 15.1] shows that the proportion of clauses with 2sg subjects in women's and men's speech are almost identical. It seems unlikely, therefore, that women's use of *sore* to express empathy is a consequence of a more general tendency. Women do not seem to orient their talk around their addressee significantly more than men do. Let us consider, then, the possibility that the distribution of *sore* is better understood in terms of how the quality of empathy fits into a local understanding of women's and men's social roles. This discussion will require us to expand the analysis beyond the minimal linguistic context examined so far, to include wider contextual information of an ethnographic nature.

Source: Meyerhoff (1999: 231–232)

1 To what extent do you consider this a quantitative or a qualitative analysis of the use of *sore* 'sorry'?
2 How would you suggest improving either the quantitative or qualitative components of this analysis?

References

Cheshire, Jenny. 2013. Grammaticalisation in social context: The emergence of a new English pronoun. *Journal of Sociolinguistics* 17: 608–633.

Cornish, Joe (dir.) 2011. *Attack the Block.* Studio Canal Features.

Creswell, John W. and Vicki L. Plano Clark. 2011. *Designing and Conducting Mixed Methods Research.* 2nd edition. Thousand Oaks, CA: Sage Publications.

Cukor-Avila, Patricia and Guy Bailey. 2011. The interaction of transmission and diffusion in the spread of linguistic forms. *University of Pennsylvania Working Papers in Linguistics*, vol. 17.2, *Selected Papers from NWAV 39*. Available at http://repository.upenn.edu/pwpl/vol17/iss2/6 (last accessed 5 November 2014).

Eckert, Penelope. 2011. Language and power in the preadolescent heterosexual market. *American Speech* 86: 85–97.

Hazen, Kirk. 2002. Identity and language variation in a rural community. *Language* 78: 240–257.

Johnson, R. Burke, Anthony J. Onwuegbuzie and Lisa A. Turner. 2007. Towards a definition of mixed methods research. *Journal of Mixed Methods Research* 1: 112–133.

Johnstone, Barbara and Scott F. Kiesling. 2008. Indexicality and experience: Exploring the meanings of /aw/-monphthongization in Pittsburgh. *Journal of Sociolinguistics* 12: 5–33.

Labov, William. 2001. *Principles of Linguistic Change: Social Factors*. Oxford: Blackwell.

Meyerhoff, Miriam. 1999. Sorry in the Pacific: Defining communities, defining practices. *Language in Society* 28: 225–238.

Rickford, John R. and Faye McNair-Knox. 1992. Addressee and topic-influenced style shift: A quantitative sociolinguistic study. In Douglas Biber and Edward Finegan (eds) *Sociolinguistic Perspectives on Register*. New York and Oxford: Oxford University Press, 235–276.

Further reading

Creswell, John W. and Vicki L. Plano Clark. 2011. *Designing and Conducting Mixed Methods Research*. 2nd edition. Thousand Oaks, CA: Sage Publications.

Johnson, R. Burke, Anthony J. Onwuegbuzie and Lisa A. Turner. 2007. Towards a definition of mixed methods research. *Journal of Mixed Methods Research* 1: 112–133.

Johnstone, Barbara. 2000. *Qualitative Methods in Sociolinguistics*. New York and Oxford: Oxford University Press.

Paltridge, Brian. 2006. *Discourse Analysis: An Introduction*. London: Continuum.

16 Writing up your research

In this chapter, we introduce you to a particular academic genre: the research paper. We review the main parts of a research paper and raise awareness of some of the characteristics of these different parts. We can give you only limited advice on referencing and writing style but there are some good sources of advice that you can turn to, e.g. Anderson and Poole (2001) or Swales and Feak (2000, 2004). Frequently, departments have their own style sheets that they would like their students to use and you should follow those in the first instance.

What is a research paper?

A research paper is a piece of writing that is based on original research. It is clearly structured with section headings, similar to an experimental or data-based research article (cf. Swales 2004: 213f). A research paper typically consists of introduction, literature review, methods, results, discussion, conclusion and reference list. The sections may overlap to a greater or lesser extent but should all recognisably be present. There may also be an abstract at the beginning of the paper and an appendix at the end. Introduction, literature review and methods usually constitute about one third of the paper, and results, discussion, conclusion make up the rest.

Introduction

The introduction gives an overview and explanation of what you are trying to achieve in your research paper. It is meant to draw the reader into the topic and convince them that what you will outline in the paper is original and interesting. For example, consider how Potter and Phillips (2008: 586) start their article on British-Barbadian migrants: "This research is based on an analysis of the narratives provided by second-generation transnational British-Barbadian ('Bajan-Brit') migrants to the land of their parents, who reported that indigenous Barbadians frequently accuse them of being mad."

This is a great first sentence, and it certainly draws the reader into the narrative. Swales' (1990) CARS (Create a Research Space) model usefully illustrates the various moves that many introductions of research articles consist of and the different ways in which they can be realised (see Figure 16.1). A move is a functional unit, so it can be realised as anything ranging from merely a clause to several sentences. He originally developed this model for research articles but it is also suitable for short assignments such as research papers. As a first step, you establish your research territory: generally in what area is the paper located and what is it about? Citations are required here! Then you establish a research niche. This second move normally starts with some kind of marker of contrast, such as *but, however* or *despite*. Justifying your research and explaining why it is important to fill this research niche is crucial: just because something has not been studied before is not reason enough to study it. You can establish a niche in various ways: by indicating a gap directly, or indirectly by counter-claiming or question raising. A research niche can also be established by continuing a research tradition, i.e. by adding to what we already know and providing a new piece of information to a specific research strand.

In a third move, you occupy the niche by stating your research question or your research goal. You may also give an overview of what you will argue and how your argumentation and the paper are structured. Figure 16.1 shows that not all steps within a move are obligatory. For example, there are different ways to create a research niche. Swales (2004) presents a revised version of the model, and move 3, in particular, is now often seen as more complex. In addition to the steps listed in Figure 16.1, this move can sometimes also include the presentation of hypotheses and definitions. Sometimes methods are briefly summarised and the value of the present research is mentioned. Some elements of recycling and fusing of material within moves is of course also always possible.

Let's have a look at an example: part of the introduction of Peter Trudgill's (2004) article "Linguistic and social typology: The Austronesian migrations and phoneme inventories" (see right-hand column of Figure 16.1). Moves have been separated by an empty line for easy recognition. This is not normally done in research papers, however. So how is Trudgill's introduction organised? First, he establishes the general research territory of linguistic and social typology. He claims centrality by saying "that there is a challenging issue for linguistic typology", and he then continues by making a generalisation about what linguistic-typological studies have found, while at the same time reviewing this literature very generally. The word *but* marks the beginning of the next move. A research gap is being established: there are no explanations for why "particular languages select particular structures and not others". Thus, he uses step 1B to make this second move.

Finally, he occupies the research niche by proposing "a legitimate sociolinguistic viewpoint" and by developing a thesis concerning potentially relevant social

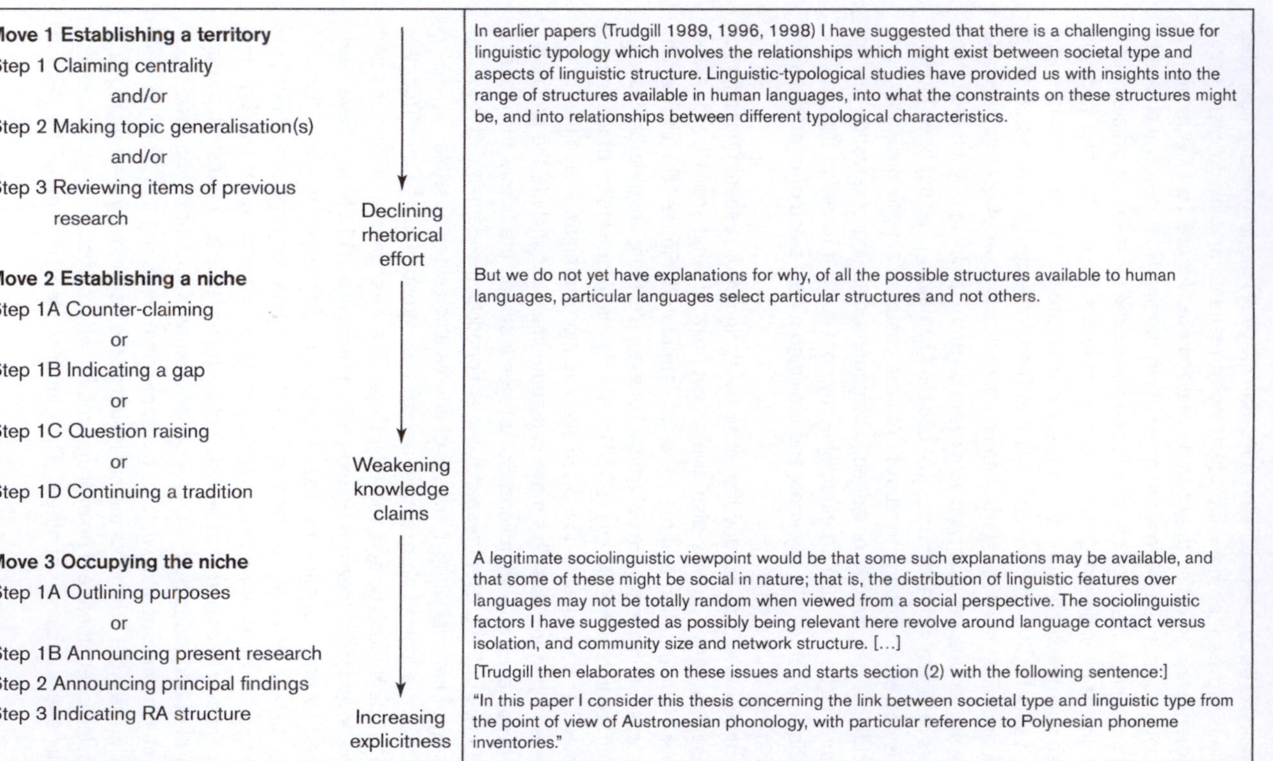

Move 1 Establishing a territory
Step 1 Claiming centrality
and/or
Step 2 Making topic generalisation(s)
and/or
Step 3 Reviewing items of previous research
Declining rhetorical effort
In earlier papers (Trudgill 1989, 1996, 1998) I have suggested that there is a challenging issue for linguistic typology which involves the relationships which might exist between societal type and aspects of linguistic structure. Linguistic-typological studies have provided us with insights into the range of structures available in human languages, into what the constraints on these structures might be, and into relationships between different typological characteristics.
Move 2 Establishing a niche
Step 1A Counter-claiming
or
Step 1B Indicating a gap
or
Step 1C Question raising
or
Step 1D Continuing a tradition
Weakening knowledge claims
But we do not yet have explanations for why, of all the possible structures available to human languages, particular languages select particular structures and not others.
Move 3 Occupying the niche
Step 1A Outlining purposes
or
Step 1B Announcing present research
Step 2 Announcing principal findings
Step 3 Indicating RA structure
Increasing explicitness
A legitimate sociolinguistic viewpoint would be that some such explanations may be available, and that some of these might be social in nature; that is, the distribution of linguistic features over languages may not be totally random when viewed from a social perspective. The sociolinguistic factors I have suggested as possibly being relevant here revolve around language contact versus isolation, and community size and network structure. [...]
[Trudgill then elaborates on these issues and starts section (2) with the following sentence:]
"In this paper I consider this thesis concerning the link between societal type and linguistic type from the point of view of Austronesian phonology, with particular reference to Polynesian phoneme inventories."

Figure 16.1 Swales' CARS model aligned with introduction from Trudgill (2004)

factors. After quite some elaboration on this thesis (not shown in Figure 16.1), he tells us how he aims to explore this thesis in his paper. He announces the research and its purposes (step 1A and B) without yet announcing his principal findings or outlining the article structure. Thus, there are various ways to write a good introduction; however, the three moves tend to normally occur in one form or another. You may have noticed that the first person pronoun 'I' has been used in this example. This is perfectly acceptable in academic writing, as long as you don't overuse it!

OTHER GENRES: ESSAYS

You may be most familiar with essays as a form of assessment when you are asked to write a response to a question or a problem. This is a genre that's very different from that of the research paper. Research papers are particularly suited to reporting on questions developed in a quantitative paradigm. In fact, the research paper is a genre that has evolved from the report genre in science and quantitative social science, which is why it is not well suited to presenting long discourse examples and to walking the reader through a close analysis of discourse (Johnstone 2000: 138).

A genre that is more suited to presenting qualitative and interpretive research has evolved in the humanities: the essay. While research papers start with a research question that is motivated by a particular research gap and data are used to answer the question, essays may start with an example of language, which is then unpacked and explored, through questioning, to explain why the data have occurred in the way they did. An essay, thus, in a narrower conception than that of the assessment-type genre, is "an informal exploration of a particular text" (Becker 1994: 163). After such a text has been explored in a lot of detail, essayists may make more general suggestions about how such texts or aspects of the text may normally work. Nonetheless, the research paper format can be adapted to research of a more qualitative nature, for example by fusing the results and discussion sections (see later in this chapter).

Literature review

What you have said in your introduction now needs to be put into context in the literature review. Sometimes introduction and literature review are merged, but more often than not, the literature review represents a section of its own. The literature review provides background information for the study as well as a critical look at the existing literature *relevant to your study*. For example, for a paper exploring attitudes towards swearing and how these attitudes intersect with gender, you may focus on the literature on swearing and different types of swear words, attitudes towards swearing and literature that has looked at swearing in relation to gender. You will likely have a word limit, so you do not need to summarise the etymology of the most frequently occurring swear words; nor do you have to outline the different approaches to the study of language and gender or on attitudes towards different varieties of English. Just briefly locate your research within the areas of language and gender as well as attitudes and profanity with a few key references and then focus on the literature that relates directly to your topic. While you summarise some of the previous literature, a literature review is *not* a summary. That's because you also evaluate previous work, you show relationships between different work and, most importantly, you indicate how it relates to your research question. In short, you report, relate and evaluate.

You report, briefly, the relevant key points, findings or arguments of the literature you've read. You should mostly use your own words when reporting rather than paraphrasing too closely and rather than giving a lot of quotations. A handful of *short* direct quotations, that are marked as such, will suffice. A frequent mistake of novice writers is to organise their review by book or article: one paragraph on what X said is followed by one on Y's article and then another paragraph on what Z says on the issue. That's all important but the previous literature has to be interrelated – How was the previous research similar or different in their methods, approaches, goals, assumptions and/or findings? Usually books and articles are organised into schools of thought regarding how they answer the question investigated: common answers that are united by the same approach are discussed together. If there are no answers to your question, choose a different dimension for meaningful comparison, for example by theme. Such themes could include:

- the development of ideas within your research area;
- current issues and questions;
- theoretical and methodological positions;
- views of different groups (academics, policy makers, etc.); or
- different approaches to tackle the problem, etc.

These themes can also be used to form subheadings in your literature review, which will make its structure even more transparent. Your review should have a conclusion. What is the result of your review? Such a conclusion could be (but doesn't have to be) a thesis, i.e. a statement or theory that you put forward to be proven.

While you're reporting and relating, you must also evaluate the authors' claims, noting agreement or conflict between them. Are arguments and conclusions supported by the authors' data? Are the arguments coherent? Are the methods reliable? Do not make the mistake of assuming that just because something was published in a journal or book means that it is necessarily right and without flaws. Usually things are more complex – take your time and come to your own conclusions.

When you come to phrase your criticism and create your research niche, you need to find a constructive tone. You don't want to sound petty; you're aiming for a subtle, polite and refined evaluation. So, for instance, instead of writing something like, "X is wrong because", "Y's results are flawed because they are different from A's" or lists of what Z has 'failed' to do and how her analysis is 'incorrect', 'insufficient' and 'inaccurate', criticism is conventionally framed more along the lines of: "X's argumentation does not consider . . ." or "Y's results contrast with A's . . ." or "curiously, Z concludes . . .".

Johnstone (2000: 132) gives some nice examples – from her own writing – of words and phrases that signal research gaps in the literature: explanations may be 'incomplete', or some issue may have been 'overlooked' or 'rarely studied'. You can also evaluate indirectly, by comparison with somebody else's research or your own, which may 'supplement', 'enrich', 'or provide another piece of the answer'. If you want to find out more about the purpose of a literature review, its structure and stylistic features, read the relevant chapters in Swales and Feak (2000).

Adhering to a proper academic referencing style in your paper is extremely important. The academic referencing system (in contrast to that of journalism for example) is designed in a particular way for a variety of reasons: it helps to place your work in a very specific research context, it prevents you from making unsubstantiated statements and it gives readers the opportunity to access and check all information for themselves if they need to. Often you'll be expected to refer to classic studies that were the first to make a particular point, but you don't want to get stuck with just the classics. You also need to check the recent literature to see how certain questions have developed. For example, Lakoff (1973) is a classic and pioneering study on language and gender. In this, she outlines many issues that have dominated the field since. Yet at the same time, some of the arguments made in this piece of work have since been contradicted and refined. Classic though it is, if you solely rely on Lakoff (1973) when designing and justifying your own study, you're asking for trouble – or at least complaints from your reader.

You should have obtained a good idea of how to reference from your reading of research articles. These are great models, so make sure to pay attention to reviewing and referencing while you read. We'll talk about the reference list later on. For now, we will offer just a few words on in-text referencing. It is always a good idea to over-reference initially. You can cut out references later on. Always put page numbers where possible, e.g. (Schleef 2005: 22), in whatever format your programme or the publication specifies. Refer to authors using their surname (not their first name). In most cases, you will also want to minimally give the year of publication. Only in very rare cases will writers put the title of the publication, so do this: "Eckert (1998: 185) argues that . . .", rather than this: "In her article

'Vowels and nail polish: the emergence of linguistic style in the preadolescent heterosexual marketplace' Penelope Eckert argues that . . .".

When revising your paper, it's a good idea to check that all information is accounted for as (a) your own analysis and findings (no reference), (b) as general knowledge statements (e.g. Rome is the capital of Italy; no reference) or (c) as referenced material taken from a different source. You may report a source directly (i.e. when you replicate the author's original phrase, clause or sentence(s) in quote marks) or indirectly (i.e. when you use your own words). It is your responsibility to signal clearly when something is your own analysis/finding. You can do this by using phrases like: "my review of the literature would suggest . . ." or "in this paper, it is argued that . . .". Have a look at the useful information from the University of Alberta on the "layout of linguistic manuscripts and in-line citations" (search the phrase in quote marks). Failure to give direct or indirect sources is considered plagiarism and can have serious consequences for your academic career.

Finally, three more pieces of advice to help you meet your deadline:

1. Don't try to read everything. Some well-chosen pieces may be quite sufficient. Literature is good if it relates directly to your research question and provides answers for it.
2. Write while reading. Don't do all the readings and then try to write the review. Read, try to find thematic undercurrents in the literature while reading and then report, relate, evaluate in small article groups as soon as possible.
3. Record bibliographic information from the start; it'll increase the likelihood that your reference list is complete and consistent!

Methods

In this section, you describe and reflect on methods used. Readers need to know what methods the study is based on and why you made certain choices as opposed to others. This section should be detailed enough so that someone reading your research paper could replicate your study exactly as you did it. Your methods section should answer the following questions:

- How did data collection proceed? (Where was data collected, who did it and who participated in the study, how many participants, how much data, when was it collected and how?)
- What tools and materials did you use? How were they prepared and why did they take the form they did?
- How was data processed after it was collected? Was it transcribed? Was it coded? If so, how? Give examples. Who did this? How accurate was it? What are the characteristics of your sample?

- How did data analysis proceed? Did you analyse data statistically? If so, how and why did you use the test you did? What factors and what data were included in the analysis? If you have conducted a qualitative analysis, how did you decide what to focus on, what to include and exclude?

One final point: methods sections are normally written in the past tense and you should do this even when you have not finished data collection and analysis yet.

Results

In this section, you present your results, clearly and up front. Results should be comprehensible on their own. Briefly describe the main findings but leave your discussion of the data and *extensive* comparison with other work for the discussion section. The exception to this is if you decide to merge the results and discussion sections, which, for shorter papers, makes a good deal of sense.

Even a quantitative study requires some qualitative analysis. What we mean by this is that long lists of numbers (even if they are in tables) may not be the best way to report your results. Instead, it may be more meaningful to your readers if you process the data, giving averages or drawing graphs. Data presentation will, to a certain extent, depend on your analysis, and you should organize it in such a way that makes your analysis clear. For example, if you have posed research questions at the beginning of your paper, you could structure your results section around those questions and answer each in turn, making sure to clearly state the evidence for your answer to each one. To clearly state your evidence means going beyond statements like "Table X shows that . . ."; you want to direct the reader to the piece of data in Table X that leads you to your conclusion. Make sure to label tables and figures informatively and to number them consecutively. When referring to a specific figure or a specific table, *figure* and *table* are often capitalised, e.g. "The data are summarised in Table 2".

Discussion and conclusion

Swales (2004: 235f) compares three studies that have looked at the structure of the 'ending matter' or 'after the results' section. Although different disciplines seem to have different traditions, a relatively clear three-part structure emerges:

1. The main research outcome is summarised.
2. The outcome is then explained, evaluated and interpreted often with reference to the research question.
3. Research conclusions and theoretical implications are drawn from the study, which may include a discussion of the study's limitations and future research.

The discussion section is where you review your results. Then you get to explain what your results may mean and what their implications are. So this is when you can pull together all the different strings in your analysis, answer any remaining research questions and discuss how your results fit into the bigger picture. This may involve going back to previous work and explaining what is new and important about your results. You might discuss what consequences your findings may have for existing theories and proposals or you may discuss potential generalisations that your findings may offer. Alternatively, you could organise a discussion around your own or others' predictions: have they been confirmed or contradicted? In whatever way you decide to explain your results, while ruling out other explanations, make sure to present evidence in favour of your interpretation. This is a difficult section to write because you will have to finish telling a story that you started in your results section, a story that involves linking your argumentation and results to the niche you established initially.

What you should not do is make a series of unconnected statements about how pieces of your results relate to a host of different research articles. For your work to have impact, it needs a coherent story that clearly relates to your research question(s). Some self-evaluation of your own study may be appropriate here. What are its potential shortcomings? You could also anticipate objections that other scholars may have towards your research. While it's nice to be realistic and honest, there's no need to go overboard with this. You want to close on a positive note!

A conclusion section often ties the whole project together. It usually summarises the main findings very briefly. Then it takes a step back and tells the reader what your results mean in the big scheme of things. What have you achieved and why is this important? How do your results, previous research and your explanation go together? Where does this particular line of research stand now after you've conducted your study? What should other research follow up on?

Let's have another look at Peter Trudgill's (2004: 316–318) article for an excellent example of a conclusion. First he summarises his results clearly and to the point.

> In the absence of a large-scale database of evidence on this topic, taken from different language families in different parts of the world, any conclusions to be produced here can be only suggestive and tentative. However, it seems that we have reached the following preliminary conclusions concerning contact, isolation, community size, and tendencies involving phoneme inventories:
>
> (i) In cases where there is long-term language contact involving child-language acquisition, high degrees of language contact may lead to larger phoneme inventories, as a result of borrowing, as suggested by Nichols.
>
> [points (ii) to (v) cut out]

He then proceeds to offer a generalisation, concludes and finishes the article:

> In the case of the Polynesian languages with very small inventories, we can point to a process whereby increasing isolation and diminution in community size [. . .] was accompanied by ever smaller phoneme inventories, as per points (iii) and (v). As points (iii) and (v) show, however, the correct generalisation is not that such languages will necessarily have very small inventories but that they will be more likely to have EITHER very small inventories OR very large ones. [. . .] The factors of isolation and small community size can quite simply lead to the development of UNUSUAL phonological systems, as has also been suggested by Nettle (1999: 147): these systems may be either unusually small, as in the case of South Island Maori and Hawai'ian [sic], or unusually large, as in the case of !Xũ and Yele.

OTHER GENRES: DISSERTATIONS/THESES

A small portion of PhD theses these days follow the same structure as research articles, and if they do, they are ten to 15 times longer (Swales 2004: 107), so when the research article structure is adapted to this genre, everything can expand and provide more detail.

More common these days in linguistics, and the Humanities and Social Sciences in general, is a topic-based structure: Introduction → (Literature Review) → (Theoretical Framework) → Method → Topic: Analysis – Discussion → Topic: Analysis – Discussion → Topic: Analysis – Discussion → Conclusion (after Bunton 1998: 114; quoted in Swales 2004). Other disciplines often show specific structural preferences, see Swales (2004) for more on this.

Short dissertations and theses, such as BA and MA dissertations and theses, often follow the same structure as research articles. Sometimes they are topic-based (Samraj 2001).

Dissertations and theses may also include some additional front matter: a coversheet, a declaration regarding plagiarism (dependent on institution), dedication, acknowledgements and preface (all optional), a table of contents, list of figures, list of tables, list of abbreviations and an optional glossary.

Reference list and appendix

At the end of your paper, you will list all references and, if appropriate, have an appendix. Make sure to follow your lecturer's guidelines for referencing. The reference list has to be (1) complete (i.e. articles, book chapters, books, etc. mentioned in the text have to be listed in the reference list; equally, all references in the list have to occur in the text) and (2) consistent (i.e. all references have to be presented in the same style). For example, all book titles should either be capitalised throughout or not. Publication dates have to be given at the same point in each reference, etc.

Traditions differ regarding whether the reference list precedes or follows an appendix. Your appendix may include additional data, interview schedules or questionnaires. Material in the appendix normally does not count towards the final word count, so you needn't worry much about space limits; do not, however, put material here that is essential for an understanding of the paper. Essential tables, graphs, text should go into the main text, not the appendix.

Revise, edit, choose a title and write an abstract

It's a good idea to revise and edit your paper throughout the writing process and then again once you have a full draft of the paper ready. Revising and editing are not the same thing. Revising your paper means rethinking your argumentation and content and conducting major rewrites of the paper. You may also have to cut it down to the specified length.

When revising, you might want to consider whether you have overgeneralised your findings. What you have found to be true for your data may not be true for all people in the community you have investigated. It's easy to find yourself overgeneralising when you are immersed in the community or data you've been studying. If you've been looking at the speech of teenagers, you might find yourself writing statements about 'teenagers' in general, when what you really have data on is 'the participants in this study' or 'these adolescents'. Sometimes overgeneralisation slips in through your use of tenses; the present tense can often be read as a claim about generalisability.

Try not to leave all your write-up to the very end – if you start writing your introduction and literature review while you are researching the literature, and start writing the methods section while designing your research tools, etc., you'll have more time for analysing and revising your finished product. Another good reason for doing this is that seeing your argumentation on paper can help you spot inconsistencies and problems in your research design or argumentation. You might try reading some of the literature relevant to your study focusing on the structure, argumentation and writing conventions used in them, e.g. see what aspects of an article map onto the sections identified in this chapter. This can help develop an awareness and feeling for effective academic writing.

We recommend that you leave about a week to revise and then edit the paper, i.e. fix grammatical and stylistic mistakes, number examples, tables and graphs consecutively, and format the paper according to your guidelines.

Finally, find a good title. In a few phrases or words, it should convey what your paper is about: your question and your argument. If it's snappy and memorable as well, even better! Most research articles also feature an abstract, which appears at the beginning of the paper. An abstract is a 150- to 250-word summary of the research. It briefly refers to all sections of the paper, summarises findings and explains their significance. It is not part of the argumentative thread of the article and it should be able to stand on its own. Research papers do not normally have an abstract: you can ask whether your course convenor expects you to write one for a term paper.

THINGS PEOPLE OFTEN FORGET TO CHECK

When editing your paper, double-check once again that you use the correct formatting and that your paper is free of typos, grammatical errors and continuity errors, i.e. make sure the text is consistent with itself throughout. For example:

- Is everything numbered correctly and consecutively: tables, figures, sections?
- Are all cross-references correct, e.g. within the text, between table of contents and text, between text references and a complete and consistent reference list?
- Are numbers in tables correct and listed to the same number of decimal places?
- Do you use abbreviations consistently?
- Will it be clear to readers what the numbers in tables and graphs mean? Are they clearly labelled? For example, are numbers raw values, percentages or weightings? Is it clear how p-values were arrived at?

Writing a research paper is like telling a story. There are conventions that people have come to expect will be satisfied and that they are looking for as readers. This chapter has outlined in detail the steps you can use to plan your write-up; the companion website has a shorter, cheat-sheet version of much of the same information, one that stresses the narrative quality of a research report. Like telling a story, writing up your research should not only give your audience some pleasure but it should also be a satisfying experience for you.

EXERCISES

Exercise 1

Consider this introduction, excerpted from King and Nadasdi (1999). Divide this introduction into moves 1, 2 and 3 and identify the steps taken to realise these moves. Also pay attention to the general tone of the introduction. What linguistic features are used to signal the different moves and what tense is used in this introduction?

> Most recent research on codeswitching has been conducted from one of two perspectives: grammatical or interactional. The search for grammatical constraints on intrasentential codeswitching exemplifies the grammatical perspective (e.g. Poplack 1980, DiSciullo et al. 1986, Poplack et al. 1989, Myers-Scotton 1993, Belazi et al. 1994, Mahootian & Santorini 1996), while the study of the social meaning of particular codeswitches exemplifies the interactional perspective (e.g. Gumperz 1982, Heller 1982, 1988, 1994). The present article concentrates instead on the role of codeswitching in the organization of discourse; specifically, it is concerned with how codeswitching figures in the expression of evidentiality in French-English bilingual discourse. Following Auer 1995, we argue that codeswitching can be analyzed at the level of discourse, relatively independently of any grammatical properties of codeswitching or of the immediate social context in which it is embedded. We do turn, however, to consideration of the sociolinguistic situation in order to explain inter- and intra-community variation.
>
> Source: King and Nadasdi (1999: 355)

Exercise 2

Consider the short reference list below. There are at least seven inconsistencies in this list. Find them.

References

Britain, David (2005). The dying dialects of England? In Bertacca, A. (Ed.), *Historical linguistic studies of spoken English.* Pisa: Edizioni Plus. 35-46.

Bybee, Joan (2001). *Phonology and language use.* Cambridge: Cambridge University Press.

Cheshire, Jenny, Kerswill, Paul, Fox, Sue & Torgersen, Eivind (2011). Contact, the feature pool and the speech community: the emergence of Multicultural London English. *Journal of Sociolinguistics* 15: 151-196.

Holmes, Janet (1997). Setting new standards: sound changes and gender in New Zealand English. *English World-Wide* 18: 107-142.

Milroy, Lesley (2007). Off the shelf or under the counter? On the social dynamics of sound changes. In Cain, C. M. & Russom, G. (Eds.), *Managing chaos: strategies for identifying change in English. Studies in the history of the English Language III.* Berlin and New York: Mouton de Gruyter. 149-172.

Labov, W. (2010). *Principles of linguistic change: cognitive and cultural factors.* Oxford: Wiley-Blackwell.

Roberts, Julie. 2006. As old becomes new: glottalization in Vermont. *American Speech* 81: 227-249.

Schleef, Erik, Meyerhoff, Miriam & Lynn Clark (2011). Teenagers' acquisition of variation: a comparison of locally-born and migrant teens' realisation of English (ing) in Edinburgh and London. *English World-Wide* 32: 206-236.

Schleef, Erik (2013). Glottal replacement of /t/ in two British capitals: Effects of word frequency and morphological compositionality. *Language Variation and Change* 25: 201-223.

Tagliamonte, Sali (2002). Comparative sociolinguistics. In Chambers, J. K., Trudgill, P. & Schilling-Estes, N. (Eds.), *The handbook of language variation and change.* Oxford: Blackwell.

Trudgill, Peter (1974). *The Social Differentiation of English in Norwich.* Cambridge: Cambridge University Press.

References

Anderson, Jonathan and Millicent Poole. 2001. *Assignment and Thesis Writing.* 4th edition. Brisbane: John Wiley & Sons Australia, Ltd.

Becker, Alton L. 1994. Repetition and otherness: An essay. In Barbara Johnstone (ed.) *Repetition in Discourse: Interdisciplinary Perspectives.* Vol. II. Norwood, NJ: Ablex, 162–175.

Bunton, David Rowland. 1998. Linguistic and textual problems in Ph.D and M.Phil theses: An analysis of genre moves and metatext. Unpublished Ph.D thesis, University of Hong Kong.

Johnstone, Barbara. 2000. *Qualitative Methods in Sociolinguistics.* New York and Oxford: Oxford University Press.

King, Ruth and Terry Nadasdi. 1999. The expression of evidentiality in French-English bilingual discourse. *Language in Society* 28: 355–365.

Lakoff, Robin. 1973. Language and woman's place. *Language in Society* 2: 45–80.

Potter, Robert B. and Joan Phillips. 2008. "Mad dogs and transnational migrants?" Bajan-Brit second-generation migrants and accusations of madness. *Annals of the Association of America Geographers* 96: 586–600.

Samraj, Betty. 2001. The influences of discipline upon genre. Presentation at AAAL, St. Louis, March.

Swales, John M. 1990. *Genre Analysis: English in Academic and Research Settings.* Cambridge: Cambridge University Press.

Swales, John M. 2004. *Research Genres: Explorations and Applications.* Cambridge: Cambridge University Press.

Swales, John M. and Christine B. Feak. 2000. *English in Today's Research World: A Writing Guide.* Ann Arbor, MI: University of Michigan Press.

Swales, John M. and Christine B. Feak. 2004. *Academic Writing for Graduate Students. Second Edition: Essential Tasks and Skills.* Ann Arbor, MI: University of Michigan Press.

Trudgill, Peter. 2004. Linguistic and social typology: The Austronesian migrations and phoneme inventories. *Linguistic Typology* 8: 305–320.

Further reading

Anderson, Jonathan and Millicent Poole. 2001. *Assignment and Thesis Writing.* 4th Edition. Brisbane: John Wiley & Sons Australia, Ltd.

Baglione, Lisa A. 2012. *Writing a Research Paper in Political Science: A Practical Guide to Inquiry, Structure, and Methods.* Thousand Oaks, CA: Sage.

Swales, John M. and Christine B. Feak. 2000. *English in Today's Research World: A Writing Guide.* Ann Arbor, MI: University of Michigan Press.

Swales, John M. and Christine B. Feak. 2004. *Academic Writing for Graduate Students. Second Edition: Essential Tasks and Skills.* Ann Arbor, MI: University of Michigan Press.

Wray, Alison and Aileen Bloomer. 2012. *Projects in Linguistics and Language Studies.* 3rd edition. Abingdon and New York: Routledge.

Index